CITY OF STRANGERS

CITY of STRANGERS

Gulf Migration and the
Indian Community in Bahrain

ANDREW M. GARDNER

ILR PRESS
an imprint of
CORNELL UNIVERSITY PRESS
Ithaca and London

Copyright © 2010 by Cornell University

All rights reserved. Except for brief quotations in a review, this book, or parts thereof, must not be reproduced in any form without permission in writing from the publisher. For information, address Cornell University Press, Sage House, 512 East State Street, Ithaca, New York 14850.

First published 2010 by Cornell University Press
First printing, Cornell Paperbacks, 2010

Printed in the United States of America

Library of Congress Cataloging-in-Publication Data

Gardner, Andrew, 1969–
  City of strangers : Gulf migration and the Indian community in Bahrain / Andrew M. Gardner.
    p. cm.
  Includes bibliographical references and index.
  ISBN 978-0-8014-4882-9 (cloth : alk. paper) — ISBN 978-0-8014-7602-0 (pbk. : alk. paper)
  1. Foreign workers, East Indian—Bahrain. 2. East Indians—Bahrain. 3. Foreign workers, East Indian—Violence against—Bahrain. 4. East Indians—Violence against—Bahrain. 5. India—Emigration and immigration. 6. Bahrain—Emigration and immigration. 7. Bahrain—Ethnic relations. 8. Ethnology—Bahrain. I. Title.
    HD8668.G37 2010
    331.62'5405365—dc22   2010002267

Cornell University Press strives to use environmentally responsible suppliers and materials to the fullest extent possible in the publishing of its books. Such materials include vegetable-based, low-VOC inks and acid-free papers that are recycled, totally chlorine-free, or partly composed of nonwood fibers. For further information, visit our website at www.cornellpress.cornell.edu.

Cloth printing   10 9 8 7 6 5 4 3 2 1
Paperback printing   10 9 8 7 6 5 4 3 2 1

*For S. K. and my parents,
Gordon and Janice Gardner*

CONTENTS

Acknowledgments ix

1. Introduction: Structural Violence and Transnational Migration in the Gulf States 1
2. Pearls, Oil, and the British Empire: A Short History of Bahrain 24
3. Foreign Labor in Peril: The Indian Transnational Proletariat 49
4. Strategic Transnationalism: The Indian Diasporic Elite 71
5. The Public Sphere: Social Clubs and Voluntary Associations in the Indian Community 96
6. Contested Identities, Contested Positions: English-Language Newspapers and the Public Sphere 118
7. The Invigorated State: Transnationalism, Citizen, and State 136
8. Conclusion: Bahrain at the Vanguard of Change in the Gulf 159

Notes 165

References 175

Index 185

ACKNOWLEDGMENTS

In anthropological parlance, "key informants" are those individuals native to the communities we study who emerge as integral to the anthropologist's inquiry. Although I found many individuals willing to share their time and thoughts with me, I hesitate to call them "informants," for that title somehow seems too formal and oddly traitorous to stand for these relationships. There were many individuals whose contributions were essential to the writing of this book, but those who proved most key were foremost my friends, and our afternoons and evenings spent drinking coffee, carousing through the nightlife of Bahrain, sharing a meal, walking along the corniche, or smoking sheesha yielded a lively intellectual atmosphere that made my time on the island all the more enjoyable. With that caveat in mind, I foremost thank S.K. for taking me under his wing. A pharmacist by training, he was born with a seemingly boundless desire to make the world a better place, a trait readily apparent in his unyielding penchant for service to those less fortunate. This book would not have been possible without his help. I also thank Ashish Gorde and Dhafi al-Mannai, both good friends, and Naman Arora, a student at the Indian School who somehow found the time to serve as my field assistant. Many others helped me along the way: Dr. R. K. Hebsur, Pragati, Mohammed, Earsil, Veena, Joel, Timothy, Aisha, Suresh, Vani, and all the students in the 2003 ILA English course I taught.

Shortly before arriving in Bahrain I met with Dr. Sharon Nagy, a cultural anthropologist interested in many of the same issues that brought me to the island. What could have ended up as a difficult relationship—two ethnographers with the same interests on a small island—ended up just the opposite. Nagy's mentorship, guidance, and friendship have been an enduring and invaluable part of my life since arriving in Bahrain.

Many others offered valuable suggestions and critiques to an early version of this book. Special thanks go to Michael Bonine, Michele Gamburd, Mark Nichter, Tim Finan, Diane Austin, Katherine Holmsen, Aomar Boum, Rylan Higgins, Erin Dean, Tresa Thomas, Karen Barnett, Monica Dehart, Neha Vora, Attiya Ahmed, Noora Lori, James Onley and the many others who read early portions of this book. My colleagues at Qatar University—and particularly Drs. Ali Al Shawi and Kaltham Alghanim—have opened my eyes to the complexities of Gulf society. Fran Benson at Cornell University Press helped pull the book into shape, and several anonymous reviewers provided fantastic and insightful suggestions for the manuscript. Most important, Dr. Linda Green oversaw the research underpinning this book and helped me better understand my mission as an anthropologist. I hope she can see her mark on this work.

This book would not have been possible without institutional support from a variety of sources. Special thanks go to the Fulbright Program and, in particular, the Cultural Affairs Office at the U.S. embassy in Bahrain. Equally important was the Bahrain Training Institute, which, in conjunction with the Fulbright Program, arranged to sponsor my research on the island for 2002 and 2003. I am also grateful to the Wenner-Gren Foundation for its financial assistance in 2002 and 2003. During writing and revision I depended on the Raymond Thompson Fund and the Haury Fund at the University of Arizona, as well as a course release at the University of Puget Sound. Research in Qatar, ongoing at the date of publication, informs portions of this book. That research was supported by Georgetown University's Center for International and Regional Studies' Migrant Labor in the Persian Gulf research grant program, the Qatar National Research Fund's Undergraduate Research Experience Program, and Qatar University's Faculty Start-up grant program.

A version of chapter 3 was published in *Deported: Removal and the Regulation of Human Mobility,* edited by Nicholas DeGenova and Nathalie Peutz, pp. 196–223. Copyright 2010, Duke University Press. All rights reserved. Reprinted by permission of the publisher. Short portions of chapters 1 and 2 also were published in *Deported*. Most of chapter 4 was previously published as "Strategic Transnationalism: The Indian Diasporic Elite in Contemporary Bahrain," *City and Society* 20 (1): 54–78.

Kristin Giordano, my intrepid wife, gave me her undying support and encouragement during the many years of research and preparation behind this book. She also joined me in the field. Her perspectives on life as a foreign woman in Bahrain have leaked into my analysis, and her photographs from our time in Bahrain are the better of those that appear in this book. Finally, I thank my parents, Gordon and Janice Gardner, who tirelessly supported the long and wandering journey that led me to anthropology and, eventually, to this book.

CITY OF STRANGERS

1 INTRODUCTION

Structural Violence and Transnational Migration in the Gulf States

In the early months of 2006, newspaper headlines in the Kingdom of Bahrain reported that police, officials from the Indian embassy, and a collection of human rights activists, after receiving a tip from an undisclosed source, had converged on a scrap yard in the suburb of Hamad Town, a government-constructed quarter in the Manama suburbs where significant numbers of the citizenry's lower middle class make their home. The owner of the garage and scrap yard, it seems, had sold a work visa to an Indian laborer by the name of Karunanidhi for BD1,200 (1,200 dinars), the equivalent of US$3,189. Although many of the details remain unclear, indications suggest that Karunanidhi then paid another individual to replace him at the work site, a move that angered the owner of the establishment and issuer of the work visa. The Bahraini owner grabbed Karunanidhi—in other words, moved him by force—and put him under an overturned bathtub in the scrap yard. He then parked his jeep over the bathtub, trapping Karunanidhi underneath, locked the vehicle, and departed for Manama, the central and singular urban center on the small island. In Manama, the scrap yard owner found his way to the flat that Karunanidhi rented with a large group of other Indian men and somehow kidnapped six of the Indian laborer's roommates. Returning to the scrap yard with the men, he locked them in a large freezer, where they remained until the loose amalgamation of help—the aforementioned police force, officials, and activists—came to their rescue. All the men were freed, although their fate in the agencies and courts that govern the foreign population on the island remains in limbo. The scrap yard owner was briefly jailed and then released.

In the Gulf newspapers that carried this story, many of the articles and letters framed the case as atypical—a sponsor "gone bad"—or as the worst that might be faced by a member of the large transnational labor force on the island, while seeking a better life in the petroleum-rich nations of the Arabian Peninsula. In 2002 and 2003, however, I spent a year in Bahrain collecting ethnographic data that sought to explore the intricate matrix of relations between citizens and foreigners on the island. I spent countless hours in the labor camps, most of which are located on the distant periphery of the city, and in the decrepit urban flats, like the one described in Karunanidhi's story, that now comprise much of the central city. The story I have just related—from February 2006—fits seamlessly into the tapestry woven by the many migration narratives I heard on those evenings in the labor camps and urban flats. These narratives, along with the newspaper clippings I have collected since departing the field, abound with accounts of stabbings, murders, rape, deportation, confinement, physical abuse, confidence games, extortion, suicides, suicides under suspicious circumstances, workplace injuries, debilitating illness, and more. Moreover, although there are certainly religious, gender, and class aspects to this violence, the most reliable pattern underpinning these events pits citizens against foreign laborers.

Sadly, reliable statistical data concerning the scope of this violence are not available.[1] In the hallway outside my university office, however, I have a large bulletin board, perhaps four feet by six feet, on which I maintain a testament to the comprehensive violence committed against Indian laborers in Bahrain. The board, comprising a subset of the newspaper clippings I amassed from the local papers during my year in Bahrain, hints at the scope of the almost daily violence that plagues the Indian population of some 140,000 who make their home, however temporary, on the island. In light of this small edifice to the Indian experience in the Gulf, the case with which I began this volume is but one episode in the ongoing, commonplace experience of foreigners on the small island, and hence is in my mind far from anecdotal. Rather, the case of Karunanidhi and his time under a junkyard bathtub is symptomatic of the *structural violence* endemic to the system by which the large transnational labor force that currently works in the Gulf is managed and controlled in Bahrain and all the Gulf states.

Unpacking and applying the concept of structural violence is one of the principal tasks of this book. To be clear from the outset, however, in lodging the experiences of the men and women I encountered in the larger

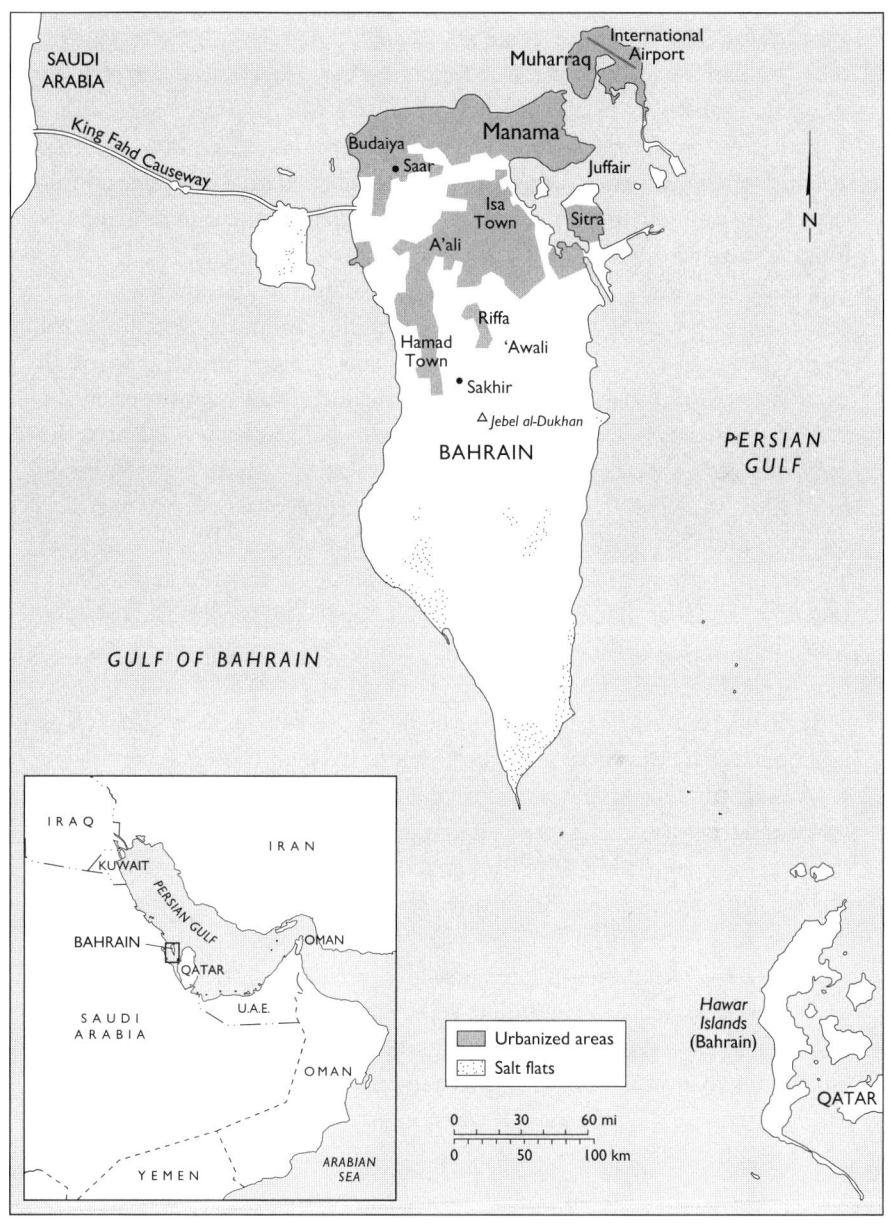

Figure 1.1. Map of Bahrain.

rubric of structural violence, I do not intend to imply that we should ignore the agency exerted in the scenario I've just described, or in the scenarios that litter this book: we ought not ignore the basic fact that these scenarios are composed of humans choosing to abuse, exploit, maim, and dominate other humans. Rather, I seek to couple that basic fact with an analysis of the structural forces that cause, permit, encourage, or are in some other way involved in the production of violence between citizen and foreigner in Bahrain. In the final accounting, the episodic violence levied against foreigners in Bahrain becomes one facet of the more comprehensive structural forces that govern foreign labor in the Gulf states.

The central mission of the anthropologist remains explication, and typically the explication of lives distant and different from those of the intended reader. The conceptual framework of structural violence, which I explore in detail, provides an analytic foundation from which I work outward in scope and, to some degree, backward in time. From that foundation I peer at the decisions and contexts that brought the men and women I came to know from India to the Gulf, at their experiences upon arrival in Bahrain, and at the strategies they deploy against the difficulties they face while abroad. I also examine the contours of the Bahraini state itself, the ongoing articulation of a particular idea of modernity in the Gulf, and the intricacies of the concept of citizenship as they have evolved in dialectic with the extraordinary flow of foreign labor to the island.

Perhaps the greatest danger with the thesis this book presents rests in its potential to fall in lockstep with the Orientalist punditry recently resurgent in Western public discourse. I am particularly concerned with potential misreadings of the theses presented here that suggest that the source of the structural violence I describe somehow inheres in the culture or character of the peoples of the Gulf. Instead, the political economic framework at the core of my analysis should make clear that although the structural violence I describe draws on the particular history and cultural framework of the Bahraini people, its ultimate source has more to do with the extension and expansion of a global labor market and neoliberal ideology to the Gulf states than with any particular qualities of Bahraini culture. The fact that structural violence seems to accompany the increasing proliferation of transnational movement should be a point familiar to scholars whose work concerns the United States' southern border, or African migration to Europe, or the countless other movements that have come to typify the contemporary historical juncture.

Ethnography and Structural Violence

For much of its early history, the discipline of anthropology was principally concerned with the forces and social components that constructed and replicated harmonious and stable societies. For Émile Durkheim and other functionalists, the organic analogy provided the foundation for their understanding of society: particular aspects of society—religion, an educational system, family and kinship, and so forth—were viewed as analogous to organs of the body, working together to produce a static equilibrium. In functionalist analysis, each of those social components plays some particular role in the survival and replication of the social whole. Deviance, violence, and other nefarious social forces were seen as abnormal, as a breakdown in the status quo, or as circumstances produced by an unusual set of external conditions.

In that light, the shift of the anthropological lens to power and violence can be seen as the culmination of a disciplinary corrective, one that moves away from idealistic portraits of harmonious social forms and directly addresses the dilemmas, social problems, and rampant poverty observable in the contemporary world. The exertion of power and the resulting violence that oftentimes accompanies it are no longer portrayed as strange or extraordinary circumstances but rather have become essential focal points in the analytic mission of contemporary anthropology. In addition to positing ruptures and social dissonance as a seemingly constant facet of human life, this corrective also challenged the underlying functionalist premise that societies were best comprehended as unconnected, discrete social wholes. Eric Wolf, Sidney Mintz, and a strong cohort of other anthropologists working in the second half of the twentieth century built upon a political economic framework in arguing that change and interaction, often on a global scale, were central facets of the historical period. These approaches remain key in understanding the transnational context of the contemporary era.

Many of these ideas were distilled by William Roseberry, a scholar who envisioned an anthropology that manifests "an intellectual commitment to the understanding, analysis, and explication of the relations and structures of power in, through, and against which ordinary people live their lives.... The routes toward an analysis of power can be various, from the political-economic analysis of the development of capitalism in a specific place, to the symbolic analysis of the exercise of power in a colonial state, to a life history of a person who experiences power from a particular position, in a particular way" (Roseberry 1996, 6).

The concept of structural violence provides one of many possible pathways to these goals. First purveyed by Johan Galtung (1969) as a way of connecting the poverty and inequality experienced by legions in the world to the intricate mechanics of the global political economy, the concept's key components remain in place today. That extreme poverty and social marginalization characterize the lives of those peoples traditionally found in the anthropological lens has been observed by Farmer (2004, 307) but was perhaps most eloquently stated by Bourgois when he said that, "with few exceptions, the traditional, noble, 'exotic' subjects of anthropology have today emerged as the most malnourished, politically repressed, economically exploited humans on earth" (1991, 113). As a conceptual framework, structural violence provides a tool for connecting the everyday violence of those conditions with their systematic and broad sources.

As Farmer states, the concept of structural violence is configured to examine the social machinery of oppression (2004, 307). Within this larger framework there are slight variations in focus. For Philippe Bourgois and Paul Farmer, the focus remains squarely upon the political economic relations that render these structural, violent results. For Nancy Scheper-Hughes, structural violence points to more discursive and ideological terrain—to the processes by which everyday violence is normalized and naturalized in public consciousness. She targets "the invisible social machinery of inequality that reproduce social relations of exclusion and marginalization via ideologies, stigmas, and dangerous discourses...attendant to race, class, sex, and other invidious distinctions" (Scheper-Hughes 2004, 13). Alternatively, for Daniel Goldstein (2004) the violent lynchings he observed in Cochabamba City, Bolivia, were best understood through their performative function as public spectacles through which community and collectivity were delineated. In spite of these differences, these and the many other texts concerned with theorizing violence are a testament to the diverse paths to the analysis of power sketched by William Roseberry. All share a concern for power, inequality, and the backdrop of a global, capitalist political economy that renders a particular terrain of suffering.

Discussions of structural violence often elide Eric Wolf's contribution to the topic—a contribution that I find particularly clear. In his final book, Wolf described power in terms of four valences, or modalities, woven into social relations. The first is the power that individuals bring to their interactions with other individuals in the world. The second is the "power manifested in interactions and transactions among people and refers to the ability of an *ego* to impose its will in social action upon an *alter*" (Wolf 1999, 5). For Wolf, the third modality of power consists of the ability to manipulate and control the contexts and settings in which those interactions occur, a mode he refers to as organizational or tactical power. Working outward in scope, he concludes with a description of structural power, or "the power manifest in relationships that not only operates within settings and domains but also organizes and orchestrates the settings themselves" (5). It is this notion of power, and particularly the notion of a set of forces *orchestrating* relations between foreigners and citizens, that guides my analysis in this book.[2]

Wolf's valenced conception of power provides the impetus for the theoretical revision I use in this book. For the progenitors of the concept, structural violence is typically distinguishable from other forms of violence, and particularly from the everyday, interpersonal violence that purportedly inheres more closely to the agency of those who deliver that violence. This rendition of structural violence is entirely useful: it is adept at connecting broad structural forces and political economic conditions to the suffering that we increasingly encounter in the regions and places where many anthropologists work.[3] The same rendition of structural violence helps delineate the forces that push many of the men and women described in this book out of India and across the Arabian Sea, for their journey and the suffering they often endure while abroad are, certainly, part of a coping strategy connected to forces well beyond the ambit of their everyday lives. But Wolf's notion of the orchestration at work in this process also provides an opportunity to connect the everyday, interpersonal violence and suffering many of the foreign workers in the Gulf states endure with the structural arrangements that so intricately construct, limit, and govern their existence in the Gulf. This marriage of Wolf's notion of structural power with structural violence opens another path to examine "how power operates not only on the global scale but in the daily lives of the people with whom anthropologists work" (Green 2004, 319).

Social Research in the Gulf States

My interest in transnational migration first bloomed during a two-week stay in Jeddah, the cosmopolitan hub of Saudi Arabia perched on the shores of the Red Sea. There I was the junior member of a team of ethnographers commissioned to examine the impact of the 1991–92 Iraqi conflict on the

Bedouin nomads of the Kingdom of Saudi Arabia's Eastern Province. When the team arrived in Jeddah, we discovered that the various bureaucracies overseeing our work had yet to procure the money and documents necessary for our trip to the remote deserts to the east. The government offices seemed to close around one in the afternoon—or at least the individuals we needed to speak with were absent after that—so in the afternoons I wandered the center of the city, strolling through the winding streets and alleys of the central souk, or marketplace, and basked in the air-conditioned environs of the modern shopping malls that had arisen around the aging center of the city.

In those first days in the Middle East, I was astounded by how infrequently I encountered Saudis in Saudi Arabia. In the stores of the souk I met Indian, Pakistani, and Bangladeshi merchants; in the hotel the Filipino concierges greeted me in English. One evening, near the city center and in search of an Internet connection, I found my way to a large bowling alley and, just before the doors were locked for the evening prayer, I dodged inside. There I found myself amid the playoffs of a Filipino bowling league. By the time we left Jeddah for the deserts to the east, I had met men from a dozen different nations, all there to make a better life for themselves and their families back home. Yet my first look into the world of Gulf migration hardly ended at the city limits. In the weeks that followed, we spent our days on the dirt tracks that lace all points of the eastern deserts together, building an ethnographic foundation for a project I later described in two articles (Gardner 2004; Gardner and Finan 2004). Here we found migrant laborers alone on the sands of the desert, enmeshed in the livelihood systems of the Bedouin nomads, tending herds of sheep, goats, or camels for Bedouin families now relocated to nearby towns.

It was a small set of memorable experiences—speaking with two Sudanese men alone at a gas station waypoint in the middle of the great eastern deserts of Arabia, and then again with a particular pair of Indian shopkeepers of central Jeddah—that first spurred my interest in this flow of transnational labor. In its original form, the research proposal I configured to the Fulbright Program proposed a project in the Kingdom of Saudi Arabia. After two or three months of work on the proposal, I began communicating with my professional contacts in the kingdom, and they rapidly noted the naiveté of the document I had constructed: they informed me that the Saudi government would never allow this research to be conducted. Under the guidance of my advisers I reworked the proposal for Oman. Meanwhile, on the heels of two months of intensive language training in the United Arab Emirates, I prepared a second proposal to the

Wenner-Gren Foundation to conduct research in Dubai, the cosmopolitan and transnational apex of the contemporary Gulf (and a city where, according to my contacts in Bahrain, expatriates outnumber citizens ten to one).

Despite the fact that my proposal was initially approved by the U.S. Fulbright Program, a month later I received word that the program's regional administrators were unable to find an institution in Oman willing to sponsor this particular research. Rather than decline the proposal altogether, a senior administrator had taken a personal interest in my project, and through her efforts the Fulbright Program "shopped" my proposal to the other petroleum-rich Gulf nations, all of which hosted large foreign communities. Two months before my slated departure—and amid my comprehensive exams—I was informed that although the University of Bahrain had also declined to sponsor my research, the director of the Bahrain Training Institute (a former Fulbrighter himself) would provide institutional sponsorship for my study.[4] In that same window of time, I received word from Wenner-Gren that they too had approved my proposal for research in the United Arab Emirates. After a brief discussion with them about the status of my Fulbright proposal, I reconfigured the Wenner-Gren proposal to cover some of the ancillary operating costs and expenditures not covered by the Fulbright grant and secured their permission to conduct my research in Bahrain. With less than two months to spare, I began checking out books from the library about Bahrain and pored over the brief chapter on Bahrain in the Lonely Planet travel guide.

Although my literature review prior to departure was piecemeal, I was surprised to discover that I was not the first to follow this circuitous path to Bahrain. In the early 1980s, Robert Lee Franklin, an anthropology student at Harvard, configured a research project to be conducted in Iran. When the revolution broke out, he shifted his destination to Bahrain, a safe haven in the Gulf where he might study the large Shi'ite community, many of whose members continue to identify themselves as ethnically Persian. Amid the tensions between the Sunni leadership and the Shi'ite majority (ongoing to this day), the government of Bahrain deemed this topic too sensitive. Franklin reconfigured his research project and emerged with "a study of the foreign communities in Bahrain, and of the Indian community in particular" (1985, 1), producing what is to date the sole ethnographic portrait of the Indian community in the Kingdom of Bahrain.

It was only upon my return from the Gulf, and through the slow process of preparing my conclusions, that I came to realize how the story of my own research project fits within the larger framework of the social

Figure 1.2. South Asian laborers fill the streets of Manama's central souk on Friday afternoons. Photograph by Kristin Giordano.

sciences in the Gulf. This framework can be grasped as a set of three interrelated factors that, together, are responsible for the dearth of ethnographically informed literature concerning the transnational populations in the Gulf states (see also Dresch 2005, 1). First, many of the nations in the Gulf have a reputation, partly deserved, for being inhospitable to social science research. As my own experiences suggest, funding and support—and particularly support from local institutions—remain relatively difficult to secure. Combined with the fact that few of the Gulf states release basic demographic data concerning the scope and constitution of the foreign populations at work there, the handful of scholars who remain focused on transnationalism in the region have struggled to construct a basic foundation from which research might build.

Second, the nations of the contemporary Gulf have long been viewed as an exception to the norm of the Middle East. As wealthy, highly urbanized, and cosmopolitan global crossroads where transmigrant populations constitute a majority of the workforce and, in some instances, an absolute majority of the population, the sociocultural matrix of the Gulf states fits poorly with the popular image of Middle Eastern heritage and culture, a portrayal that recycles Orientalist tropes through its typical focus on the rural Bedouin traditions of the region. The fact that the stagnant cultural images of camel herds, woolen tents, and coffee pots predominate in the way the Gulf states represent themselves only further confuses the issue and yields some insight into the processes of auto-Orientalism that accompany Asia's increasingly dense interconnections with the global system (see Mazzarella 2003, 138–45).[5] Rather than view the contemporary Gulf as an opportunity to redirect Middle East studies, many scholars seem content with the ongoing marginalization of the Gulf states in the literature. Study of the Gulf states remains overshadowed by work on the Levant and North Africa, and what analyses of the Gulf do exist are dominated by political scientists, economists, and security specialists, all to the exclusion of a robust and detailed analysis of everyday life in the cities of the Gulf.

Finally, the extraordinarily transnational character of Gulf societies has produced a unique set of difficulties in the development of a cohesive social science literature. On the one hand, the foreign populations in the Gulf states are itinerant and rapidly shifting. Both these conditions quickly render synchronic portrayals of Gulf society obsolete, as the basic geography of the global labor supply streaming to the Gulf has continued to shift rapidly over the past decades. At the same time, ethnographic literature concerned with those populations at work in the Gulf is often distributed across the transnational divide. A small handful of scholars have explored the lived experiences of transnational laborers in the Gulf states (Longva 1997; Nagy 1998; Khalaf and Alkobaisi 1999; Leonard 2002, 2003; Strobl 2009). More common are ethnographically informed works that peer at the experiences of those in the Gulf from the communities and regions from which they come (e.g., Gamburd 2000; Osella and Osella 2000a, 2000b; Silvey 2004).

All of these factors have conspired to marginalize social scientific analyses of the Gulf. The dearth of ethnographically informed work has also truncated its contribution to the burgeoning literature concerning transnationalism and globalization. These latter topics have emerged as central in anthropology and related social sciences, yet the bulk of the ethnographies and case studies that inform that literature concern populations and processes with one endpoint in the developed and democratic states of the global north. For vast numbers of people in the contemporary world, however, the Gulf states represent the singular and most important transnational node in their livelihood strategies. Estimates from 1997 suggest that the Gulf Cooperation Council states host well over 10 million foreign workers (Kapiszewski 2001, 39; 2006, 4). The transnational movement behind this number involves millions and millions of families and countless communities in South Asia, Africa, and other points around the globe. Foreign labor constitutes a majority of the workforce in all the Gulf states, and an absolute majority of the population in Kuwait, Qatar, and the United Arab Emirates. Moreover, the movement of people to and from the Gulf states was produced in dialectic with the processes and forces that have now lodged the cities of the Arabian coast as truly global cities—as central nodes in the Asian financescape and as important locations in the production of global culture. Raising the profile of the Gulf peoples and cities in the ongoing assembly of a literature concerned with transnationalism can be seen as another undergirding purpose of the ethnography presented here.

LANGUAGE AND FIELDWORK IN BAHRAIN

Seminal anthropologist Bronislaw Malinowski's call to render the "verbal contour of native thought as precisely as possible" represented a watershed moment in the development of a codified set of anthropological methods (1922, 23). Gone were the days of the armchair anthropologists and their theorizing, reliant as it was on the secondhand observations of missionaries and colonial emissaries. Soon the days of anthropology from the colonial verandah, an enterprise that brought only fleeting contact with the peoples anthropologists sought to study, would also end. Malinowski's sentiment, reinforced by W. H. R. Rivers and Franz Boas, emerged as central to the journey anthropologists take, a journey outside the synergy of the anthropologist's native language and thought, and into the mental worlds of those they wish to know. The conviction that language is central to the sentiments, expressions, emotions, thoughts, and behavior of human beings remains a cornerstone to the discipline. The case of my work in Bahrain is a caveat to this tenet, but a challenge to its underlying premise—that the boundaries of language neatly coincide with the boundaries of culture. In Bahrain, a regional hub of transnational migratory conduits for centuries, complex and varied patterns of language use mark the island as a bellwether to linguistic shifts now endemic to capitalism's expansion around the globe.

The official language of the Kingdom of Bahrain is Arabic. Although I was never fluent, my own abilities in that language were at their zenith upon arrival on the island. Yet from my first moments on the island, my greetings in Arabic commonly drew an appreciative smile from locals, followed by a reply in English. In fact, English is commonly spoken in many of the transnational spaces and places where foreigners and citizens interact. The prevalence of English certainly owes much to the dominion of the British Empire, for Bahrain played a central role in what James Onley (2007) has described as British India's "informal empire." The bureaucratic hallways of the quasi-colonial apparatus brought English to the island. Furthermore, because Bahrain's relations with the British Empire were managed through British India, Bahrain also drew colonial transmigrants from South Asia. Indians arrived to serve as clerks, accountants, quartermasters, and security guards in the second wave of migration at the turn of the nineteenth century. The language of that bureaucracy and those early colonial transmigrants carried English to the streets of Manama.

In the 1950s and 1960s, as Bahrain parlayed its role as the nexus of relations between the Gulf and the West into its position as the center of Gulf finance and management, the predominance of English was again reinforced. The nation's movement into the English-speaking financescapes of the now-global political economy coincided with the increasing reach of global mediascapes: English and American television programs, movies, and news permeated the lives of those on the island.[6] Today, the impact of global culture on Bahrain is pervasive. In my year in Bahrain, the sounds of the street included Eminem's Detroit-based rap and the mesmerizing buzz of British-born Panjabi MC's "Mundian to Bach Ke," featuring Brooklyn-born Jay-Z and a prominent sample from the television show *Knight Rider*, the David Hasselhoff series that so captivated my younger brother in the early 1980s. LaserVision, the DVD store around the corner from my flat, was widely known to have one of the best collections of new American movies, and at night cars from around the island blocked the narrow streets around its entrance as Bahrainis and expatriates selected the latest releases from the United States and other points abroad.

Although the predominance of English owes much to the historical processes I've described, perhaps the strongest argument rests in the transnational milieu itself. In a context in which nearly half the population are foreign-born expatriates, including Indians, Bangladeshis, Pakistanis, Sri Lankans, Filipinos, Indonesians, Nepalese, South Africans, Egyptians, Britishers (as they are called on the island), Americans, and countless others, English is increasingly the basic means of communication among foreign communities. All members of the professional class of the Indian diaspora speak English, and its influence now reaches into the laboring class. Midway through my time in Bahrain, I volunteered to teach an introductory English course to Indian laborers as part of the community service organized by the Indian Ladies Association. Before the first class was held, dozens of laborers had to be turned away, and for the eight-week duration my classroom was always full.

At the same time, the predominance of English on the island should not eclipse the other important and interesting patterns of language use concurrent with the processes I've described. Bahrain, like all the states of the Gulf Cooperation Council, is ruled by a Sunni elite.[7] Only in Bahrain, however, does that Sunni elite rule over a Shi'ite majority, many of whom trace their familial heritage to Iran. Powerful Shi'ite families still foster their Persian identity, and Persian is widely spoken within this subcommunity. Moreover, the long-standing connections between Bahrain and the Indian Subcontinent have lodged both Hindi and Malayalam in the linguistic palette of contemporary Bahrain. The popularity of Hindi movies and other media, the historic presence of Hindi-speaking bureaucrats and merchants, and the presence of Hindi- or Malayalam-speaking housemaids and nannies in Bahraini households have pushed these languages to prominence as well.

Even within the expatriate labor camps (where the largest and poorest contingent of the Indian community lives), rapid changes and linguistic struggle seem to be characteristic. The majority of Indian laborers who arrived over the last two decades come from the southern state of Kerala, where Malayalam is the predominant language, and few of them are entirely fluent in Hindi. Upon arrival, many begin to pick up bits of Arabic and English in order to communicate with sponsors, bosses, managers, and customers. Owing to the Keralites' numerical prominence within the larger Indian community, those from other Indian states might begin to learn Malayalam. Malayalam is predominant enough that many Bahraini government documents have been published in Arabic, English, and Malayalam.[8]

Among the elite classes of the Indian diaspora, altogether different forces are driving linguistic change. Unlike the transnational working class, most members of the diasporic elite arrive on the island with families in tow, and regardless of their state of origin their children are taught in English and Hindi at the various Indian schools on the island. Often their mother tongue is consciously spoken in the household—the only refuge from the confusing plurality of languages in the city outside. Conversely, a handful of the most powerful Indian families have attempted to master Arabic as part of their attempt to secure Bahraini citizenship.[9]

In the complex linguistic terrain of the contemporary Gulf, I ended up conducting a majority of my interviews in English. If I used a translator, that translator was also Indian, so in the final form all the interviews were recorded in some version of English. I toyed with the idea of cleaning up the grammar and syntax of these quotes to better fit the American ear, but in the end I decided to reproduce the quotations much as I received them. Reading over the interviews, there are few junctures where the meaning is not clear, and with the larger topics of transnationalism and globalization lurking behind this ethnography, the point is this: the "verbal contour of native thought," to again quote Malinowski, is in linguistic flux, a process wrought by the transnational processes described here. The inability to communicate, the struggle to learn the necessary bits and pieces of three or four different languages—these processes characterize the mental worlds of all inhabitants of the small island, and particularly those of the many diasporic communities that make their home in the city.

Research Methods

Like most anthropologists before me, those first weeks in the field were a bewildering experience. I spent many of my nights alone in my small flat, or, alternatively, on long walks through the city. Peering into shop windows or restaurants, I saw men from around the world immersed in conversations, yelling and laughing, arguing, engaged in life. Outside that window I was not only outside their "culture," but I was also beleaguered by my anthropological lens, whose gaze is at once on others and on oneself. By day I struggled with real dilemmas of conducting research in Bahrain: my visa status, arranged by the Fulbright Program and the Bahrain Training Institute (my host institution), was classified as a tourist/visitor, forcing me periodically to fly to Qatar and back for renewal. This situation was finally remedied after four trips to and from the airport in Doha. With nothing but a temporary visitor's visa, I was unable to obtain the Central Population Register card, or CPR, the keystone to one's bureaucratic identity on the island and necessary for day-to-day activities such as paying bills, purchasing a mobile phone, and securing utilities.

All of these problems were eventually solved, and it was only then that I began to realize that the issues I had faced—the feelings of homesickness, the struggles to work through the government's bureaucracy, the feeling of being an outsider to the thousands of urban lives going on around me—were actually an important form of participant observation unique to the transnational milieu I was studying. On an island like Bahrain, where hundreds of laborers and professionals from around the world arrive and depart every day, the experience of finding one's way into the cultures and communities of the island is as much a part of the transnational experience as actually "belonging."

My participant observation included numerous other activities. Shortly after arriving on the island, I joined the Manama Toastmasters, a cosmopolitan group of mostly professionals who sought to improve their "leadership skills, self-confidence and communication through public speaking," a journey they take in English.[10] I also joined the Riffa chapter of the Lions Club, a group of mostly Muslim Indian and Pakistani men (and several women) committed to improving the health and welfare of those less fortunate. I spent countless hours at the many Indian social clubs on the island, including the first and largest of them all, the Indian Club. I attended numerous parties and events organized by these clubs for the laborers, and in conjunction with the Indian Ladies Association I taught the aforementioned introductory English course to expatriate Indian laborers. Eventually, these associations and institutions emerged as one of the focal points of my research on the island.

I also got to know many of the expatriate instructors at the Bahrain Training Institute, who, in somewhat ironic fashion, serve on the frontlines of the Ministry of Labor and Social Affairs' attempts to forge an educated and skilled workforce capable of replacing the large contingents of foreigners on the island. Through all these channels, I seemed to have an endless list of people to interview, most of whom belonged to the diaspora's middle and upper class—the successful businessmen and, less frequently, professional women, as well as the merchant families with long-standing ties to the island. All of these interviews were conducted in English. In my first visits with participants I used a semistructured interview format that explored a sequence of topics, including the basis of their decision to migrate, recollections of their arrival in Bahrain, a description of their participation and membership in social clubs and other organizations, the primary challenges they face, narratives about their experiences of periodic trips back to India, and their aspirations for the future. The bulk of the interviews I recorded were what Karen Leonard (1999, 45) calls "experience narratives," emphasizing family and individual migration experiences.

Follow-up interviews were often unstructured and focused on particular gaps in my understanding of their individual and collective experiences.

My contact with the laboring class was much more difficult to achieve. At the beginning of my time in Bahrain, I spoke with several custodians and cafeteria staff at the Bahrain Training Institute. However, my failed attempts to befriend and interview Salma Bala, the maven of Indian expatriate activism on the island at that time, left me adrift for the better part of a month. Two months into my fieldwork I met a young Tamil pharmacist named Santosh.[11] Through his own ingenuity and desire, he had reconfigured his elected position at one of the Indian social clubs on the island into a social service position. He spent many of his evenings visiting labor camps, dealing directly with the sorts of problems laborers encounter in the difficult environment of Bahrain. Our friendship rapidly bloomed, and once or twice a week I would accompany him to the labor camps. Here too I conducted interviews based on the "experience narratives" template, and I worked closely with Santosh to refine the interview guide we used in the camps. We met with these men in the evenings after they had returned, tired and hungry, from a long day of labor in the hot sun. Typically we sat with ten or twelve men, and after explaining the purpose of the project and reviewing our promise of confidentiality, we sought one particular individual to interview. Upon returning to the same camp, we would occasionally continue talking with the same individual; other times, we sought a new individual interested in sharing his migration experience. Typically many men would gather around us in the course of the conversation, and what often began as an individual interview would eventually end in the form of a focus group. All in all, few of these interviews were conducted in English: I relied on Santosh's linguistic facility to work through the Tamil, Malayalam, Kannada, Hindi, and other languages we encountered in these trips. Although we offered no remuneration for participation in these interviews, we often brought a large bag of rice and two-dozen packets of fruit juice for the men as a token of our gratitude.

While most of my contact with the laboring class of the Indian diaspora drew upon Santosh's network of contacts, I also had the chance to teach the aforementioned introductory English course, sponsored by the Indian Ladies Association, to approximately forty men and women who, roughly, fit into the laboring class of the Indian community. My students—clerks, storekeepers, concierges, drivers, electricians—were economically one step above the manual laborers I encountered in the camps, and all were eager to improve their English. Any notion that teaching the course was a chore

Figure 1.3. Interview at a labor camp. Photographer unknown.

was cast aside at our first meeting. The students arrived in the evening, always punctual, and often after a ten- or twelve-hour workday. Our conversations in class and afterward provided me with another set of perspectives on the dilemmas and tribulations of Indian transmigration.

Finally, I interviewed numerous Bahrainis during my time on the island. Some of these interviews were with government officials charged with some aspect of managing the bureaucratic structure of migration. Other interviews were with Bahrainis from all walks of life. I had a small group of Bahraini friends with whom I regularly spent time—we hung around the horse track on the weekend, meandered through the malls and markets of the island by evening, or wandered out to the southern deserts and beaches on Friday afternoons. Their perspectives on work and life on the island came to play a central role in my portrayal of the dilemmas faced by citizen-youth (a topic explored at length in chap. 7). With most of these individuals, I employed unstructured interviews that explored their perspectives on the presence of such a large migrant population in their midst, their perceptions of the effect of this population on Bahraini society and culture, and the government's efforts to "localize" the workforce.

Most of the individuals with whom I spoke were men. The flow of transnational labor to the small island is far from gender balanced: the great majority of the arrivals from India are men, both single and married, who arrive with the idea of staying a few years, sending money home, and saving for a wedding, a business, farmland, or a sibling's education. This is not to say that women do not arrive to work on the island, for many do. One of the largest occupational segments of the foreign female expatriate population is made up of domestic workers, estimated to number between 30,000 and 50,000 in Bahrain (Strobl 2009). Although I spoke with and observed these women on several occasions, direct access to the population of domestic workers is difficult to secure, for their time and movements are the most strictly controlled. Some Indian women arrive on the island as professionals—employees like any other—and some arrive on a spousal visa. Many members of these latter categories play powerful social and professional roles within the diaspora through their occupations, churches, temples, schools, social clubs, and voluntary associations. I also befriended and spoke with numerous second-generation Indian women, the daughters of families that had made their home on the island for decades or longer. My opportunities to meet and interview Bahraini women were few, although through my contacts at the University of Bahrain I was able to meet a handful of female students. Our interactions fell short of public meetings, however; instead, we had long discussions over our mobile phones, taking advantage of the freedoms offered by this new technology.

Although many of the men and women I spoke with insisted that their comments were "on the record," I have given them pseudonyms, with the exception of those holding official posts at the various embassies and Bahraini government offices, or other public positions. In part, these pseudonyms are to protect the participants from potential repercussions, be it from their Bahraini sponsors, other members of the expatriate community, their employers, or, in some cases, their families and friends. This issue is particularly critical to the Indian laborers. A question to an Indian laborer regarding the problems encountered in the workplace, for example, would often be followed by silence, a furtive look over the shoulder to make sure no one outside their close circle of friends was present, and then an answer. The reasons for the clandestine character of the interviews should be evident well before the conclusion of this book: for many of these men, their livelihoods and those of their families hang by a thin thread and, more specifically, are heavily dependent on the goodwill of their citizen-sponsor. My presence in the labor camps was unusual, to say the least, and the anonymity guaranteed to the men who shared their stories with me only partly redresses the risks they took in simply speaking with me.

In the final accounting, I conducted a total of sixty-six formal, semi-structured interviews. Eight of these were with women. Most were also with individuals of Indian descent, although they may have possessed a Canadian, Bahraini, Australian, American, or other passport. Of the remainder of that total, seven of these full interviews were with Bahraini citizens, and five were with individuals from other transmigrant communities on the island. Together, these migration "experience narratives" are the foundation of my ethnographic data. I have also made significant use of my field notes, which include the details of interactions, conversations, and shorter interviews with hundreds of other individuals on the island. I regularly attended meetings and other social gatherings, and the minutiae of those experiences, also recorded in my field notes, pervade this study. I maintained a set of clippings from two newspapers on the island, both of which provided a wealth of detail about the transmigrant experience. Finally, I have continued to correspond with many of the individuals I met during my stay on the island, and in that sense, I am still collecting data.

AN OVERVIEW OF THE CHAPTERS

In chapter 2, I posit the history of Asian transmigration to Bahrain as composed of three distinct periods. For centuries, South Asian merchants were well entrenched on the island, moving pearls (Bahrain's principal pre-oil export) eastward and various foodstuffs from the Subcontinent to the Gulf. Second, beginning in the late 1800s, the British colonial apparatus drew increasing numbers of Indian bureaucrats and, later, engineers to the island. Finally, following the OPEC embargo, Bahrain implemented a vast number of infrastructural modernization projects and drew labor from South Asia to complete these projects. Underpinning these changes and expansion of the conduits connecting South Asia and Bahrain is the continuity of the *kafala* system, a historic arrangement and practice that, while grounded in Islamic Law, was codified through the practice of indentured servitude that typified the pearling mode of production. Understanding the history of the *kafala* system helps us better comprehend its contemporary structure and expression—a story that takes up many of the following chapters. The genealogy of the *kafala* also helps explain the emergence of the public sector as the domain of the citizenry and the private sector as the domain of the foreign population, a binary that recurs in my analysis of the machinery of structural violence in Bahrain.

Chapter 3 begins with another story of violence levied by citizens against the poorest of the Indian laborers. I use this story as a springboard toward a more comprehensive portrayal of deportation and the production of "illegality" as both an everyday aspect of a foreign laborer's life and also as an *industry* from which citizen-sponsors profit. Deportation (and more specifically, deportability) also provides an entry point into the multifaceted and systemic aspects of the structure of dominance constructed by citizens and the state to govern the foreign population on the island. Using several more migration narratives, I map the machinery of the structural violence that shapes the experience of this transnational proletariat. That machinery includes the preestablished debts with which most transmigrants arrive, the sponsor's control of the worker's passport, the linguistic and cultural barriers maintained by citizens and state, and the governance of workers' movement on the island.

Although the majority of the Indian population on the island work as manual laborers or low-level clerks (a *transnational proletariat*), there is a substantial and highly visible diasporic middle class as well. In chapter 4, I explore how the structural violence I have portrayed as shaping the lives of this transnational proletariat also shapes the lives of this middle class. I ask whether members of this latter group—who have more resources, more strategic options, and more cultural capital—are able to mitigate the impact of this dominance. Through a detailed presentation of the narratives I collected in Bahrain, I conclude that although members of the middle class face a different set of pressures, this *diasporic elite* also faces the structural violence endemic to the matrix of the kafala.

In the difficult context of Bahrain, foreign workers generally face a repressive and fairly comprehensive form of dominance. Individually, of course, they strategically respond and challenge the limitations imposed on them. They also, however, work collectively. In chapter 5 I consider the role of the wide variety of diasporic social clubs and voluntary organizations in achieving these goals. Although outright political activity by the diasporic communities is prohibited, these various social clubs—regional clubs such as the Kerala Samjam, national clubs such as the Indian Club, and voluntary associations such as the Lions Club and Toastmasters—provide a basic social fabric for individuals to connect with other individuals, to collectively solve the various dilemmas they face, and to reach out to the poorest members of the Indian transnational proletariat.

My analysis of those clubs and associations provides one angle on the complex public sphere rendered by the heterogeneous demographics and rapid change in the region. I continue mining that vein in chapter 6, a chapter devoted to the English-language newspapers on the island. Citizens, foreigners, and the state use the English-language newspapers as a public forum to promote a particular vision of Bahrain's future, to establish and negotiate their own collective identities, and to assert particular frameworks for understanding the dilemmas both foreigners and citizens face. These newspapers reveal the frictions generated by the complex and heterogeneous cultural space of contemporary Bahrain.

In chapter 7, the final ethnographically informed chapter, I turn to an analysis of the Bahraini citizenry. Because I devote the bulk of this volume to the experiences of foreigners on the island, I risk leaving the reader with a shallow and undeserved portrayal of the Bahraini citizen as nothing more than the vessel through which this structural violence against foreign workers is deployed. In this chapter I examine that citizenry, principally along the lines of class and sect, in order to better understand who exactly is being served by the migration industry on the island. My examination proposes that the citizenry's lives have been reshaped by the presence of a large transnational population in Bahrain. I conclude this chapter with an analysis that suggests that the long-standing association of the public sector with native workers and the private sector with foreign workers, along with the structural arrangements of the kafala system, can be understood as part of the nation's struggle against and resistance to the calculus of globalization. These arrangements, while certainly producing a systemic and structural violence that impacts foreigners on the island, are at the same time a mechanism that allows the state and its citizenry to host (and profit from) the global economy without submitting to its logic.

Concluding Remarks

As an ethnographic text, this book focuses on a particular group of people at a particular point in time. The core of my ethnographic data comes from 2002 and 2003. From that foundation, however, I incorporate events and occurrences from the years that followed my fieldwork into my analysis. I also use the experiences of these Indian men and women to examine and explore the structure of the Bahraini citizenry and state. At the current juncture, the most pressing need in the Gulf is for more research—more investigations into different communities and different aspects of the experiences of transnational migrants in the region, more inquiry into the impact of the global economic downturn on these migration flows, more investigation of the citizens' attitudes about the foreign presence in the region.

Although there is still much work to be done, the experiences of the Indian men and women in Bahrain are strongly representative of the experiences of South Asians in all the Gulf Cooperation Council states. The stories I have heard from South Asian men and women in Saudi Arabia (2000), the United Arab Emirates (2002), and Qatar (2008–present) would fit seamlessly into this book.

I am less secure with the argument that one might extrapolate the experiences of these Indian transmigrants to populations from sending states outside of South Asia. In early 2009, for example, I began spending some of my weekends visiting a particular labor camp on the outskirts of Doha, Qatar. All the men in this camp work for a single company. Roughly half the men are Egyptian, whereas the other half are Asian—from Sri Lanka, Nepal, India, Bangladesh, and the Philippines. The friction between these two contingents is palpable, and my South Asian contacts in the camp have described at length the perceived advantages of foreign workers who share a language, religion, ethnicity, and (to some degree) culture with the citizens of the country. As my contacts report, the Egyptian men, all of whom work in the same positions as their South Asian counterparts, receive higher pay and more benefits, and enjoy more freedoms than their South Asian counterparts. To date there is little ethnographically grounded work to help us understand the experiences of these other communities, but anecdotal evidence suggests significant differences in the experiences of other foreign contingents in the Gulf states. Even this anecdotal evidence, however, suggests a substantially different migration experience than that of the South Asian men and women described in this book.

Finally, Bahrain has recently announced its intention to dismantle portions of the sponsorship system. What has widely been reported as a wholesale scrapping of the sponsorship system seems, on closer inspection, to consist solely of a reallocation of the right to release workers from their contracted job from the sponsor himself to the state.[12] Even so, this change will represent an important incremental step in restructuring the dynamics of the labor force in Bahrain. As the leading proponent of this change, Bahrain's labor minister faces staunch resistance from the business community and other powerful groups on the island, and the debates surrounding the proposed change are ongoing as this book goes to press. In the concluding chapter of this book, I explore these recent developments at more length.

2   PEARLS, OIL, AND THE BRITISH EMPIRE

A Short History of Bahrain

In setting out to explore the context of interactions between Indian transmigrants and citizen-hosts on the island of Bahrain, I begin with a quick overview of the history of the transnational conduits that, over hundreds of years, have carried South Asians from their homes to the Gulf. In the remainder of the chapter I present a more in-depth analysis of Bahrain's complex history. Still, the points I make in this chapter are fairly straightforward. First, the processes one might identify as transnational have a long history on the island—long enough that they precede the solidification of the nation-state by many centuries.[1] Second, although Bahrain shares much with the other petroleum-rich states of the Arabian Peninsula, that commonality should not obscure the particular history of the island's place in the regional and global political economy. Finally, this particular history, and the social relations that comprise it, played an important role in shaping the structure of contemporary relations among the peoples of Bahrain, including both citizen and foreigner.

Finally, a brief comment about some of the terminology that I use in describing particular components of the Indian community in Bahrain: as Sarah Mahler has observed, anthropologists concerned with people on the move need to remain attentive to the differential access individuals have, and their differential participation in, the transnational processes and social fields we study (1998, 81–82; see also George 2000, 148–49). The basic bifurcation between the working and professional classes, as described by Karen Leonard (2002, 214) in her work on the Indian diaspora in the United Arab Emirates, becomes the basis for my use of the terms *diasporic elite* and *transnational proletariat,* terms that I imagine are unfamiliar and perhaps unwelcome additions to the growing lexicon of appellations used to describe people on the move. By *transnational proletariat* I mean the Indian foreign laborers in the working class, usually men, alone, with families behind them in India. Their gaze remains fixed on their home in India, and they are transnational in the sense that their social fields, collectively and individually, are spread between two nations but free of neither. Conversely, I switch to *diasporic elite* to describe the middle and upper classes of the Indian community on the island. These professionals, skilled workers, engineers, educators, and merchants typically bring their families with them to Bahrain. Their tenure on the island may be short or long, but as a community their history is now centuries old. Their long-standing presence in Bahrain, and the disparate ties they maintain with points around the globe, doesn't necessarily make them less transnational than their impoverished countrymen on the island, but it does conform to the basic pattern of a diasporic, if not cosmopolitan, existence. These terms, and the division they connote, are mentioned only in passing in this chapter, but they emerge as central to the structure of my analysis in the chapters to come.

An Overview of Transnational Labor in Bahrain

The Middle East is a major destination in the global migration of labor. The principal receptors of these migration flows are the Gulf Cooperation Council (GCC) states—Kuwait, Saudi Arabia, Bahrain, Qatar, United Arab Emirates, and Oman. Together, these states host a foreign population of well over 10 million men and women, a figure that must be gauged in comparison with a total population, including foreigners and citizens, of over 30 million (Kapiszewski 2001, 39; 2006, 4). As these figures suggest, the petroleum-rich states of the Arabian Peninsula are an important juncture in the transnational migration of labor, a node in the transmigratory network that, looking outward from South Asia, certainly belongs in the same constellation as western Europe and North America. These figures also suggest a noteworthy and unique aspect about the migratory waypoints on the Arabian Peninsula, for the proportions of foreigners to citizens are astoundingly large. In all the GCC states, foreign labor comprises a majority of the total workforce, and in several states (Kuwait, United Arab Emirates, and Qatar) foreign workers comprise an absolute majority of the population. As James Clifford observed well over a decade ago, diasporic culture and its language are beginning to challenge "the binary relation of *minority* communities with *majority* societies" (1994, 311). In the cities of the Arabian littoral, that challenge is both discursive and demographic, for foreigners numerically predominate in many of the public spaces of the cities, they work behind the counters of businesses and shops at the foot of the tall glass skyscrapers of central Manama, and they crowd the narrow streets of the souk on Friday afternoon. The sheer scope of these foreign populations has fundamentally altered the social fabric of the urban agglomerations that dot the shores of the Gulf waters and has also shaped the social and political structures of all the Gulf states (Longva 1997, 2000, 2005; Louër 2008).

Although the sources of these migration flows, and hence the demography of foreign labor in the Gulf states, have varied significantly over time, since the 1970s South Asian transmigrants have come to dominate these Indian Ocean conduits. In general terms, the history of the South Asian presence in the Gulf can be divided into three overlapping periods. For much of known history, merchants from the Indian Subcontinent maintained a strong presence in the Gulf, moving cloth, rice, and other foodstuffs, spices, and a variety of other materials westward to the Gulf, and sending pearls—the region's primary export for many centuries—back along that same route (Palgrave 1982; al-Muraikhi 1991; Slot 1993; Buckingham 1971; Carter 2005). Members of powerful South Asian merchant families, the vestiges of which still maintain a presence in the cities of the contemporary Gulf, often served as bankers and financiers to the ruling families or strongest tribes in the region, and those Indian merchant families' long-standing presence in the region constituted the historical framework for the migratory conduits that today connect the Arabian Peninsula with the ports of the Indian Subcontinent.

The British presence in the region forged a larger and more sustained connection to the Indian Subcontinent, and hence forms the second of these three periods. After devastating several Gulf ports with its navy, Britain imposed the 1820 General Treaty of Peace, an event that gave international recognition to the Sunni rulers of Bahrain and what later became known as the Trucial States (now the United Arab Emirates). Although the island was never a formal colony, its eventual status as a British protectorate, combined with the tenor and scope of Britain's relations with the island's indigenous peoples, placed the island squarely in the ambit of the British Empire. For many decades, Britain's relations with the region's rulers and governors were administered via British India's colonial bureaucracy. With each passing decade, the British Crown extended its involvement in the region, encouraging the rulers of Eastern Arabia to form government departments and institutions modeled on the European state (customs, education, public works, municipalities, police, secular courts, hospitals, and the like). Many of these new departments and institutions were run or supervised by British colonial civil servants (often from India) in the private employ of the rulers. These new departments and institutions also drew increasing numbers of low-level Indian bureaucrats from the Subcontinent to the cities of the Gulf. British representatives in the Gulf also fostered the transmigration of private entrepreneurs to serve this growing population of quasi-colonial bureaucrats and to contribute to the ongoing construction of a Western-style private sector. In essence, then, the second wave of South Asian migrants arrived on the coattails of the British Crown. Many of the established families I came to know during my fieldwork on the island—members of the diasporic elite in Bahrain—arrived as part of this second migration flow. Their fathers or grandfathers crossed the Indian Ocean to work for the burgeoning number of government bureaucracies and institutions or, equally likely, to engage in various entrepreneurial activities in service of the increasingly wealthy population in the region.

The latest chapter in the history of migration from South Asia to the Arabian Peninsula began in the 1960s, gathered speed in the 1970s, and in many ways continues to this day. The development of the oil industry throughout the region, in conjunction with vast increases in the global demand for that oil, filled government coffers and led all of the Gulf states to establish a variety of modernization plans, including infrastructural projects (new highways, bridges, buildings, museums, universities, mosques, and so forth) as well as new bureaucracies, expanded state apparatuses, and comprehensive welfare systems. Although the impetus for these projects was already in place at the end of the 1960s, the oil embargo of the 1970s, by increasing state wealth manifold, fueled a dramatic increase in the number and scope of these projects. At this historic juncture, South Asian migration to the Gulf grew rapidly. The type of South Asian passing through these migratory conduits also shifted. In the past, transmigrants to the Gulf were typically skilled workers or entrepreneurs. While the flow of these transmigrants continued, the new arrivals were predominantly unskilled laborers. These men filled new positions generated by the increasing number of infrastructural projects on the island.

These historical factors explain the increasing flow of transmigrants to the island, but scholars have provided a number of other explanations for why South Asia in particular came to play a predominant role in providing labor to the Gulf. South Asia contained a comparatively inexpensive supply of educated and trained clerks, supervisors, and assistants (Holden 1966; Kapiszewski 2001, 4, 62; Azhar 1999, 101; Weiner 1986), and many of them spoke, read, and wrote English—the language of the growing transnational private sector. In addition, and in comparison with the established flows of Arab migrants to the Gulf, South Asian laborers usually arrived unaccompanied by families, and hence the costs of reproducing that labor supply were largely borne by the sending states. As other scholars have suggested, the fact that many South Asian transmigrants were neither Arab nor Muslim also made for a more pliable and docile workforce (Nakhleh 1976, 77; Weiner 1986, 53–54), or, from another angle, a population that the citizenry was more willing to exploit. Through this confluence of forces, and building on long-established connections generated through both mercantile and imperial relations, the South Asian presence in the GCC states grew rapidly over the last decades of the twentieth century. Although remnants of the first two periods of the South Asian migration to the island can still be discerned today, it is this last component—the transnational proletariat—that has come to numerically dominate the South Asian populations in the cities of the Gulf.

My own ethnographic work, combined with that of the handful of other scholars with experience investigating one or both ends of the migratory conduits that connect the Gulf states to South Asia and points farther abroad, suggests a series of patterns that characterize the transmigrant experience in the GCC states (Longva 1997, 2000, 2005; Nagy 1998; Leonard 2002, 2003; Khalaf and Alkobaisi 1999; Gamburd 2000). Foremost, these are "guest worker" populations. Although there are a few notable exceptions, naturalization is neither encouraged nor readily possible.[2] Both discursively and practically, Gulf states and Gulf citizens alike reinforce the temporary nature of these transmigrants' tenure in the GCC states, even though many foreigners stay for years, for a lifetime, or in the case of some families, for generations. In spite of both the size and long tenure of many foreign populations in the Gulf states, South Asians forge lives largely separate from the host society: in Bahrain, for example, the transnational proletariat dwell in decrepit apartment buildings in the central urban slums now largely abandoned by the citizenry, or bunk in labor camps on the semi-industrial periphery of the city. Families of the diasporic elite send their children to separate schools (e.g., the Indian School, the New Indian School, the Pakistani School) and join social clubs specific to their home nations or regions (e.g., the Young Goans Club, the Pakistani Club). Intermarriage between citizens and noncitizens is uncommon, and

Figure 2.1. Luggage on its way from the airport to a labor camp. Photograph by Andrew Gardner.

many of the elite Indian families I spoke with—families that, in some cases, have been in Bahrain for several generations—had never been invited to a Bahraini house. As Longva (1997) remarks in her acute analysis of relations in Kuwait, interactions in these plural societies are largely confined to the arena of work.

Another pattern that characterizes the transmigrant experience pertains to the kafala system. Excepting those who arrive illegally—a point I examine in detail in the coming chapters—all South Asian workers arrive through the kafala (sponsorship) system, the framework by which transnational migration in the GCC states is organized and controlled.[3] Through the kafala system, individual foreign workers are linked to a particular job and, more importantly, to a particular citizen or corporate sponsor (a *kafeel*). This relationship has a contractual facet in the sense that the men and women who cross the Indian Ocean to work in the Gulf sign contracts that oblige them to work, typically, for two years at a set level of pay. These contracts also oblige the sponsors to pay a certain rate, to cover travel costs, to provide a vacation period, and so forth. As I argue in the following chapters, by binding foreign workers to individual citizens, the kafala system is the keystone in the systemic and structural violence levied against foreign workers in the Gulf. At the current juncture, it suffices to say that the kafala relation represents a central concern in the lifeworlds of most of the foreign workers I interviewed, and as such it plays a predominant role in patterning their experience abroad. At the same time, there are significant and substantial changes on the near horizon in Bahrain, for the kingdom has recently announced plans to dismantle portions of the sponsorship system. These changes are discussed in the final chapter of this book.

There are also gendered, ethnic, national, regional, linguistic, and religious patterns to the migratory conduits between South Asia and the Gulf. The vast majority of transmigrants in the Gulf states are men. Indeed, on a Friday afternoon, when many foreign workers have at least some portion of the day free, the central streets of Manama are overtaken by South Asian men. Female transmigrants, both fewer in number and less visible, are also present in the Gulf. The largest contingent serves as domestic workers, a vocation generally seen as one of the poorest paid and most vulnerable components of the foreign population (Longva 1997, 70; Kapiszewski 2001, 181–82; Strobl 2009).[4] At the other end of the socioeconomic spectrum, many professional women arrive from Asia to work in various capacities for the transnational corporations that serve the region; other women arrive on a family visa reserved for foreign workers meeting the minimum income threshold.[5]

The various national and ethnic groups that migrate to the island find their way—or are slotted—into particular types of work: Indians, Pakistanis, and Bangladeshis work in construction and the service sector, Filipinos work as concierges and run beauty parlors, whereas Indonesian and Sri Lankan women work as housemaids. In part, the association of particular national and ethnic groups with particular sorts of work can be explained by chain migration and the labor brokerage system: brokers serving one portion of the workforce utilize connections they've established in particular regions of South Asia. At the same time, chain migration—the process by which one transmigrant from one particular place uses his or her knowledge and contacts to pave the way for additional transmigrants—also structures the workforce in this manner. Finally, and perhaps as a result of these processes, employers in the region come to believe that particular sorts of people—specific ethnicities or nationalities—are "naturally" better for certain sorts of positions and hire accordingly. Altogether, these interlocked processes have forged a workforce deeply patterned by ethnicity and nationality. These patterns, and the processes undergirding them, characterize all the states of the GCC.[6]

What I have omitted in this chapter are the historical factors and socioeconomic processes that have generated this abundant and willing labor force in South Asia. In comparison to the ethnographic literature concerned with foreign workers *in* the Gulf, this literature is relatively large (Gamburd 2000; Osella and Osella 2000a, 2000b; Kurien 2002; Silvey 2004; Pertierra 1994; Sekhar 1996; Nair 1999; Nambiar 1995; Brochmann 1993; Eelens, Schampers, and Speckman 1992). I have also omitted the growing literature that traces the complicity of the United States and western Europe in maintaining these Gulf regimes and, hence, in maintaining the particular order that shapes the lives of foreigners and citizens alike. Holloway (1994), for example, argues that the nature of the contemporary state requires understanding its particular place in global capitalist relations (see also Sharma and Gupta 2006). Although these factors are certainly essential in providing a complete map of the structural forces that produce the episodic violence foreign workers face in Bahrain, they are beyond the scope of the analysis I provide here.

Early History

The state of Bahrain is a collection of low, geographically unremarkable islands off the eastern coast of Saudi Arabia.[7] The two largest islands, Awal and the smaller Muharraq, are separated by a shallow bay that was once traversable by human and donkey at low tide. For millennia Bahrain served as an entrepôt on the maritime trade routes between Asia and the continents to the west. In the third millennium BC the island was known as Dilmun. Its strategic location on the route between Mesopotamia and the Indus Valley, combined with an abundance of freshwater springs found on the island and in the shallow waters that surround it, enhanced the island's mythos—it is Edenic Bahrain to which wise men and heroes are transported to live out an eternity in the epic of Gilgamesh. The island was also known to the Greek Empire: an admiral under the command of Alexander the Great purportedly visited Tylos (the Greek name for Bahrain), and Pliny made note of the island's renowned pearl beds. Islam arrived in 640 AD, but the religious continuity that followed did little to steady the fate of the small island, which, at the fringes of various empires, continued to change hands in the passing centuries.

The Omanis, building on their strategic location at the mouth of the Gulf, captured the islands in the fifteenth century, and they are responsible for Arad Fort, a large fortress that today has been refurbished as a national and iconic emblem of Bahrain's long history. The next century belonged to the Portuguese. Their fleets conquered ports from the Strait of Hormuz north to those on the southern fringe of the Mesopotamian delta. Historians have remarked on the peculiarity of Portuguese control—noteworthy for how little influence these outposts had upon the people, culture, artwork, and architecture beyond the fortress walls (Khuri 1980, 16). Perhaps as a result of this insularity, the Portuguese were driven from the island in 1602 by the indigenous population, and the rebellion's merchant-leader appealed to the Persian Empire for protection (Lorimer 1908, 836; Khuri 1980, 17).[8]

The Persian grasp on the island was not firm, and the Omani fleet regained control of the islands for a brief period in the eighteenth century. The Persians returned in 1753, but they did so amid a climate of relative chaos. The Arabian Gulf was a notoriously difficult, if lucrative, mercantile venue. Caught on the seams of empires, the ports on the Arabian side of the Gulf often functioned as maritime city-states—as important trading bazaars connecting the inland tribes with the production of the East, and also as sovereign entities capable of collecting fees from passing boats. By the eighteenth century, the English had expanded eastward into Asia, but the Gulf remained beyond their sphere of control. The primary arm of their imperial enterprise, the English East India Company, had become aware of Bahrain and its riches from Portuguese deserters as early as 1613, but had been unable to locate the island and its surrounding pearl beds (Lorimer 1908, 838).

In 1782, perceiving weakness in Persia's position in Bahrain, the 'Utub (a maritime Arab tribal confederation from Zubara in western Qatar and Kuwait) descended on Bahrain by sea. The 'Utubi combatants defeated the Persian forces in the field, and those of the local sheikh's forces still alive retreated to the fort. The 'Utub plundered the market town of Manama, and after taking possession of a Persian vessel, they retired en masse to their home port on the Qatari coast. After a failed counterattack by the Persian fleet, the Kuwaiti 'Utub intercepted a Persian messenger upon the seas, and they turned south to assist their tribal brethren. This time, upon arriving in Manama, they seized the town and burned it. The Persian troops retreated to the citadel, where they withstood a two-month siege by the 'Utubi forces, which now included the Zubara contingent as well. The citadel—and Bahrain as a whole—eventually fell to this Zubara clan, otherwise known as the Khalifa family (Lorimer 1908, 839).

The island that the Khalifa branch of the 'Utub came to rule was already a transnational hodgepodge of peoples. The axes of difference among these various groups recur throughout this book; perhaps the most important to our purposes here are the sectarian differences. The 'Utub, and more specifically the Khalifa, were a Sunni conglomeration of extended families that maintained a strong tribal ethos, in stark contrast to the nontribal Shi'a they came to rule.[9] As a mercantile hub for the region, Bahrain also included significant populations of Persians (also, for the most part, Shi'ite), Basra Arabs, Hindus, and Jews. In many ways, the arrival of the Khalifa seemed merely another chapter in the island's long and tumultuous political history. The arrival of the British, however, brought this era of changing political control to an end.

One final note on Bahrain's early history: on the outskirts of contemporary Manama, the capital city and international hub that has spread south to encompass nearly all of the hinterland villages of the island, one can still see the remnants of the famous Bahraini burial mounds, or *tumili*—fields of small dirt hillocks stretching as far as the eye can see. Although many of these graveyards have been destroyed by construction projects, estimates as to their original number reach 150,000 (Clarke 1981, 69). Even today, the vast scope of these remains suggests something unfamiliar to those of us from the New World, for they yield a clue as to the sheer number of lives that have been lived on the small island. That many of those lives were connected to other places along the Gulf littoral, the Arabian Sea, and the northeastern reaches of Africa is difficult to gauge against the permanence of their rest in the southern plains of the small island. The early historical sources we have for Bahrain, however, clearly portray a city, people, and marketplace intricately connected to the emergent global system. And for much of the island's history, the lives that passed on the island intersected with the lucrative trade wrought by the pearl beds surrounding the island.

Pearls in the Global Ecumene

That the fates of entire peoples, communities, and states might be buffeted by a single commodity was a point clearly developed by Sidney Mintz (1985) in his exploration of the intricate connections among sugar, nascent capitalism, and the colonization of the New World, and reinforced by Wolf's (1982) more expansive consideration of the development of a world system. Bahrain, under a variety of designations, appears in the numerous historical documents that chart the earliest years of Eric Wolf's revision of world system theory,[10] and the islands' mythic notoriety had much to do with the rich pearl beds that surround it. Greek accounts noted the presence of "fish eyes," as pearls were known, and later accounts mark their presence in the markets of Manama.[11] By the nineteenth century, when the small island had become thoroughly enmeshed in the mercantile trade routes of the Indian Ocean world, Bahrain emerged as the principal pearl market in the Arabian Gulf (Lorimer 1908, 245). The pearls of the Gulf were considered higher in quality than those of Ceylon (Buckingham 1971, 456), and they made their way to markets on several continents. Many of the earliest historical accounts spend time describing the minutiae of this livelihood (Buckingham 1971, 454–57; see also al-Muraikhi 1991, 77–90).

During the period after the Persian defeat in Bahrain, pearling vessels were principally controlled by the Sunni tribesmen of the island—members of the ruling al-Khalifa clan as well as the handful of other Sunni tribes that made their home on the island (Khuri 1980, 36; Franklin 1985, 75). The Khalifa rulers extracted revenue through a system of levies on the industry (Farah 1985, 5). Boats plied the waters around the islands, and the pearling crews, composed of both Arabs and slaves of African origin, worked the bottom of the sea in depths exceeding seventy feet.[12] Work was seasonal: the boats spent just over four months on the seas around Bahrain, beginning in June when the sea is hot and calm. Working vessels returned to the island only occasionally to replenish supplies. At the conclusion of the pearling season, crews passed the winter months in idle anticipation of the next season (Buckingham 1971, 456–57). Divers shared in the profits obtained by the sale of pearls, each receiving an advance at the beginning of the season and a second advance during the off-season. Both payments were debited against future earnings, oftentimes forging a growing chasm of debt and servitude into which future generations of the laboring class were born.

The work of pearling itself was difficult. A typical pearling dhow held a crew of sixty, including the divers, pullers, ship's boys, captain's mate, and captain (Jenner 1984, 27).[13] The captain sailed the dhow to the chosen location, and the anchor was lowered. Divers quickly descended to the bottom, accompanied by two ropes, one with a stone weight, the other with a collection bag. After collecting ten or twelve oysters from the sea bottom, the diver surfaced while the pullers retrieved the haul. The divers worked in shifts, and after a sequence of ten dives, the diver warmed himself by the fire while another took his shift. The pearl merchant's vessel traveled among the dhows of his fleet, and the merchant courted buyers one at a time on the deck of his vessel.

The importance of the pearl industry precedes available historical accounts. By the eighteenth century, Bahrain was a central hub in regional commerce. The pearl trade was certainly the cornerstone of the island's position, but the gleam of the pearl often obscures other important attractions of the island. Bahrain functioned as a source of fresh water for passing ships. The islands contained numerous freshwater springs, and the shallow waters around the island also bubbled with fresh water, for which the local population configured technologies for extracting the fresh water from saline (Buckingham 1971, 456–57). The interior of Bahrain, by all accounts, was a veritable garden. In his trip to Bahrain in the early nineteenth century, Buckingham observed "no less than three hundred villages scattered over the small island, and every portion of the soil is cultivated; producing dates, figs, citrons, peaches, and a species of almond, called *loazi,* the outer husk of which is eaten as well as the kernel" (452).

Agricultural production was, for the most part, a Shi'ite activity, and although their interior villages were connected to the booming port of Manama by trade, they were disconnected from the wealth derived from the pearl industry (Khuri 1980, 36). Palgrave, in the colonial discourse typical of the nineteenth and twentieth centuries, states that the "fifty or sixty hamlets that lie scattered in its interior [do not] keep up much communication with the thriving emporium on the north-west, and hence their inhabitants bear an almost savage look, indicative of an uncultivated mind, the result of isolation" (1982, 210). These "uncultivated" minds were responsible for much of the agricultural production on the island and were hence part of the reason that the emporium to the northwest thrived in its role as a gateway to the populations of the eastern peninsula.

The Sunni inhabitants of the island controlled the production of pearls, but the distribution of this commodity brought diverse populations to the island. In the seventeenth century, Venetians, Jews from Aleppo, and Banias from Gujarat were the chief exporters of Gulf pearls (Slot 1993, 498). By the early 1800s, however, the bulk found their way to the markets of the Indian Subcontinent (Buckingham 1971, 454). As pearls reached the markets of India, products of the Subcontinent flowed back to the markets of Bahrain along the same lines of trade; a short list included "cotton and silk fabrics, embroideries, rice, spices, coffee, sugar and tea, fiber ropes, timber, metals, iron and sundry gewgaws all coming from India" (al-Muraikhi 1991, 106). With a reliable mercantile connection to the Subcontinent, Bahrain rose from an important entrepôt to the preeminent emporium of the western Gulf (Lorimer 1908, 245). The success of the Indian merchants in this equation enhanced their power on the island. By the end of the nineteenth century, they controlled the customs port and served as personal bankers to the ruling family. From the 1890s to 1965, the Indian rupee served as Bahrain's principal currency.

After many centuries at the crossroads of regional trade routes, and with its increasingly solidified mercantile connections to the Indian Subcontinent and to the Arabian Peninsula's interior, the port of Manama was widely recognized as a heterogeneous and multicultural trading hub. As Palgrave ably noted in his 1862–63 travel diary,

> The arrival of strangers, many or few, from north or south, is an every hour occurrence here; and a passing look, or a chance "good morrow," was all the notice taken of us by the many who thronged the landing place.... Mixed with the indigenous population are numerous strangers and settlers, some of whom have been established here for many generations back, attracted from other lands either by the profits of commerce or of the pearl fishery, and still retaining more or less of the physiognomy and garb of their native countries. Thus the gay-coloured close-cut dress of the southern Persian, the saffron-stained vest of 'Oman, the white robe of the Nejd, and the striped gown of Baghdad, are often to be seen mingling with the light garments of Bahreyn, its blue and red turban, its white silk-fringed cloth worn Banian fashion round the waist, and its frock-like overall; while a small but unmistakable colony of Indians, merchants by profession, and mainly from Guzerat, Cutch, and their vicinity, keep up here all their peculiarities of costume and manner, and live among the motley crowd, "among them, but not of them." (Palgrave 1982, 205–12)

The historical record repeatedly remarks on the heterogeneous character of the island. Certainly a plethora of different cultural and ethnic groups made their home on the island. Some arrived by choice, such as the Indian merchants, and others by force, such as the African slaves who worked the sea bottom for the bounty of pearls. Moreover, the indigenous population, if one can even be delineated, included a variety of groups demarcated not only by the Sunni/Shi'a schism but also by regional affiliation, such as those with a genealogical connection to Persia or the eastern districts of Saudi Arabia. In most cases, the pluralism of the social milieu did not extend to the local level: villages were homogeneous, and within the port city of Manama, specific quarters became the home of particular groups.

Nor should this portrait of premodern Bahrain be conceived as a sort of static social arrangement. The booming pearl industry of the late nineteenth century reshaped society on the island. As the connections to the pearl markets of India solidified, agricultural land in the hinterlands of the main island was abandoned. "Production for internal consumption continued," Nelida Fuccaro states, but the "export of agricultural produce, especially dates, decreased considerably as the local agricultural workforce increasingly became absorbed in fishing and pearling controlled by the new tribal elites" (2000, 54). The industry thrived as the market for pearls and other luxury goods expanded in the decade following the First World War.[14]

In 1893, however, in Japan, Kokichi Mikimoto, the son of a noodle vendor, patented a process for cultivating pearls. After he spent another twelve years perfecting the process, cultured pearls began to make their way into the global market as Japan's first successful export. In Bahrain, the impact of this technological shift was slow, and the industry continued to thrive in the 1920s. When the U.S. stock market collapsed in 1929, however, demand for luxury goods dwindled, and in the early 1930s, with the global prominence of the cultured pearl, the Bahrain industry collapsed (Zahlan 1989, 22).

Although the pearl trade in Bahrain all but vanished in the decades that followed the global collapse of the industry, the legacy of the relations of pearl production established over the course of centuries lingered on. Like the pearl beds, petroleum provided the basis for an essentially extractive industry; the tributary relations between the Sunni royal family and the captains of the pearling dhows were in some sense replicated with oil production, albeit under the guise of legitimacy provided by the quasi-colonial bureaucracy now present on the island. Furthermore, the indentured servitude and circle of debt that characterized relations between pearl boat captains and the divers constituted an early rendition of the contemporary kafala system. Like the pearl divers of the last century, transmigrant laborers today arrive with a burden of debt that is difficult to escape. Finally, for many centuries Bahrain's lucrative pearl industry drew foreign traders, merchants, and laborers to the island. The petroleum era, while drawing new groups of individuals from afar, was nonetheless only the latest chapter in a long history of transregional migration through Bahrain.

THE ARRIVAL OF BRITISH IMPERIALISM

The British entry into the Gulf region, premised upon the strength of their maritime forces, was a gradual one. The arrival of the Khalifa Arabs to Bahrain, of course, marked a significant milestone in Bahraini history, but in the larger context of the Gulf their arrival was but one chapter in the history of tribal relations in the region—a set of relations carried from desert to sea. With the long-standing presence of the Persians, the 'Utubi Arabs, the Omanis, and the famous "pirates" of the lower Gulf (the tribes of what today are the United Arab Emirates), the Arabian Gulf of the eighteenth century has been characterized as a veritable "free-for-all attack and counterattack, alliance and counter-alliance" in which ports and territory frequently shifted hands (Franklin 1985, 64).

In entering this regional stage, the British sought legitimacy through the eradication of these attacks and counterattacks, or of "piracy," the nomenclature used by the Europeans to describe the fiercely competitive economic warfare waged by the various ports of the Gulf (Franklin 1985, 61; Onley 2004, 31, 36–37). Piracy, although often portrayed as a guerilla response to the encroachment of the Portuguese, French, English, and Dutch, also relates to the gradual erosion of the Persian Empire and the stability it granted to mercantile activity in the region, to the increasing volume of trade in the region, to the rise of the fundamentalist Wahhabis (Saudis), who waged war on Indian shipping during 1797–1819, and most importantly, to the fact that British definitions of piracy often included the Arab enforcement of a "protection fee" system that mirrored the relationship between caravan routes and tribal homelands on the peninsula (Khuri 1980, 19–21; Onley 2004, 36–37, 42–43).

The British, after devastating several ports through naval attacks in December 1819, imposed an antipiracy treaty on the rulers of what came to be known as the Trucial States (now the United Arab Emirates) in early 1820, to which Bahrain was admitted at its ruler's request. The local rulers promised to abstain from all forms of maritime raiding, including piracy, in return for Britain's promise to protect them from this raiding and arbitrate any disputes arising from it (Onley 2004, 31, 36). This treaty, known as the General Treaty of Peace, yielded international recognition to the rulers and their families, and thereby reinforced their positions as the hereditary leaders of their respective sheikhdoms (Zahlan 1989, 7–8; Onley 2004, 66).[15] Responsibility for the enforcement of this and subsequent treaties was given to Britain's Gulf Resident in Bushehr, who took his orders from the government of India (Onley 2007, 14–20). The Gulf Resident maintained a representative in Bahrain who reported to him on a regular basis. In the nineteenth century, this man was a locally recruited Indian or Arab merchant with the title of Native Agent, whereas in the twentieth century he was a Briton with the title of Political Agent (Onley 2007, 136–88). Through this agency, Bahrain emerged as a vital node in what Onley calls British India's "informal empire."

A calculated move by many accounts, the presence of the British Residents and Agents in the Gulf served multiple ends. Britain's growing involvement in the region was ostensibly based on the protection of trade routes to India and the East. In practice, the British political presence also enabled a British company, the British India Steam Navigation Company, to dominate the vital long-distance trade between India and Gulf ports, particularly Basra, Bahrain, Dubai, and Muscat (Landen 1967, 99–101). Furthermore, the stabilization of borders and regimes in the region turned group competition inward rather than outward (Franklin 1985, 66).

Through exclusive agreements signed between the local rulers and the government of India in the late nineteenth century, Britain took control of the external relations of the Gulf sheikhdoms, turning them into British "protected states" (Onley 2007, 21–29). This move would become the window for Britain's increasing involvement in the internal affairs of the port cities and their surrounding territories. The British concerns expanded to include "port facilities, pearl production, exports and imports, and a general political order that stimulated international trade" (Khuri 1980, 86). In Bahrain, direct connections to the markets of India and other ports far afield drew increasing numbers of merchants and traders to the city: Germans, other Europeans, and a contingent of fifty Jewish pearl merchants who had arrived in the 1890s sought the protection of the British Agent on the island (Khuri 1980, 86).[16] The Agent's extraterritorial jurisdiction in Bahrain, granted by the Exclusive Agreements of 1880 and 1892, allowed him to try all legal cases involving foreigners in Bahrain and to try with a Bahraini judge all cases between foreigners and Bahrainis (Onley 2007, 119–27). The former were tried in the British Agency Court, whereas the latter were tried in the Joint Court. Over a century ago, then, we can see traces of the dual system that continues to characterize the arrangements in all of the contemporary Gulf nations.

As the jurisdiction of the British Resident and his Agents expanded, power was centralized in the court system. The British Agency Court was formally established in 1919, with the Joint Court being established soon after. A secular court for Bahrainis was also established in the 1920s, run by a British colonial civil servant privately employed by the ruler of Bahrain: Sir Charles Belgrave, who oversaw the creation of the modern government of Bahrain, with its departments and institutions, between 1926 and 1957

(Khuri 1980, 89–90). Councils and governing bodies were established, eclipsing the indigenous institutions of leadership.[17] The degree of involvement by the British in Bahrain outpaced British efforts among the other fledgling states of the western Arabian Gulf. In Bahrain, the British became involved in the minutiae of everyday internal affairs, and in 1946, the political residency—the locus of the British Empire's regional presence—moved from Bushehr to Bahrain. British air force, naval, and army bases were established on the island in 1932, 1935, and 1961, respectively, and numerous British commercial firms located their regional headquarters in Manama (Franklin 1985, 86; Zahlan 1989, 49).

Petroleum and the Global Political Economy

In his comprehensive analysis of the Gulf region during the British era, Lorimer explains Bahrain's strategic importance to the British imperial interests in the region. He also spends some effort describing the pearl industry and concludes by stating that should the pearl beds fail, "the Shaikhdom would shortly be reduced to comparative insignificance" (1908, 245). Some twenty-two years after his book was published, the pearl market did collapse. The veracity of the argument underlying Lorimer's prediction, however, remains in question, for the international collapse of the pearl market neatly coincided with the discovery of oil in Bahrain.

In October 1931, Bahrain's first oil well was drilled at Jebel al-Dukhan, the sole mountain on the main island. Seven months later, the well began to produce 9,000 barrels of oil a day, and the region's petroleum era was under way (Zahlan 1989, 51). Larger discoveries followed, but few of them were in Bahrain. Nonetheless, with a sufficient supply of petroleum, as well as the economic benefits of its stature as the epicenter of the British presence in the Gulf, Bahrain boomed in the decades that followed the discovery of oil. In fact, for much of the twentieth century, Bahrain paced modernization in the Arabian Gulf even as the coffers of nearby nations began to surpass its own.[18]

The British, who by then were managing all external affairs of the small island nation (as well as a sizable portion of the internal affairs), granted one-third of the oil royalties to the Khalifa leadership (Franklin 1985, 87). These monies, and the jobs produced by the growth of the oil industry, stimulated the local economy and wrought fundamental changes in Bahraini society. To sketch a basic outline of the impact, one can point to the physical relocation of many families out of the central districts and into the newly constructed suburbs of Manama; one can note the education of women, as well as their entry into the labor market; one can point to the government's construction of universities, hospitals, schools, roads, palaces, mosques, and other infrastructural components that, together, conditioned fundamental changes in the day-to-day activity of most Bahrainis, and, furthermore, changed the locations of that activity; one can also note that more frequent travel by Bahrainis, for both work and pleasure, increased contact between Bahrainis and foreigners.

At the same time, many Bahrainis had difficulty accessing the wealth generated by the industry. Most of the jobs in the oil industry, particularly in its earliest decades, went to foreigners, and often to Indian nationals (Franklin 1985, 88). As already described, Indians had been on the island in significant numbers for centuries. With the rapid development of the petroleum industry, and with the continuing expansion of the British-managed government bureaucracy, the need for trained professionals and the assorted clerks, supervisors, and assistants who spoke English far surpassed the supply of educated and trained Bahrainis (Holden 1966, 176; Kapiszewski 2001, 4).[19] Moreover, those citizens who did gain a foothold in the industries on the island often departed for other pursuits. As Seccombe and Lawless (1986, 111–12) state, many of the Bahrainis who gained formal or informal training under the foreign-run industries on the island quickly found their way to other alternatives — establishing their own businesses, working in the private sector, or themselves migrating to work in nearby countries. As a result of this confluence of factors, the flow of foreign labor to the island increased steadily over the middle decades of the twentieth century, and the wealth generated by Bahrain's petroleum industry coexisted with significant periods of unemployment for citizens.

In 1971, the year Britain withdrew its military from the Gulf and terminated its nineteenth-century treaties with the Gulf rulers, Bahrain declared its independence from Britain. Two years later, the OPEC embargo resulted in the overnight quadrupling of the income generated by petroleum (Zahlan 1989, 61–62). Independent and instantly wealthy, Bahrain experienced a quickening in its pace of development. At this juncture in history the flow of labor to the region reached unforeseen highs: between 1971 and 1981, the population of non-Bahrainis jumped from 37,885 to 112,378 (Directorate of Statistics 1999, 16). Put another way, in 1971 one out of every five individuals on the island was a noncitizen foreigner. Ten years later, one out of every three individuals on the island was a foreign worker.

Not only did the number of foreigners working in Bahrain grow but the sources of that labor shifted rapidly in the 1970s. In particular, inter-Arab labor migration was rapidly eclipsed by the arrival of South Asian laborers from India, Bangladesh, Pakistan, the Philippines, Indonesia, and numerous other nations of the Indian Ocean. This shift in labor is frequently linked to the OPEC embargo, an event that, as noted, multiplied the island nation's income practically overnight and hastened the establishment of large development projects, and hence fueled a demand for labor that the citizenry itself could not meet (Azhar 1999, 101; Weiner 1986). Although the laborers arriving from South Asia in the 1970s were certainly filling positions that Bahrainis were unwilling or unable to take, the simple correlation between this flow of transnational labor and the demand in the Gulf labor markets has been closely examined and challenged by other scholars. Emile Nakhleh, for example, observes that six years after its inception, the Bahrain Petroleum Company began to extensively employ Indians and Iranians in response to the 1938 labor strike by citizen-employees (1976, 77). Other research suggests that the British government precariously balanced its interests in maintaining good relations with the royal family, minimizing or altogether excluding foreign interests from gaining a foothold, and finding a productive and capable workforce for developing oil production and other related industries on the island (Seccombe and Lawless 1986, 94–96). Labor from the Indian Subcontinent threaded the complexities of these demands: beyond providing a capable, trained, and inexpensive labor force, Indian laborers were already British subjects and, from the perspective of the island's Sunni leadership, less politically volatile than Arab or Persian labor (Seccombe and Lawless 1986). The idea that these new labor forces were politically docile and less culturally troublesome than non-Bahraini Arab laborers is a recurring theme in analyses of the historical context of transmigration to the Gulf (Nakhleh 1976, 77; Weiner 1986, 53–54).

Although the petroleum reserves in Bahrain were, in the end, the smallest in the Gulf, Bahrain continues to rely on oil for a substantial portion of its national income. Estimates vary significantly, from 50 percent to 77 percent of the state's total income (Seikaly 2001, 179; Wright 2008; Ali 2009), but even these figures fail to convey the intricacy of this dependency, for many of the island nation's diversification projects depend heavily on petroleum and gas in their productive capacities. Nonetheless, the Kingdom of Bahrain has arrived in the twenty-first century with a collection of economic strategies aimed at diversifying its economy. The nation's commercial and financial sectors, while increasingly eclipsed by the metropolis of Dubai to the south, continue to draw global corporate entities to the island. The nation's bureaucracy—itself a complex negotiation of the island's quasi-colonial legacy and the vested interests of the ruling Sunni sect—continues to keep pace with change and reform in the Gulf. The stellar wealth of nearby nations is absent in Bahrain, however, and the harsh reality of a diminishing resource base, the "golden bubble" that financed the rapid changes of the past century, is better known in Bahrain than in any of the petroleum nations of the Gulf littoral.

Bahrain in a Regional Context

Much of the scholarship concerned with the petroleum states of the Arabian Gulf portrays them as a fairly homogeneous set of neighbors. Ample evidence supports this fact. The Sunni ruling families of several of these modern states share an overlapping genealogy, and even the common folk of today's Gulf states trace familial connections across multiple national borders. Five of the six nations of the GCC are Sunni-ruled, but only in Bahrain does that Sunni leadership rule over a Shi'ite majority.[20] In her seminal attack against the Orientalist portrayal of the "Islamic" city as a conglomeration of particular morphological features, Janet Abu-Lughod (1987) describes the "feel" of the cities of the Middle East—the spatial and personal semiotics indicative of the divide between public and semiprivate urban space (169). One might easily add to this rendering the sound of calls to prayer, the smell of *sheesha,* the tight winding streets of the older quarters, or the minarets that reach from low neighborhoods to the sky. The cities of the Gulf littoral also have a common feel to them, with long waterfront corniches, modern highways connecting the rhizome-like network of traffic circles, each with a monument at its center. The cities themselves are a testament to these similarities: all of these neighboring nations are principally urban, with great majorities of the population dwelling in and around the cities of the region.

All of these cities are highly transnational. In all the nations of the GCC, foreigners constitute a majority of the total workforce. In Kuwait, Qatar, and the United Arab Emirates they constitute an absolute majority of the population. Dubai, the cosmopolitan hub of the United Arab Emirates, is now 90 percent foreign. The cities of the Gulf are busy with development. Suburbs sprawl into the desert, and the airports hum with international traffic. Monumental architecture proliferates: the world's tallest building

(Burj Dubai) now stands in the Emirates, and newly constructed luxury neighborhoods in the shape of palm trees (and visible from space) have emerged off the coast of Dubai. Bahrain, like its GCC neighbors, periodically announces plans for astonishingly massive new developments and projects. Throughout the Gulf, gleaming new buildings appear with great frequency, and the sound of construction is a constant backdrop to life in the cities of the GCC nations.

All of the Gulf states possess significant reserves of petroleum and hence significant sources of wealth. On the coasts of Saudi are cities of iron that reach out to the sea. Refineries dot the western shores of the Arabian Gulf, and for every stratotanker that rounds the Strait of Hormuz and passes into the open ocean, millions of dollars flow into the countries of the Gulf. Beginning with the discovery of oil beside Jebel al-Dukhan, the "mountain of smoke" south of Manama, and gaining momentum in the 1970s when the embargo quadrupled petroleum income overnight, the pace of change in the Gulf has shaped similar societies with similar results. The Sunni leadership of these nations invested heavily in the public sector. Although great portions of the private sector came to depend on human capital from abroad, the hallways of the expanding government bureaucracy became the bastion of the citizenry. This particular relation to the state, described at length in the penultimate chapter of this book, is a bond shared by the citizens of all the petroleum-rich nations of the GCC.

There is also a connection among Gulf Arabs—a bounded, mutual identity shared by those who dwell in the oil-rich nations of the Gulf, a communal identity more localized than the often-noted bond of the *umma*, or Muslim world. The boundaries of that communality basically fit *al-khaleej*, or the Gulf Arab states (Dresch 2005, 1). Beyond the domain of lineage shared by some members of the Gulf society, this affiliation is built on the parallel economies of the region. The citizenry of these Gulf nations have, together, undergone massive transformations in the past decades. The wealth derived from the oil reserves forged large public sectors: educational opportunities were expanded, housing programs were created, health systems to serve all citizens were constructed. Although the diverse components of the Gulf states' citizenry have benefited unequally from these developments, the large public sectors and the entitlements they provide are widely recognized as essential components of the ruling families' ability to maintain their hegemony through the distribution of wealth via the conduits of the state (Champion 1999; Kapiszewski 2001, 5–9; Longva 1997, 46–52). This set of relations—of tribal relations organized within the bureaucracy of the state—is one facet of the shared experience of the citizenry of the Gulf states.

The flow of foreign labor to the Gulf began during the British era, but the wealth produced by rising oil prices in the 1970s expedited modernization plans, and in all the nations of the Gulf foreigners arrived in huge numbers to perform the myriad tasks of building "modern" nations. This large foreign workforce, then, is another aspect of the shared experience of the Gulf nations. Indigenousness and nationalism, the strange bedfellows of the contemporary Gulf, exist in dialectic with the highly transnational demographics of the region. In the urban milieu of the Gulf, citizens are often minorities in their own land. In Longva's ethnography of citizen/foreigner relations in contemporary Kuwait, one informant described his feelings as follows: "Imagine seeing strangers everywhere around you, including in your own homes. We used to know all the Kuwaitis, and to trust each other. In the old days, when someone made a promise, you knew he would keep it. We are like a big family. Now, everyone is a stranger. You don't know whom to trust anymore" (1997, 124–25). This feeling of a society besieged by rapid, external change is another condition shared by all the petroleum-rich GCC nations, and the sense of belonging to the state incorporates ethnic, racial, religious, and tribal boundaries under the rubric of citizenship.

The similarities among Gulf nations are substantial, and the components I describe here are the basis for some mutuality in the identities purveyed by the inhabitants of the region. There are, however, many noteworthy differences. Perhaps most important, oil was discovered first in Bahrain. Hence, the benefits of that wealth—including a variety of social programs, job opportunities within a large state bureaucracy, low-cost loans for houses, land grants, and much more—began to accrue in Bahrain first. The first schools in the Gulf region were created in Bahrain, and the citizenry has long prided itself on its position as a beacon of modernization in the Gulf. Its position in relation to the other Gulf states as the primary hub for British imperial activity and transnational corporations facilitated its position at the forefront of the region's integration with the global political economy.

The island's declining oil reserves (and hence its declining wealth) have in some ways undermined Bahrain's role as pacesetter for modernization in the region. In Dubai to the south, taller buildings rise by the month, more wealth courses through the economy, and unlike Bahrain and the other smaller urban conglomerations of the Gulf littoral, Dubai has emerged as a true global city in the region.[21] Yet Bahrain's declining resources have forced the nation to cope with the difficult task of economic diversification, and in this sense the small island nation again sets the pace in the Gulf, for the Bahraini state today faces a set of conditions that all the nations of the GCC will sooner or later share. In terms of the policy environment forged during and after the British era, Bahrain again led the other Gulf nations in devising alternatives to petroleum dependency. These projects resulted in the refinery, the aluminum industry, and other industrial production, as well as a booming financial sector. More recently, Bahrain has instigated a set of labor reform policies that again place it at the forefront of change in the Gulf.

This attempt to turn away from direct dependence on petroleum, while not fully successful to date, depended heavily on the island's experience as the hub for the quasi-colonial activity in the region. The British constructed an air force base on Muharraq, a naval base in Jufair (southeast of Manama), and an army base in Hamala (in western Bahrain), in addition to multiple other projects; the construction of Awali, an "American"-style compound on the island, only enhanced the island's position as expatriate friendly. As Gulf-wide oil production increased, Bahrain emerged as a service center to the activities of the surrounding nations: the relative security and openness of Bahrain attracted a wide variety of financial, administrative, and service offices to the island.[22] In the parlance of *al-khaleej*, the Bahrainis are the "beggars of the Gulf," a sentiment that is often also commonly phrased as the "Indians of the Gulf." The lessons learned as both beggars and handmaidens to the British imperialists, however, proved essential to Bahrainis in developing their nation as the service and financial hub to the more conservative surrounding nations (see Zahlan 1989, 83).

In the twenty-first century, Bahrain retains its reputation as one of the most hospitable of the Gulf nations. The foreigners with whom I spoke—many of whom had experience in the other nearby Arab countries—repeatedly said that Bahrain was the easiest adjustment for expatriates: you can wear shorts in public without fear of the *mutaween* (the religious police of Saudi Arabia), one man remarked; you can practice your religion at one of the handful of churches and temples discreetly tucked about the city, others stated. In general, my informants reported, the Bahrainis are particularly worldly and educated. Hindi music booms from the passing cars filled with Bahraini teenagers, observed a friend as we walked down a busy boulevard, and the audience of the Bollywood films I attended was an even mix of Indians and Bahrainis. And, as other expatriates noted, you can get a drink at one of the many bars on the island.

This liberalism is peculiar to Bahrain. On weekends, teenagers and families from nearby countries stream into Bahrain over the causeway that connects the island to the mainland. Bahrain is a weekend destination for those from more conservative environs: the hotel bars fill with European expatriates, Indians and Filipinos, Saudi men, Bahrainis, and individuals from all the other regions of the globe who visit, live, or work in this transnational city-state. International corporations (many of which do business in Saudi Arabia) often choose to locate their regional headquarters in Bahrain. The island's relative liberalism, wrought by its long transnational history and its intricate connection to Britain, is the primary attraction. Yet it is an uneasy liberalism—both a lifeline to the nation's economy and a target for the more conservative and disenfranchised elements of Bahraini society.

Transnational Bahrain

To the claim that Bahrain has a long history of hosting the processes now called transnationalism is the obvious response that much of this history preceded the existence of the nation-state. As in other regions of the globe, here nations were something quickly constructed and, in many senses, something foreign and imperial imposed on the more geographically fluid tribal structure characteristic of the Arabian Peninsula. There are good arguments to this end: that the lines drawn by colonial powers were mostly a matter of convenience, part of the predilection of a bureaucratic empire that needed to organize the people and terrain it encountered, and to do so in a particular fashion before it could proceed to conquer and exploit. Or one could convolute the terms of the argument and instead take the ebb and flow of peoples and powers across Bahrain's shores—from the Mesopotamian chapter lost to history, through the arrival of the Greeks, of Islam, of the Portuguese, of the Omanis, of the Ottomans, of the Persians, and of the maritime Arab tribes of the Gulf's western shores—as evidence enough that change, rather than stability, was the norm for islands between two seas. Instead, the arrival of the British, the legitimacy they conferred on the Khalifa family, and the continuity of those provisions suggest that it was the constancy of change that came to an end with Britain's Treaty of Peace.

What has come to be called transnationalism in the contemporary literature casts one eye to the role of the nation-state and the corporations, economies, and cultural flows that transcend them. The other eye—and this is the métier of the anthropologist—sifts through the contextual factors of these individuals whose lives are stretched between two or more states, and in this context I find the basis for the argument presented in this chapter: that the historic relations of production configured in the past provided a template for managing the dramatically large flows of foreign labor to the island. The shape of the Bahraini state, the expectations of the citizenry, and the experience of Indian foreign workers on the island today echo the island's experience of British imperialism, the tribal legacy of its leadership, its role as a maritime mercantile hub, and the relations of production forged by the exploitation of the pearl beds surrounding the island.

The processes underlying the contemporary transnational movement of peoples around the globe are not new. For much of known history, Bahrain functioned as an important node in regional and Indian Ocean circuits. Although never a true empire, it was often an important jewel in others' crowns. At particular junctures in history, Bahrain stood alone, or functioned as a mercantile city-state for the seafarers of the Gulf. Throughout this history, the mix of peoples that composed the island's population reflected the heterogeneity of these long-distance connections. In the chapters that follow, I turn to the Indian diaspora—the largest of the foreign populations working on the island today. This Indian community, outsiders to the tribal relations of the Arab leadership, is nonetheless one of the most historically important populations in the kingdom. Their lives on this island have been shaped by the complex history of interactions between foreigner and citizen—a history in which the agency of the Sunni leadership, as well as the Shi'ite population, forged a particular set of relations with the global political economy of oil production, with the quasi-colonial administration long present on the island, and with the nearby nations of the Gulf.

3 FOREIGN LABOR IN PERIL

The Indian Transnational Proletariat

During the final weeks of my time in Bahrain, I visited a labor camp in the distant reaches of outer Muharraq, beyond the airport and just a short walk from the waters of the Gulf. Here amid the dirt streets and walled compounds of the lower- and middle-class Bahrainis was a masonry tile factory. A group of thirty or forty transnational laborers, mostly Indian, lived and worked on the job site, where they prepared large flat bricks for some of the myriad construction projects on the island. On our arrival, we knocked at the large metal gate and were quickly ushered inside, while the men furtively glanced up and down the street. As the interview progressed, the men eventually described their problems with their Bahraini neighbors. Over the last two years, they said, they had curtailed their trips to the small "cold store" (island nomenclature for a convenience store) on the corner. The store itself was only a five-minute walk from the compound, but over the previous months teenagers in the neighborhood had repeatedly attacked the men on their walk to the store, and more recently they had begun to throw bricks and stones over the high wall of the workers' compound. The men's descriptions of these violent encounters resonated with descriptions from other camps, where men had described roving gangs of Bahrainis burgling their camps, stealing air conditioners and other valuables, and threatening them with violence. Indeed, everyday violence seemed characteristic of many of the men's existence in Bahrain.

An article in the English-language newspaper, appearing some months later, reported a similar incident in great detail:

> Fire damaged part of a labour camp, in Naim, after three Bahraini teenagers burst in and set fire to the workers' clothes. It was the third

time that they had raided the same building in one night. When the youths broke in the first time they beat up one of the workers, who required hospital treatment for his injuries. They returned half-an-hour later and stole the labourers' safety shoes. However, when they went back the third time they piled up the workers' clothes, doused the pile in kerosene and set it on fire. The labourers managed to put out the blaze, but only after it had destroyed their air-conditioner, refrigerator and carpets.

"It all started when the Bahrainis barged in the labourers' residence at 10 pm," said Bangladeshi mechanic Mubarak Muslim Mia, 27, who lives in the building. "They entered one of the rooms exclaiming that they are Bahrainis and have a right to be anywhere they want to be. One of the residents asked them what they wanted, barging in so late at night, but the Bahrainis shouted at him and beat him up really bad. We rushed him off to the hospital to get treatment for cuts in his hand."

Almost 100 Indian and Bangladeshi workers live in the building. They work for various companies, but split the cost of the rent amongst themselves. However, they did not immediately report the matter to the police to avoid a confrontation with nearby residents. They even kept quiet when the teenagers came back 30 minutes later and stole their safety shoes. "Each shoe costs around BD7 or BD8—this might not be much, but it is a fortune for people like us," said Mr. Mia. "We did not want to go to the police right then because we thought that it would stop there. We did not want to get in trouble with the people from the neighborhood."

However, half-an-hour later the culprits re-entered the building and took workers' clothes out of a cupboard before soaking them with kerosene normally used for cooking. They then set the pile on fire. "We fought to extinguish the fire, but our clothes were fully charred," said Mr. Mia. "The air-conditioner, refrigerator and carpets were all lost to the flames and we immediately went to the police."

The incident happened last Tuesday, but the workers are still without air-conditioning and a refrigerator while summer temperatures hit 40C. It is understood that three youths were arrested, but have since been released from custody. "We are poor people, it is not easy for us to gather enough money to buy new equipment," said Mr. Mia. "The air conditioner costs BD120, fridge BD70 and our clothes almost the same amount. We are at the end of the month and are left with no money at all. We do not know why these people treat us like this. We never harmed them, why would they harm us?"[1]

Why indeed? Why might teenage boys from the neighborhood harbor a grudge against the impoverished foreign workers who make the tiles that pave the sidewalks and courts of the modern city? And what circumstances conspire to allow three young men to fearlessly confront and abuse a group of nearly a hundred able-bodied laborers? And if these conditions are common to transnational laborers on the island, why does the flow of this labor to Gulf states continue unabated? At the outset of this book, I argued that the concept of structural violence provided a key analytic tool for understanding the lives of foreign workers in Bahrain. As that concept suggests, the idea of these Bahraini teenagers as individual agents of violence is merely a starting point for an expansive analysis of the social, cultural, political, and economic forces that are complicit in the production of this violence. In this chapter, I begin to examine the mechanics of the structural violence endured by the transnational proletariat. That violence, and its structural properties, can be conceived in terms of the forces, policies, arrangements, and ideas that together orchestrate the interactions between foreign workers and citizens.

Describing that set of arrangements—a complex and multifaceted set of forces that are systemic in nature—poses some difficulty. Somewhat arbitrarily, I begin with a critical analysis of illegality. I seek to demonstrate how deportation, and the threat of deportation, becomes a principal fulcrum in the systemic abuse and exploitation of foreign workers in Bahrain. Drawing heavily on the ethnographic data I collected from Indian members of this transnational proletariat, I pay close attention to the production of illegality—in other words, how the arrangements and norms of this system *produce* illegal workers. In turn, my analysis of illegality and the threat of deportation becomes one component of a larger explication of the *kafala*, or the sponsorship system that plays an instrumental role in orchestrating the experiences of foreign labor on the island.

ILLEGALITY AND DEPORTATION IN BAHRAIN

The study of illegality, deportation, and removal can be seen as part of the ongoing articulation of an anthropology attentive to transnational processes. Transnationalism is a broad concept that incorporates analysis of the movement of people, capital, and culture across the boundaries of the nation-state. For well over a century, the Western tradition portrayed the nation-state as a fundamental and intrinsic component of contemporary social organization. Transnational theorists, however, assume no absolute permanency or a priori status to the nation-state as an organizational form; rather, amid the contemporary era of global interconnection, these theorists envision nation-states as engaged in an ongoing struggle to assert the predominance that was once assumed. States are seen as agents jostling for position amid the global flows of people, capital, and culture. Attention to illegality, deportation, and removal focuses the anthropological lens on the processes by which states seek to control the movement of people in particular. In the contemporary world, and by the logic of the nation-state, many people transgress the contemporary order—they are not where they belong. Illegality, deportation, and other forms of removal are tools the state uses to control and govern the transnational movement of people. The ethnographic examination of these processes provides new perspectives on the changing power of the state and the lived experience of people on the move.

The portrait of an "illegal" worker one perceives through the public discourse in Bahrain is strikingly similar to that purveyed here in the United States: an individual somehow finds his or her way across a discrete border of the nation and finds employment in the country. In doing so, the person avoids visa fees, documentation, and, more generally, the purview of the state. In Bahrain, this portrait of the illegal worker meshes with the sectarian imbalance of power on the island, for these workers are also portrayed as taking jobs from the underemployed Bahrainis, who are typically Shi'ite. This characterization confounds the government's attempts to persuade or compel its citizens to enter the private-sector workforce (a set of policies and directives collectively referred to as Bahrainization). Moreover, as an individual outside the systemic controls of the kafala, an illegal laborer is also seen as a cultural threat, for he (or she) is outside the purview of the citizen-sponsor. Although the purported threat of the large foreign population to the cultural integrity of the Bahraini nation is of much interest and debate on the island, the common portrayal of an "illegal" foreign worker that I have presented is largely a fiction. In part, it represents a projection of European and American norms on the Gulf migration discourse. It also reflects the situation in neighboring Saudi Arabia, where an unknown number of individuals arrive on a hajj visa (for religious pilgrimage to Mecca) and stay illegally to work. Both of these explanations—sneaking across the border or arriving under false pretenses—elide the circumstances that broadly produce illegal workers in the Gulf Cooperation Council states. For most transmigrant laborers in Bahrain, the path to illegality is a strategic response to the systemic abuse enabled, if not codified, by the kafala. Furthermore, this path is largely contingent on the passivity of the state in enforcing existing labor laws.

All the illegal Indian laborers I encountered in Bahrain described an almost identical set of circumstances. This uniformity became apparent to me midway through my time on the island. With the help of a network of friends I had assembled in my first months in Bahrain, I arranged an interview with a group of struggling Indian laborers, several of whom were illegal. We sat in their living quarters, an unfinished cinder-block garage belonging to the men's employer. The men lived six to a room. Rats scurried across the rafters overhead, and a sick Indian laborer—now unable to work—coughed in the back bunk-room. One of the men described his path to illegality for me: "I came here as a mason, but the company that took my visa, they didn't pay me. The other workers approached the Labor Department . . . and they [the workers] complained about the company, but by that point they hadn't received any salary for five months. Me and him [pointing to another man] didn't wait that long—we left the company and found work here. The other workers never did get their money. Since we left early, we were illegal, and now we're afraid to approach the Labor Ministry." Several weeks later I journeyed to the back of the souk for another set of interviews. Behind the dense maze in the souk, crowds of South Asian men moved through the streets, in and out of doorways, and disappeared down the small alleys that lead to apartments out of view. The neighborhood, now largely abandoned by the Bahrainis, is widely known as an urban locus for illegal transmigrants. Santosh and I found our way to the apartment we sought, and there I heard another version of the same story:

> I came to Bahrain as a welder in a car carriage repair shop. For four and a half months, I received no salary, so I filed a case. Then I finally left the company. My case is now in the courts—I filed a case against my sponsor. The case states that he did not pay me four and a half months' salary. I filed the case in the beginning of 1998, and there has been no progress [as of July 2003]. . . . As an illegal worker, I do have worries. I have a paper that I received from the court, and now I am afraid to go to the police about this paper. I don't want to have to go to jail for being an illegal worker, and that is why I can't go to the

courts anymore or ask the police for help. I will wait for amnesty. If amnesty came tomorrow, I would go.

Over the years, some of the standard companies would employ me regularly for some period of time. With those standard companies, there was no problem with the payment—they never withheld my salary. Some companies hired me for a week, some hired me for six months. Others hired me for two months. The standard companies hire for the longest period, and they pay regularly. Some of the other companies pay during the early stages, but then they stop. They pay for the first four months or so, then for the last two months they stop. They cheat us. Of all twenty companies, only five were good to the workers the entire time. The other fifteen cheated me, cheated us.

Building on his long stay on the island, this transmigrant was able to put his most recent experiences in context. His description points directly to the process by which illegality is produced—most commonly, by a sponsor simply refusing to pay the wages contractually specified, and the subsequent departure of the transmigrant from the sole job at which he may legally work. His experience also suggests the systemic character of this abuse. Over and over again, this transmigrant faced the same dilemma: should he continue to work in the hopes of eventually receiving his wages from the sponsor, or should he depart the sole job at which he can legally work for employment in the black market? He now awaits an "amnesty," one of the periods in which monetary penalties and jail time associated with illegality are temporarily suspended in the hopes that illegal workers will voluntarily return home.[2] His experiences establish many of the central experiential points that recur throughout this chapter: the kafala locks individuals to a particular job and a particular sponsor—to the very person who profits from the transmigrant's labor on the island. This aspect of the kafala is the cornerstone of the orchestration of the extremely unequal relations between foreigners and citizens, and hence a cornerstone in the mechanics of structural violence observable in Bahrain.

These vignettes focus on the relationship between foreign workers and their sponsor, or *kafeel*, in the creation of illegal workers. In terms of structural violence, the experiences of the workers reveal the systemic pressures in operation on the island—an interconnected set of factors that overdetermine the violence and abuse I identified at the beginning of the chapter. These men also speak to the ever-present fear and vulnerability caused by their illegal status, a lived experience of vulnerability connected to the everyday surveillance of public spaces by citizen-sponsors (De Genova 2002, 438; Willen 2007). The next narrative moves beyond the complex relationship between foreign worker and sponsor, and begins to look at the complicity of the state itself, the arrangement of labor, and other contextual factors that orchestrate the experiences of foreigners on the island.

I met Vijay near the end of my fieldwork in Bahrain. Santosh, my friend and translator for many of my forays to the labor camps, had been assisting Vijay in working through his dilemmas with the Bahraini court system and the immigration office, as well as with the other related problems described here. The three of us sat in a squalid, cramped room in a central neighborhood that, over the previous decades, had been abandoned by the Bahrainis to the legion of foreign laborers who arrive daily to work on the island. My notes from the interview capture the central thread of Vijay's experience abroad:

> Vijay told me that he had been a tailor in Pondicherry, India. Actually, he was a master tailor, he clarified—the supervisor of the showroom. It was a good job. But then some of his friends left for the Persian Gulf, for places like Dubai, Bahrain, Kuwait, and Jeddah. Then some of them came back. They had lots of money. More than that, they were respected. People on the street, people at the teashop—they looked upon these return-migrants in a particular way. Vijay wanted that respect.
>
> His friends suggested he call a labor broker in Madras, and he did. After some discussion, he agreed to pay 45,000 rupees—that's about US$1,000—for a visa and a job at a garment factory. He was going to Bahrain. It was a two-year contract, and he'd earn 45 dinars a month (about $120). He noted that he didn't really know what a dinar was worth when he made the deal, but the figure was close to what his friends had reported from their own experiences. He would be out of debt in a year [considering the size of the debt he had just incurred and the monthly wages promised by the contract he had just signed], and then he could start to make some real money.
>
> Coming up with the 45,000 rupees wasn't easy. He had a little bit saved. He borrowed some with interest from a moneylender. He got a little bit from his father. To make up for what was left, the family pawned his mother's jewelry. Then he got on a plane—his first ever.
>
> He realized something was wrong right away. He arrived at the airport in Bahrain at two in the afternoon, but no one was there to pick

him up. So he just sat and waited. The airport was air-conditioned, and he was cold. He had no food and no money. Someone from the company finally came for him at midnight and took Vijay straight to the garment factory. The rest of the workers were just getting off their shift, so he rode to the camp with them. He had a cot in a small bedroom. There were six other men in the room. They gathered around him and asked him why he came to Bahrain. They told him that the company was very bad, that they had to work until midnight, that the company didn't always pay their wages, and that they certainly didn't receive overtime pay.

He called his father, and his father told him to weather the difficulties. It wasn't a lifetime, said his father—just two years. He couldn't understand a lot of what was going on around him, because he only spoke two South Indian languages. He tried to learn some Arabic and Hindi at night at the camp. He began to meet others in the camp, and he discovered the other men faced a similar set of dilemmas [in that they were trapped in these circumstances with a debt held by a labor broker in their home country]. When the plant manager would come around, they'd argue with him. The manager was also an Indian—a Gujarati, Vijay noted. None of the workers were allowed to talk directly to the Bahraini sponsor, and their arguments with the manager went nowhere.

So they decided to wait until they had paid off their debts. They worked long hours, well into the night, and they received no additional pay. A year went by, and most of the workers had paid off their visa-related debts. They began to slow down production on the floor. As a result, the Bahraini boss fired the Indian manager. On the day he was dismissed, the manager gathered all the workers together and told them that if they went on strike they might be able to get their overtime money and back pay. They walked out at midnight the next day, pooled their money, and rented a bus. There were 180 of them. The group from the Indian state of Andhra Pradesh decided to back out. Then there were 110. The next morning they went to the Ministry of Labor and stood outside.[3]

A man finally came out and gave them a piece of paper. The writing was in Arabic, and none of the men could read it, but the man told them to bring it back to the company and they would get their salary and overtime. They showed it to the company man the next day, but he called the police. Although frightened by the arrival of the police, the men were told that the officers only wanted to arrest the manager. The manager escaped by flying back to India the next day. The company gave the men their back salary, but not their overtime, and they worked for five more months. Three weeks before the Ramadan holidays, the new manager told them that there wouldn't be any holiday for them. He said they would have to work every day.

They struck again and went back to the Ministry of Labor. The Ministry officials were upset, and they made them return to the camp. The men waited at the camp for two days. Then the company closed the canteen. They had no food. The company turned off the electricity, so they had no air-conditioning. Then the company turned off the water. A Ministry official came on the fourth day, and he told the men that this was now a matter for the courts. Then a Bahraini lawyer came. She took 1,200 dinars from them—that's $3,000, or 10 dinars from each man.

The men were only allowed to go to the court in small groups. The judge asked them if they wanted to go on with the case. If they did, they had to keep working for the company. If they dropped the case, they could get papers to find another job. The company owner returned the passports to the men who dropped the case. Vijay decided not to drop the case. The factory closed. He no longer had a source of income. He became an "illegal" worker. He has no ticket home, but he found a job installing air-conditioning ducts. It's under the table, as we say in the United States. If he crosses paths with the police, however, he'll have to go to jail and pay a fine of 10 dinars per month—that's about US$25. He's stuck. He heard rumors that a government-sponsored amnesty period might be granted next year. If he's able to save enough money, he'll buy a ticket home then.

With Vijay's story, we have an abundance of detail that allows us to better explicate the forces at work in the production of illegality in Bahrain. In addition to the fundamental fact that Vijay was exploited and underpaid, consider the multiple other issues with which he struggled: before his sojourn in the Gulf, Vijay had no clear idea about the exchange rate; the debt he incurred for travel to the Gulf was borne by his family as a whole, and the pressure to stay in place came, in part, from his own family ("His father told him to weather the difficulties"). Vijay was unable to communicate with many of the other workers in the camp, and he could not speak Arabic. He was unable to parse the documents and court orders, and unable to understand the court proceedings. He had no direct access to his sponsor, and dissent was channeled through a foreign manager. The court system and police force did little to resolve the situation, and in the final accounting the state was seemingly complicit in the making of his circumstances. By the end of the narrative, Vijay is an illegal worker. Although his relationship with his sponsor was central to this condition, numerous other forces conspired to produce these circumstances.

MAPPING THE STRUCTURE OF VIOLENCE

To recapitulate, the kafala is the Gulf-wide sponsorship system by which the large transnational populations at work in the Gulf states are organized, managed, and controlled. The kafala is the sponsorship system itself; *kafeel* is the Arabic singular noun for the individual sponsor with whom each arriving foreign worker is associated. To continue building my argument that the kafala itself is key to understanding the structural violence levied against foreign workers in Bahrain, I analyze three aspects of the kafala: its connection to the larger global political economy, the practical and instrumental underpinnings of the kafala itself, and the slippage between the kafala as a cultural practice and as a legal arrangement. I then describe four facets of this system of exploitation and control that surfaced repeatedly in my interviews with Indian men and women on the island: the transnational character of the contracts and debt incurred in their sojourn to the Gulf; the control of the foreign workers' passports by the kafeel; the linguistic and cultural barriers that limit their strategic responses to the dilemmas they face; and the spatial aspects of this system of dominance. As a comprehensive system for controlling foreign workers on the island, the kafala clearly resembles what Bales (2004, 2005) has called "contract slavery." I sketch the connections between the kafala and the new slavery that Bales has ably described.

First, in calling the systemic control levied against foreign workers in Bahrain a form of structural violence, I point to the global political/economic forces and, more specifically, the poverty, economic marginalization, and environmental degradation that push men and women from India to the Gulf. The stories from my ethnographic data—of farmland drying up, of the inability of poor Indian families to pay for the education or marriage of sons and daughters—constitute one piece of the puzzle posed by calling this control a form of structural violence. Furthermore, in seeking a remedy through employment abroad, Indian laborers and their families typically pay thousands of dollars for the right to work in the Gulf; the first two or three years of labor are often devoted simply to paying back the debts they and their families incurred. Although significant portions of these payments move across the transnational divide to the kafeel, or sponsor, the debt itself remains in India and, typically, with the transmigrant's family. The transnational character of this debt becomes a fulcrum for abuse: a labor strike or individual resistance to the conditions of employment in Bahrain puts distant Indian families and key productive resources at great risk.

Second, I point to a variety of practical and instrumental aspects that enable this structural violence against foreign workers. The vast majority of the transnational manual laborers I spoke with had yielded their passports to their sponsor upon arrival. Hence their ability to physically leave the island as one potential response to violence and exploitation is controlled by the kafeel, who is, at the same time, the individual or entity positioned to profit from the workers' presence. Moreover, under the terms of recent edicts, only sponsors or their citizen-proxies can deal with the critical paperwork at the variety of government offices that contribute to the management and regulation of the large foreign populations. And although English is the language of the booming private sector on the island, all government agencies, including the court system, operate in Arabic. Combined with the fact that most laborers reside in labor camps located in the distant urban periphery and thus are far from the government offices and embassies to which they might appeal in times of difficulty, Indian transmigrants are systematically handicapped from challenging the dilemmas and problems they encounter in Bahrain.

Finally, the kafala is a system only partly codified in law. As the anthropologist Ahn Longva has observed, in the Gulf nations the kafala emerged in the twentieth century as an outgrowth of a cultural practice used to organize labor on the pearling dhows that plied the waters of the Persian Gulf (1997, 106–7). Enmeshed in this notion of the kafala as a cultural practice, citizens often balance the systemic abuse levied against foreign workers with notions of the kafeel's responsibility for potential moral and cultural transgressions that the sponsored foreigner might commit, a notion that posits foreign workers as a polluting presence (Peutz 2006, 223, 231; Douglas 2002). These vague interconnections also suggest links among deportation, illegality, and the welfare state, for citizens are not just protecting their cultural traditions, or even a certain set of political rights (Isin 2002)—they are also protecting a citizenship that confers an abundance of material benefits (Walters 2002, 279). Although the underlying moral discourse is frequently cited by citizen-sponsors as a balancing factor in their relationships with foreigners, I echo Longva in remarking that I know of no cases that demonstrate detrimental results to sponsors for the cultural or moral infractions of sponsored foreign workers.

Power and Transnational Debt

The foundations for the imbalance of power between citizen-sponsor and foreign worker in the Gulf are constructed well before the worker sets foot in Arabia. Over the last twenty to thirty years, the work visa that allows the foreigner to work in the petroleum-rich nations of the Arabian Peninsula has evolved from a minor aspect of the bureaucratic system—what one of my informants called a "mere formality" upon his arrival in the 1970s—to a valued commodity on the global market.[4] Whereas the men and women who arrived before the 1980s reported paying little or nothing for these visas, the men I interviewed in 2002 and 2003 often had paid well over $2,000 for the right to come to Bahrain and work. Furthermore, the dramatic rise in the market price of these visas coincided with a steady decline in the monthly wages paid to foreign unskilled laborers. Near the end of my time on the island, I began to encounter new arrivals at the labor camps who had paid thousands of dollars for a two-year work visa permitting them to work for BD30–40 a month (approximately $100)—well below the BD60–90 considered standard for manual laborers upon my arrival in 2002. Excluding calculations for the interest charged by moneylenders, and even minimizing expenditures on food, phone calls home, and other incidentals, these men cannot turn a profit until the end of their second year abroad. The risk, of course, is that the contract will not be honored—or that the laborers will not be paid at all. The sliver of potential profit that rests in the back end of these calculations depends on the goodwill and honor of the kafeel.

In gauging the structural forces that shape and condition the foreign worker's experience in the Gulf states, my interests are twofold. First, the sums of money needed to acquire these work visas are large. Vijay, for example, described a combination of sources for the sum he paid: he drew on his personal savings and borrowed some from moneylenders. His family, and more specifically his mother, pawned her gold jewelry, and Vijay borrowed the remainder from family and friends. Another young laborer described his situation: "My father is very old, and he can no longer work. My older brother is very lazy, and he's not working either. He's not smart, and he's not taking care with his life. He only earns 1,500 rupees [about $34] a month.... My family had some paddy land, but to come here we had to sell the land. There wasn't enough water in the well anyway, and the harvests were smaller and smaller each year. So that's why we decided to sell the land, and that's why I came here."

Nearly all members of the transnational proletariat described similar scenarios, sometimes with additional facets. Households may decide, for strategic financial reasons, to end one child's education so that he or she can enter the workforce and help with the burden of debt incurred by another's trip to the Gulf. Farmland and other productive resources are put up as collateral for the loans described by these laborers. The overall portrait emerging from my interviews suggests that the individual laborer is deeply enmeshed in a complex web of household relations and dependencies: he arrives in Bahrain as an emissary of a household-level strategy that places the well-being of the extended family before the transmigrant's individual interests.[5] In essence, most of the men I encountered clearly articulated that the fate of an extended family hangs in the balance. Together, these typical aspects of Gulf migration forge unequal relations between foreign workers and their sponsors, for in their actions foreign workers risk not only their own lives, well-being, and future, but also those of their families in India.

Second, not only is the balance of power between foreign worker and kafeel tipped by the simple fact that the laborer enters the relationship with a large and family-held debt; it is also tipped by the transnational character of that debt. The details of the system for moving both money and people east to the Gulf states have been well described by other scholars (Gamburd 2000; Fuglerud 1999; Kurien 2002). The $2,000 or $3,000 paid for the right to work in the Gulf is, most commonly, paid to a labor broker or agent in the sending country. That agent is entitled to some portion of the funds, but the bulk makes its way across the transnational divide to the citizen-sponsor. The citizen-sponsor pays the various fees to regularize the work visa, typically approximating $800 at the time this research was conducted. Although the money has, for the most part, moved to the Gulf, the debt itself remains in South Asia. Should a problem arise between the kafeel and foreign worker, that money remains off the bargaining table: productive land and familial savings remain at risk, and the laborer is thousands of miles away from the agent with whom he or she originally negotiated the contract to work in the Gulf.

The basic premises of the relationship help explain why the threat of removal is so effective. For Vijay and the other men who described their experiences to me, returning home is more than a poor solution to their problems: it is potentially a cataclysmic financial event. They return home to families stripped of key productive resources and burdened by the additional debt incurred in sending them to the Gulf in the first place. These forces compel the foreign worker to stay in place, to endure the suffering at the hands of exploitative and abusive sponsors, or to flee those scenarios in search of work as an illegal laborer.

Control of the Passport

Although the debt accrued in exchange for the right to work abroad builds the unequal basis for the relationship between foreign laborers and their citizen-sponsors, the widespread practice of confiscating a foreign worker's passport also plays a predominant role in shaping the outcome of many conflicts. Bahraini law explicitly forbids confiscating foreign workers' passports, yet the practice is common: all except one of the laborers I encountered had relinquished their passports to their sponsors upon arrival. And, as Vijay's narrative makes clear, this illegal practice is indirectly supported by the state. Consider again this portion of Vijay's story: "The men were only allowed to go to the court in small groups. The judge asked them if they wanted to go on with the case. If they did, they had to keep working for the company. If they dropped the case, they could get papers to find another job. The company owner returned the passports to the men that dropped the case."

In the most practical sense, the sponsor's possession of the passport prevents the laborer from departing the island: no matter how difficult the working conditions, and no matter how focused the abuse, the laborer is beholden to his or her original sponsor. Although the practice of a sponsor retaining a worker's passport is expressly forbidden by law, in Vijay's case the court ordered that the men who dropped the case against the citizen-sponsor would have their passports returned. Such an order is evidence, if not of the state's complicity in establishing the parameters of this structural violence, then at least of what Heyman and Smart describe as "some variety of symbiosis" between the state and illegal practices (1999, 1), for the court seemed content to allow the sponsor to retain the passports of those men who would not drop the case.

More than merely a mechanism for preventing labor from fleeing, control of the foreign worker's passport becomes a key mechanism for deriving additional profit from the transnational proletariat. In times of difficulty or in legal imbroglios, foreign workers are often forced to buy back their passports from their original sponsors. As an example, for several weeks I attended the meetings of the Ecumenical Council of Charity, one of the many diasporic voluntary associations that informally assist foreign workers in crisis. In January 2003 the group made contact with a Sri Lankan domestic worker, recently diagnosed with breast cancer, who was languishing in the hospital. The woman hoped to return to Sri Lanka for treatment, but her kafeel refused to release her passport until she paid him BD300 ($800). Members of the charity group spent ten minutes considering how much money the group would donate to this end. These sorts of scenarios recur in the interviews I conducted on the island, and although some workers, like Vijay, bring their cases before the court, most transmigrants end up relying on their savings, personal networks, and the charity of these informal organizations to pay off sponsors and regain their passports in time of distress. More commonly—and as was the case with Vijay's compatriots—foreign workers receive their passports only after forfeiting any claims against their original sponsor.

Linguistic and Cultural Barriers

Linguistic and cultural barriers are another set of limits to the agency of foreign workers and hence structure inequities in the workers' relations with sponsors. Consider Vijay's description of the many nights he spent trying to learn Arabic and Hindi as part of his attempt to increase his ability to understand and interrogate the system in which he was enmeshed. Although large transmigrant workforces may be made up entirely of South Asians, that is no guarantee that the laborers can speak with one another. Bahrain and the other Gulf states draw heavily from South Indian states where Hindi is not widely spoken. As one construction manager noted, most companies are careful to draw labor from a variety of different regions, for these linguistic, national, cultural, and ethnic differences help build a more fragmented and docile workforce—a workforce with less ability to organize and strike. For example, in the labor strike described by Vijay the entire contingent of laborers from the state of Andhra Pradesh broke from the strike. That these men constituted a discrete linguistic group within the camp played an instrumental role in their decision to abandon the strike.

The relative powerlessness of the transmigrant laborer is further reinforced by the policies and procedures that situate the sponsor as "mediator between the state and individual migrant" (Longva 1997, 103). As Vijay described, transmigrants often lack direct access to their official sponsor and must instead deal with proxies—often other expatriate laborers in managerial positions—in contesting their working conditions, pay, and hours. The power of the sponsor is buttressed by the inability of Indian laborers to directly interface with the state and its multiple bureaucracies: renewing a visa or switching sponsors requires the intervention and approval of the kafeel. Beyond the fact that most of these government ministries operate in Arabic, my informants remarked that by policy many of the immigration bureaucracies in the government now only serve Bahrainis, and that expatriates can no longer bring issues directly to the various ministries but must instead rely on citizen-intermediaries.[6] As one laborer described, "Twice over my ten years here my sponsor got 550 dinars [$1,460] from me for visa renewal. Both times he didn't even regularize my visa. So I paid 1,300 dinars [$3,450] to come to Bahrain, I paid 1,100 dinars [$2,920] and then 450 dinars [$1,195] recently. So that's...2,950 dinars...nearly 3,000 dinars [$7,960] for six years. Did I even earn this much? I don't know!"

Upon arrival in Bahrain, the transnational laborer enters a linguistic and cultural context in which his capacity as an agent is severely constrained. As Vijay described, many of these laborers have difficulty even speaking with their own countrymen. While Malayalam, Hindi, or English may serve them in the public spaces of the country, it is Arabic that predominates in the hallways and offices of the state bureaucracy, a fact that further fetters their ability to address the dilemmas and hurdles they face on the island. Furthermore, a set of entrenched policies and practices channel power to the kafeel: he is the foreign worker's official representative to the state and also the person who profits from his labor. Together, these arrangements and practices comprise another facet of the structural violence foreign workers encounter in Bahrain: by constraining their ability to assert their rights, to take collective action, or to put their case before the state, these policies and practices enable the violence these workers endure in their everyday lives.

Geographies and Temporalities of Dominance

In the course of conducting ethnographic interviews with members of the Indian transnational proletariat, I focused on their explanations of the

Figure 3.1. Men preparing to depart camp for their work site. Photograph by Andrew Gardner.

dilemmas and tribulations they faced in the crucible of the kafala. Much of the information they conveyed to me concerned the conditions of their workplace, the economics of their sojourn in the Gulf, and the strategies they configured to cope with problems and challenges. In the interstices of these migration narratives, however, I began to realize how their physical location in the city, as well as the tight management of their time, played a significant role in curtailing their strategic responses to the systemic pressures they faced.

Daily life in the labor camps begins at an early hour. Men typically rise at four or five in the morning to prepare food for the day. Their "duty," as it is commonly called, typically begins at 6:00 a.m., and they work until noon with a short break somewhere in that period. During the half-hour break at noon, many eat the lunch they have prepared for themselves; those without kitchen facilities at their camp (or those who don't prepare their own lunch) purchase meals from the "chiapati cars" that make the rounds of the larger work sites during the lunch hour. After their short lunch break, the men continue working until 4:30 or 5:00 in the afternoon, at which time they are transported back to the camp. In the congested streets of urban Manama, transportation to and from the work site can occupy thirty minutes or more. Arriving back at camp around 6:00 in the evening, the men cook, eat, wash, and relax. They are often asleep by 10:00 p.m.

Although these "normal" schedules typify the days of countless laborers on the island, many work different hours, and many others work even longer hours, as Vijay noted regarding his own experience in the garment factory.

The laborers work six days a week on such schedules. Friday, the second day of the weekend in Bahrain during my time there, is usually the men's day off.[7] Many of the laborers I spoke with had the entire day off; others worked a portion of that day, sometimes for overtime pay, sometimes as part of their regular duties. For those laborers who had some portion of the day free, hours were spent preparing for the coming week, washing clothing, writing letters and recording cassettes for loved ones in India, and watching VCR or DVD recordings of Indian movies. Others would journey to the souk, the central market area, where on Fridays the streets fill with laborers from around the globe. An afternoon in the souk provides a chance to visit friends and relatives, to share a leisurely stroll with co-workers, and to purchase inexpensive necessities from the many shops in the central district.

The majority of the camps I visited were far from the center of the city. Typically they were located in light industrial districts with few services, such as grocery stores, Internet cafes, hardware stores, and restaurants. These camps were poorly served by public transportation, making life all the more difficult for laborers. Some workers were unable to make the long journey to town on their day off, and many others curtailed their movements around the neighborhoods outside their compounds for fear of conflict with the predominantly Shi'ite populations that share these less desirable locations in the city. Their geographical isolation on the periphery of the city and the culture of fear that characterizes their presence in many of these neighborhoods constrained their ability to take their dilemmas to the Indian embassy, government offices, medical facilities, or the social clubs and other diasporic institutions that provide some modicum of assistance to foreign workers in crisis. Like domestic workers—many of whom are literally locked inside for much of their stay in Bahrain—members of the Indian transnational proletariat have little contact with the world outside their labor camp and workplace.[8]

As the daily schedule of the typical worker suggests, time also constrains transmigrant laborers. Work occupies most of the day, and what free time the laborer has typically occurs in the evening or the weekend—hours when all government agencies and many other services are closed. Together, then, these spatial and temporal factors prevent communication among foreign workers, mitigate their ability to cope with conflicts with sponsors, and

Figure 3.2. South Asian laborers at work. Photograph by Andrew Gardner.

generally limit the strategies they bring to bear against the difficult circumstances of laboring in the Gulf. In that sense, these factors actively contribute to the framework of the structural violence encountered by the laboring class of foreign workers on the island.

Labor Contracts, Structural Violence, and New Slavery

Kevin Bales argues that in the modern world, labor contracts often mask contemporary forms of slavery: "Contracts are offered that guarantee employment, perhaps in a workshop or factory, but when the workers are taken to their place of work they find themselves enslaved. The contract is used as an enticement to trick an individual into slavery, as well as a way of making the slavery look legitimate" (2004, 20). This contract slavery, he argues, is one facet of a "new slavery," a contemporary form of slavery in which legal ownership is avoided, purchase costs are low, profits are high, there is a glut of potential slaves, the relationship between owner and slave is typically short, the slaves are disposable, and ethnic differences are less important than in traditional slavery (15). To some degree or another, all these descriptors resonate with the experiences of the transnational proletariat in the Gulf. Bales's definition of slavery hinges on control: "it is not about owning people in the traditional sense of old slavery, but about controlling them completely" (4).

Like Bales's explication of new slavery, the relationship between Bahraini citizens and the foreign workers they sponsor is about control. Thinking about this control in structural terms — and in terms of structural violence — has pushed me to increase my scope of inquiry: What are the arrangements, both local and transnational, that foster these forms of dominance? On what aspects of the complex arrangements of transmigration to the Gulf is this dominance contingent? Unpacking the complexities of control has been my principal task here, but that task should not eclipse the fact that this structure of dominance, and the violence it encourages, has a purpose. That purpose is, of course, profit. When a poor Indian family mortgages its productive assets, pulls children from school, and pawns the mother's jewelry to come up with the thousands of dollars it takes to send a son to the Gulf, only to have him face month after month of no pay and, finally, be relegated to scrounging for illegal work, it may seem a tragic story for that family. When viewed systemically, however, this scenario suggests that we move beyond simply thinking about what services these transmigrants supply to citizens, as De Genova suggests (2002, 422). Rather, we can see the outline of what William Walters calls a "deportation industry" (2002, 266). Walters uses this concept to suggest that deportation, viewed holistically, is a "system that implicates all manner of agents — not just police and immigration officials, but airline executives, pilots, stewards, and other passengers" (266). In Bahrain, and through the mechanism of the kafala, the list of agents must also include the multitude of individual citizen-sponsors on the island, all of whom operate under the tragic logic of the kafala: although there is profit for sponsors who *do* regularly pay their foreign workers (after all, they are capturing the surplus labor of these transmigrants), there is even more profit for those sponsors who fail to pay the men and women they bring to Bahrain. Looking at certain strata of the foreign laboring population, one can perceive this system as a vast transfer of wealth—one whereby thousands of families in South Asia are separated from what little wealth they have accrued, through equity or debt. That wealth is then transferred to the labor brokers, sponsors, and the state, who, in tandem, perpetuate and maintain the deportability of the laborers they bring to the island.[9]

Removal and Deportation in the Gulf Transmigrant Experience

With no path to assimilation, the Indian transnational proletariat in Bahrain is the largest component of a foreign workforce configured and controlled to buoy Bahrain's place in the booming transnational economy of the contemporary Gulf. As a system, the kafala has emerged as a fulcrum of abuse to which racial, cultural, gender, and religious bigotry cling. By vesting power in individual citizens through the kafala, the Bahraini state enables these vectors of abuse. Currently a variety of informal church organizations, voluntary associations, and other informal institutions function as the primary means by which the foreign communities address this abuse: informal and ephemeral diasporic institutions pay for the plane tickets to send the bodies of deceased workers home, to help individuals make payoffs to sponsors for releasing them to return to India, and to help publicize the most dramatic confrontations between sponsors and foreign workers. Plans are under way to dismantle certain aspects of the sponsorship system. These proposed plans face significant resistance, despite the fact that they are an incremental change at best.

What can we conclude about the role of deportation in the lives of these Indian transmigrants? It is certainly true that Bahrain and its Gulf Cooperation Council neighbors are atypical migratory waypoints, particularly when compared with the European and North American migratory conduits that predominate in the literature on transnationalism and migration. The patterns that characterize transmigrants' experiences in the Gulf, significantly different from those of immigrants to North America and western Europe, reinforce De Genova's emphatic call for research that avoids any claims of an overarching, generic immigrant experience (De Genova 2002, 424). Nonetheless, as Peutz (2006) and De Genova (2002) suggest, removal, deportation, and the threat of deportation remain integral aspects in the Gulf migrant's experience abroad. Viewing the many facets of the transmigrants' experiences through the lens of structural violence, however, demonstrates, in theoretical terms, the importance of contextualizing removal, deportation, and the threat of deportation in the larger arena of power relations that shape the migrant and transmigrant experience. Removal, deportation, and the threat of deportation provide a fine starting point for an analysis of the complex and interrelated factors that produce vulnerability among the Indian laboring community in Bahrain, but together they represent but one facet in a complex structure of dominance that shapes the experiences and systematizes the exploitation of foreign workers in the Gulf.

What is unique in the case of the Gulf is the distribution of the power in the machinery configured to manage Gulf migration. Although the state certainly plays a central role, the kafala nonetheless distributes much of the power traditionally seen as belonging to the state and its various apparatuses to individual citizens, to what Walters calls "private authorities" (2002, 268). The production of illegality, the threat of deportation, and the act of removal are powers and processes generated in the relations between individual sponsors and the foreign workers they bring to the island, processes disembedded from the "contemporary administrative practice of Western states" (Walters 2002, 266). It is this arrangement, vesting citizens with the power and responsibility to manage and control the foreign population, that encourages the sort of violence I describe throughout this book.

As should be clear, these cases of violence are far from anecdotal, and although the discursive scope of the international human rights movement has certainly reached the shores of Bahrain, the power of the foreign worker to secure basic human rights is, ironically, decreasing. Sadly, throughout the Gulf, the violence and abuse I describe have become increasingly normalized and in many ways exacerbated by the recent global economic downturn. As Nancy Scheper-Hughes argues, this normalization is a key aspect of structural violence (2004, 14). Her attention, and that of other scholars interested in identifying and describing structural violence, frequently draws on the discursive terrain that produces this normalization—on the ideas and beliefs that guide, permit, and condone individual acts of violence (Scheper-Hughes 2004; Holmes 2007). These issues are dealt with at length in the later chapters of this book. Here I focused primarily on the machinery of inequality—on the arrangement of relations between citizen and foreigner that produces these beliefs and ideas, and produces the violence I have described. These arrangements are essential to understanding the lived experience of the hundreds of thousands of men and women who depart for the Gulf in search of a better life for themselves and their families.

4 STRATEGIC TRANSNATIONALISM

The Indian Diasporic Elite

While the previous chapter described the lifeworlds of the poorest segments of the Indian community, this chapter explores the experiences of the Indian *elite* in Bahrain. The size of this segment of the diasporic community is difficult to gauge, but my estimates suggest approximately 30,000 individuals.[1] As merchants, accountants, bankers, doctors, advertising executives, and other well-paid professionals—accompanied to Bahrain by their spouses and children—these men and women work in the skyscrapers their impoverished countrymen have built. As one might expect, members of this diasporic elite lead lives significantly different in character from those of the Indian transnational proletariat. Yet is the Indian diasporic elite subject to the same structural violence that characterizes the experience of the transnational proletariat in Bahrain, or do the significant resources they bring to bear (in terms of social, cultural, and economic capital) mitigate their vulnerability to this structural violence? Albeit with certain caveats, the ethnographic data I collected suggest that the diasporic elite *do* find themselves enmeshed in webs of dominance that appear strikingly similar to those of their impoverished countrymen and countrywomen on the island. I conclude the chapter with a description of the strategic transnationalism that makes up the diasporic elite's principal response to the vulnerabilities they face during their sojourn on the island.

Transnational Theory and the Gulf States

In constructing a theoretical lens through which the social sciences might begin to unpack the complex social fields wrought by the increasing mobility of labor, social scientists have focused almost to exclusion on transmigrant populations spread across particular geographical polarities. Like the Indian laborers described in the previous chapter—most of whom, even while abroad, remain fixed on their home communities in India—the case studies that inform transnational theory typically examine lives spread across two nations. In their seminal collection, Basch, Glick, and Szanton Blanc (1994), for example, look at the institutions constructed by various groups of Caribbean and Filipino transmigrants in the United States, mostly within the greater New York City area; Smith and Guarnizo's collection (1998), while geographically diverse, nonetheless relies almost exclusively on case studies of populations with a transmigratory endpoint in the United States; Goldring (1998) examines the social fields that encompass Las Animas, Mexico, and the transmigrant community in the Bay Area; Smith (1998) describes the formidable conduits between Ticuani, Mexico, and the burgeoning Ticuanense community in Brooklyn, New York; and Matthei and Smith (1998) chart the transfer of Los Angeles gang structures through the transnational conduits binding south central Los Angeles to the Garifuna communities of the Belizean coast. Ongoing contributions to this empirical foundation, most of which are focused on these south-to-north conduits, arrive in ever-greater numbers. From this springboard, social scientists have hypothesized processes that strain or erode the foundations of the nation-state (Appadurai 1996; Kearney 1991; Hobsbawm 1990, 182–83; Ong 1999, 214), explored the social fields that cross national boundaries (Basch, Glick, and Szanton Blanc 1994; Goldring 1998), delineated a "cultural bifocality" endemic to contemporary transmigrants (Rouse 1992, 41), and periodically assessed the viability of anthropology's territorialized notion of culture (Hannerz 1996, 19–22; King 1991, 6).

In ascertaining how the case presented here fits within this larger literature on the transnational movement of people through the circuits of global capitalism, one can certainly delineate parallels between the case of the Indian transnational proletariat in Bahrain and the case studies underpinning much of the theoretical production of transnational theory. Yet in the previous chapter I described a structure of dominance rooted in the state and manifest in the habitus configuring everyday interactions between transmigrants and citizens. As a system, this structure binds and constrains transmigrant agency in particular ways: this transnational proletariat's movement back and forth across the Indian Ocean, for example, is fettered by the systemic controls exerted by a sponsorship system that ties transmigrants to an individual sponsor; their ability to move about the island and to meet, organize, and communicate with other transmigrants is strictly monitored and controlled; their status on the island holds no promise of permanency or assimilation; and their inability to engage the Bahraini legal system hampers recourse in the many dilemmas they encounter. An accounting of these differences points to a principal pattern in the transnational literature: although most of the case studies fit the polar model of home and away, most also focus on migration from the global south to the global north, and therefore to particular types of states—wealthy, democratic, and nominally open societies, some of which (like the United States) have articulated an identity ostensibly based on the assimilation and incorporation of difference.

What about populations migrating to other sorts of destinations? A handful of ethnographers have begun to explore the transmigration experiences of those moving outside the Western conduits that predominate in the literature. Leichtman, for example, presents the case of the Lebanese diaspora in Senegal, arguing that the transnational canon fails to appropriately gauge the "important role colonialism has played in influencing transnational processes in other parts of the world," an influence she describes as shaping the destinations of transmigrants, promoting particular economic hierarchies, encouraging racism, and offering or withdrawing the protections implicit in citizenship (2005, 666, 681).[2] Aihwa Ong, in her well-known work (1999), describes the flexible positions negotiated by cosmopolitan individuals tethered to multiple locations around the Pacific Rim, including (but not limited to) endpoints in North America. More specific to transnationalism on the Arabian Peninsula, Anh Longva (2000, 2005) argues that the large transnational populations in the Gulf states have played an integral role in forging the fundamental structure and logic of the state, a logic she sees as ethnocratic in nature. Gamburd's ethnography (2000) of Sri Lankan domestic workers and their time in the Gulf details the panoptic control exerted by host families over the women they hire, as well as the fleeting and contingent avenues by which these women exert agency. As ethnographers have begun to examine transnational populations moving outside the global north, analysis has charted alternative forms of the state, other regimes of repression and control, and new configurations of dominance over the trans-status subjects moving between nations. These works suggest that the ability of men and women to forge transnational lives can, under particular configurations of state and culture, be significantly more constrained than the models emanating from analyses of transnational flows with an endpoint in the global north. In this sense, then, the case study presented here is meant to join those looking at transnational movement outside the West (Leichtman 2005; Willen 2007; Ong 1999; Sarker and De 2002), and following Ong (1999, 214–15), to further illuminate the processes by which governance is extended over the mobility endemic to transnational populations in the contemporary milieu.[3]

Although this chapter is meant to complement the literature concerned with transmigration to endpoints outside the global north, I also use the data I collected to address the fundamental geographical polarity underlying much of transnational theory. Unlike the transmigrants portrayed in the vast majority of the literature, and unlike the Indian laborers described at the outset of this chapter, the Indian diasporic elite in Bahrain are, generally speaking, *not* caught between two places: their struggle has little to do with the dilemmas of maintaining a social field spanning Bahrain and India. Rather, members of the Indian diasporic elite build and maintain social fields that are rhizomic, stretching from Bahrain back to India, certainly, but also reaching to numerous other points around the globe. Although this model bears some resemblance to Ong's notion of flexible citizenship, it is the "citizenship" portion of that concept that becomes particularly problematic in the Gulf states, for members of the Indian diaspora in Bahrain rarely find sanctuary in Bahraini citizenship. Rather, they maintain social relations and an identity that are, at best, moored in the Gulf states.

THE LURE OF THE GULF

On a warm spring day in 2003, I found myself lost in the traffic circles of Saar, one of Manama's many burgeoning suburbs. I had arranged a five o'clock appointment with George, a busy manager at a dairy plant and a fellow member of the Manama Toastmasters, the international club I had recently joined. After circling the nondescript factory several times, I noticed the small sign on the side of the building, and passing through the security gate, I arrived ten minutes late for the interview. George's office was piled high with paperwork and files from his daily responsibilities, and after a long discussion about the impact of Gulf migration on his home state of Kerala, George described his own motivations for coming to Bahrain:

> I'd been working in India, in different parts of India, for about three years. And I had been working with one of the best companies, one of the best paying companies in all of India. In spite of all my hard work

and struggle when I was younger, I could only make...not more than 100 dinars [$265] a month. One hundred dinars, that used to be my salary, and I would work 16 hours [a day] sometimes, 20 hours, whatever it is. I was in sales, moving to different places, traveling and touring. It's a big, vast country. In sales, you have to get from one place to another, so there's a lot of travel. So my salary over that period, take the average, was about 100 dinars. Now when you come here to Bahrain, if you're lucky you can make two, three times that.

Six weeks later, at a manufacturing warehouse on the opposite side of town, I spoke with Deepali, a young professional, about her experience working in India:

So I started working in American Express in Delhi, and it was quite good, an international company and all that. But the money was so bad!...The pay there was equivalent to 50 dinars [$133] a month, and I was like, "what is this?" So I realized that I was living, but I was not happy. I would be sulking the whole day. I had to get up at 5:30, and change two buses to be in the office by 8:00. I'd finish at 5:00, again two buses, and reach home by 8:30, 9:00.

As George and Deepali make clear, the petroleum-rich nations of the Arabian Peninsula continue to provide economic opportunities that surpass readily available positions in India. The relative pay scales of Gulf-based and Indian-based jobs are common knowledge in professional circles and figure prominently in the long-term career strategies of many of the individuals with whom I spoke. Furthermore, the lure of the Gulf draws individuals at many different points of their career: for every young professional recently arrived on the island, I met others near the end of their career. For example, as a former officer of the Indian navy explained, he and his wife, a radiologist, saw a sojourn in Bahrain as a stepping stone to retirement: "In two years, we could save what would take us seven or eight years in India." Another Indian who originally left India for Oman on the eve of the 1991 Gulf War noted that, at the time, "for every dollar you earned in India you could earn six here in the Middle East."

Karen Leonard recently concluded that "market forces rather than individual agency are driving the expatriate workers in the Gulf" (2003, 156). As Deepali and George suggest, market forces play a key role in many decisions to come to the Gulf. Yet in the interviews I conducted with professionals and other members of the diasporic elite, other justifications for the move abroad also figured prominently in the decision process. In general, many were seeking jobs more connected to global finance, insurance, business, and other related arenas, all in the domain of what Appadurai (1996) calls the global financescape. The oil wealth of the Gulf has fostered the growth of these sectors, and Bahrain, as the regional hub for significant portions of the Gulf's financial and service industry, is one avenue into the world of transnational business. The economic gain associated with occupations in the sectors of the financescape is complemented by the possibility of transfers to other, more desirable locations (typically Europe, North America, Australia, and New Zealand). In this sense, Gulf destinations serve as a catalyst for even greater diasporic displacements (Leonard 2003, 131).

Other reasons cited by the professionals and skilled laborers I interviewed fall entirely outside the economic calculus often bound to migration. Take the case of Shahzeb, an administrator in an educational institution on the island. The son of a Pakistani (and Muslim) diplomat, Shahzeb grew up in India, where he fell in love with a young Indian (and Hindu) woman. After their controversial marriage, the young couple began to look beyond the borders of Pakistan or India for a place to begin again. The difficulties of life in either of those places, with all the incumbent pressures of a cross-national and cross-religious marriage, were in their estimation too formidable. As they described it to me, Bahrain "represented a sort of neutral ground for us. With the difficulties between Indian and Pakistan, neither place seemed ideal for settling down. Bahrain represented such a place—a neutral ground where we could begin our life anew." Another successful Indian administrator, Mariam, echoed this sentiment: "I came to Bahrain in 1981. I came not because I wanted to work—I just needed a change of scene. This is my second marriage. My first husband died in India. In India, when you get married...a widow is never looked on in the same fashion as a normal person." For Mariam, whose story I explore in more detail later in this chapter, Bahrain represented a new start beyond the pressures and confines of the socially constructed role of the Indian widow.

Along these same lines, the recent rise of the Hindu/fundamentalist BJP, a political party intertwined with the increasingly polemical relations between the Muslim and Hindu populations in India, has also pushed Muslim Indians out of India. As a wealthy Indian corporate executive described, "Hyderabad...no, India in general, is no longer a safe place for Muslims. Every year things are changing, and for Muslims it is getting worse." Like many members of the Indian diasporic elite, he is looking westward for his future: he had established residency in Chicago and, at the time of my research, was preparing to move his family in the coming year. Moreover, he was no longer maintaining a household in India.

Finally, many members of this professional class were born in Bahrain. Many of these second- and third-generation Indian transnationals are part of the historic subcommunities of the Indian diaspora in Bahrain. The largest and most influential are the Bhatias, the Hindu portion of the Sindh community, cast from their homeland in Karachi after partition. Building upon mercantile linkages already established in the Gulf, many members of the Sindh community eventually moved families and resources to Bahrain, Dubai, and other urban ports of the region. Other Indian groups with a long-standing presence in Bahrain include the Gujarati businessmen whose enterprises historically centered on the sale of gold; the Bohra community, an Indian Muslim sect with a belief system particularly configured around business (see Blank 2001); and the Dhobi community of laundrymen. Over the last two decades, these historic components of the diasporic community have been joined by the sons and daughters of the generation of engineers and professionals who arrived in the 1960s and 1970s. Together they are children between, if not without, national allegiance. As one young woman, the daughter of a construction manager, answered my questions about her "home": "Where am I from? It's a very tough question. Sometimes I felt as if I was a kite, blowing between countries, from nowhere."

To recapitulate, while Leonard suggests the centrality of market forces in the "push" factors that encourage transmigration from South Asia to the Gulf, the purported centrality of those economic calculations must be gauged against the wide variety of other reasons that factor in decision processes. Following Mahler's call (1998, 82–83) to disaggregate the transmigrant populations by class, I suggest that these noneconomic factors often play a larger role in the transmigratory calculus of the diasporic elite than in the decision processes of the transnational proletariat (see also Gamburd 2000) and, as such, serve as a marker of class. Whereas the members of the transnational proletariat by and large arrive for solely economic reasons, members of the diasporic elite find themselves in Bahrain for a panoply of reasons, including—but not limited to—those of an economic nature.

In analyzing the structural violence levied against the transnational proletariat, I have argued that the economic compulsions and the transnational debts incurred by members of this proletariat in securing work in the Gulf—are keystones in the structure of dominance that permits and even encourages episodic violence against foreign laborers in the Gulf. If we keep in mind that economic factors are only one facet of the calculus that brings members of the diasporic elite to the petroleum-rich nations of the Arabian peninsula, then the question becomes this: Are the members of the diasporic elite free from the vulnerabilities rendered by this structure of dominance? Put another way, do the variety of compulsions, both economic and non-economic, that push members of the diasporic elite out of India correlate with a degree of freedom from the structural violence their impoverished countrymen encounter in the Gulf? In the next section I explore this issue and suggest that although the diasporic elite's reasons for coming to Bahrain are diverse, once ashore their encounters with the citizenry and state are strikingly parallel to those of the transnational proletariat.

Everyday Encounters and the Exertion of Dominance

I collected the following story from Anhil, a third-generation merchant at the apex of the Indian diaspora in Bahrain:

> Walking down the street, if I see five or six Bahraini guys coming toward me, I take the other road. I just don't want to go through them—it's to that point here. If you see five or six of them coming in a group, you go around the corner and come back later... things have happened to me once or twice. I've gotten into physical fights. One time I was parking my car, and this guy wanted to park in the same spot. He tells me to move my car, and this led to an altercation. He hit me. I hit him back. And all of the sudden his friends come, and there are ten of them. And then I thought, if I keep hitting this guy back, then ten guys are going to hit me. So I just left, and he hit me a couple of more times as I was getting away. When I got home, I realized that this was the stupidest thing I did, because I was in an alley, and these guys have no respect for—I hate to say this—but they have no respect for their lives.
>
> Another time, I used to have an office downstairs here. And this road, it's all expat store owners—Indians, Filipinos. And what happens is this: we double park, and everybody knows everybody, they just come and ask us, and we just move the cars. So this Bahraini guy comes for the first time to the road, and my car was blocking the street. Normally a guy would come in and ask me to move it. He comes into my office, storms right past my secretary, and bangs

his hand on my desk telling me to move my car. And I just lost it—I told him not to bang the table. And the next thing you know, it's a big thing, and he's called the cops. The first thing the cop asks me is this: what nationality are you? I asked him what that had to do with anything. Finally I said that I was Indian, and he took my license. Then it became another big thing. I had to get my license back, and I had to pay fines for double-parking my car, which under normal circumstances in Bahrain isn't anything. I was technically wrong, but it's a law that's never enforced in Bahrain.

Incidents like this reinforce to me that the less interaction you have with Bahrainis the better.

In laying out a strategy for transnational anthropology, Aihwa Ong argues that "the anthropology of the present should analyze people's everyday actions as a form of cultural politics embedded in specific power contexts" (1999, 4). In the next two sections, I follow Ong's advice by portraying these everyday interactions between citizen and foreigner as a means of describing the "specific power contexts" that members of the Indian diaspora encounter as they move about the island. The character of these interactions, where violence is always possible and recourse by the transmigrant to legal and institutional frameworks is difficult, is part of what Franklin called the "informal nature of domination" that transmigrants face in Bahrain (1985, 104). Like Gupta, however, I see the division between the formal and informal venues as problematic: rather, through an analysis of these everyday interactions we can see the state "implicated in the minute texture of everyday life" (Gupta 2006, 211). The pattern of these everyday interactions reveals the deployment of two contradictory logics that are key to understanding the systemic violence levied against foreigners of all classes.

Elite members of the Indian diaspora, whether recent arrivals or the children of transmigrants, envision themselves as components of the transnational financescape, a term deployed by Appadurai to describe the mysterious and rapid disposition of global capital in the contemporary world (1996, 34). As highly trained human capital, elite members of the Indian diaspora contribute to key sectors of the Bahraini economy as engineers, doctors, managers, financiers, and advertising executives, and in countless other positions that the undertrained citizenry are incapable or unwilling to fill (Khalaf and Alkobaisi 1999, 284; al-Rasheed 2005, 1). In doing so, members of the diasporic elite find themselves in cadence with the version of Bahraini nationalism widely purveyed by the state and its citizenry, a blueprint that envisions Bahrain as the progressive hub of finance and service industries in the Gulf, a beacon of modernity in the region, and a tourist attraction constructed around the city as a site of consumption. Yet the hierarchical logic of this global financescape—the logic that, in many cases, drew the diasporic elite from their homeland to Bahrain—coexists with a contradictory set of power relations codified in the state and manifest in the everyday interactions between foreigner and citizen-host. In these everyday interactions, even the lowliest citizen holds power over the educated and successful transmigrant. The friction of these two competing visions is evident in a continuation of the interview with Anhil, the merchant quoted earlier. In exasperation, he appealed to the neoliberal logic edified in Bahrain's national vision: "I mean, I have a business. I run things! I import things into this country! I pay taxes! I export things! And there are very few Bahrainis who actually do that—I actually purchase things made in Bahrain and export them to other countries, and earn an income for Bahrain!"

Bourdieu (1987) uses the concept of habitus to describe the learned dispositions individuals bring to bear in social interactions. In describing the interactions between citizens and noncitizens in the petroleum-rich states of the contemporary Gulf, scholars have connected this habitus to a "master-servant mentality" (Leonard 2003, 144), often stretching back to the particular configuration of the pearling industry's indentured servitude or to the tribal structure of the Bedouin peoples (Beaugé 1986, as quoted in Longva 1997, 78). Others have connected the citizenry's habitus to the explosive period of modernization wrought by the discovery of oil, a particular configuration that Champion argues has resulted in a "mudir syndrome," using the Arabic word for "boss," where every citizen sees him or herself as entitled to a position of authority and command over the legions of foreigners at work in the Gulf states (1999, 5). These explanations may provide some perspective on the genealogy of power relations in the contemporary Gulf, but as contemporary expressions of inequality these relations are more than simply vestiges of the past: they illustrate modern forms of dominance and governance. More acutely, this structure of dominance substitutes nationality, ethnicity, religion, and citizenship for the class logic wrought by the neoliberal model, a model that is at once essential to the predominant national vision promoted by the state and, at the same time, antithetical to the ethnocratic and sectarian order of the Bahraini state.

On an individual level, transmigrants encounter these particular forms of governance as a daily matter of course: at traffic stops and accidents—alarmingly common on the island—police commonly request the nationality of those involved as the first order of business. Several of my informants remarked that altercations often devolved into citizens shouting, "I'm a Bahraini!" Newspaper articles ubiquitously list the nationality of individuals in the course of reporting: "A Pakistani barber was reportedly deported last night after stabbing a former employer"; "A Bahraini was stabbed in the back in a clash between two groups of men"; "A Moroccan woman was attacked after accepting an offer of a lift home to Juffair from a Manama hotel."[4] In everyday interactions and in the discursive terrain of the media, individuals are described in terms that locate their relationship to the state by way of their ethnicity and nationality, thereby reinforcing the bonds between what Longva (2005), in her analysis of the Kuwaiti state, describes as the ethnocratic basis of state power and meaning of citizenship. Or, as Neha Vora (2008) has aptly argued, middle-class Indians quickly develop a racial consciousness during their time in the Gulf.

The governance of the transmigrant, in the Foucauldian sense of both direct governmental control and, more obliquely, a regime of order, discipline, and organization, is constantly reinforced in these daily interactions. The effects of this governance take shape in the residential patterns that characterize life on the island. Whereas poor and middle-class members of the diaspora often live in urban enclaves—in particular neighborhoods, once Bahraini, and now abandoned to the foreign underclass—the upper segments of the diaspora often dwell in the upscale mixed neighborhoods peripheral to the city. In these locations, most of my informants stated, they had little to no interaction with Bahraini neighbors. As an Indian construction manager with an older villa in the suburb of Riffa remarked, "We have never made any Bahraini friends. I've lived in Bahrain for so many years—twenty-three, twenty-four years—but I haven't made any Bahraini friends. I don't visit their families, and I don't go to their festivals." The social activities of Indian nationals are largely confined to Indian restaurants, the many clubs and voluntary organizations dominated by the Indian diaspora, and the temples, mosques, and churches of the expatriate elite.

These separate social worlds are characteristic of the Gulf, and the governance that produces this separation helps explain the function of exclusion and dominance in a plural society (Longva 1997; Nagy 1998, 84–85; Vora 2008). In this section, however, I have also sought to connect the habitus deployed by citizens in everyday encounters to the Bahraini national project. That national project channels a neoliberal logic and is manifest in both the discursive terrain, where Bahrain is perceived and projected as a site of global consumption, a boomtown, and the financial and service hub of the

Gulf, and also in the material realm, where shopping malls and skyscrapers rise along the low shores of the island, and educated and trained human capital streams to the island in service of this vision. Yet in the everyday interactions between citizens and foreigners, the basic class logic of this neoliberal model is mitigated by the logic of citizenship, itself the conceptual nexus for racial, ethnic, religious, and gendered vectors. Understanding the terms of this contradiction, I argue, is key to understanding the everyday violence foreigners encounter on the island.

Encounters with Power: The Diasporic Elite and the *Kafala*

The habitus deployed by citizens in their everyday interactions with noncitizen transmigrants represents a key force in the subjectification of members of the Indian diaspora—both working class and elite—as servants of the Bahraini state and its citizenry. In Wolf's multivalenced notion of power, this roughly corresponds to *interactional* power, manifest in relations between individuals, and *embodied* power, in the Nietzschean sense, that draws "attention to how persons enter into a play of power" (1999, 5). Through the deployment of this power, as an expression of habitus, the achieved differences and hierarchies wrought by the neoliberal logic of global capitalism are eclipsed by the citizen/noncitizen dichotomy: whereas impoverished laborers complained of being constantly pelted with stones on their journey between their decrepit labor camp and the small grocery store a block away, Indian men of significant worth and accomplishment avoid Bahrainis on the street, endure constant ethnic slurs, and avoid any public or direct confrontation with citizens.

In his analysis of the state, Foucault noted that "relations of power, and hence the analysis that must be made of them, necessarily extend beyond the limits of the state. In two senses: first of all because the state, for all the omnipotence of its apparatuses, is far from being able to occupy the whole field of actual power relations, and further because the state can only operate on the basis of other, already existing power relations. The state is superstructural in relation to a whole series of power networks that invest the body, sexuality, the family, kinship, knowledge, technology and so forth" (1985, 64). Without denying the certain, interlocking relationship between everyday practice and the relations of power codified in the state, in the case of Bahrain we can also delineate the opposite of Foucault's point: the habitus deployed by citizens in their everyday interactions with transmigrant foreigners depends on a state apparatus configured to reinforce the hegemony of citizen over noncitizen. In other words, the habitus that citizens bring to their everyday interactions with noncitizens, and in that sense, the governance exercised over the diaspora as a whole, is itself premised on a series of structural arrangements, codified in the state, that formally reinforce the power of the citizenry over the transmigrants on the island.

As should be clear from the earlier chapters of this book, the risks and uncertainties of life in Bahrain often coalesce around the *kafala,* or sponsorship system. Unlike the working class, most members of the diasporic elite retain control of their passport. Their *kafeel,* however, whether an individual or a corporate entity, still mediates their relationship to the state. The power of the kafeel is invested in a series of procedures and documents, including the work contract, which specifies a particular period of time (typically two or three years) at a particular salary; a no-objection certificate, which clears the transmigrant to enter the country and take a job; and a residence permit, which is associated with a particular employer and a particular job. These contractual, legal, and bureaucratic aspects of the kafala are essential components by which the asymmetrical relationships between citizens and foreign workers are constructed. In essence, they channel power to the kafeel.

The following letter to the editor of one of the English newspapers in Bahrain illustrates some of the practical and bureaucratic dilemmas faced by the professional and elite members of the Indian diaspora:

> I have been working at a local further education institute as a senior lecturer in travel and tourism for almost fifteen years. During this period I am happy and proud to state that I played a pivotal role in training hundreds of Bahrainis sponsored by the Labour Ministry to take up jobs in various airlines and travel agencies.[5] On December 30, 2003, I was asked by the owner to sign a document stating that I received all my dues from the institute since my date of joining in February 1989. Since I refused, my salary for December 2003 was not paid. I threatened to take the matter to court. This type of tactic has been tried several times on me but I never succumbed to the owner's coercion.
>
> On December 30, 2003, at 6 pm the owner convened a meeting where he verbally and in writing promised to pay BD2,000 [$5,306] immediately and BD1,000 [$2,656] by mid-2004. This amount, being only one-tenth of what I should receive, was turned down. On

December 31, 2003, I lodged a complaint at the Labour Ministry and since no settlement was reached, they passed the dispute on to the courts. On January 6, 2004, the owner sent me two invoices to the tune of BD16,800 [$44,576] being sponsorship charges. A grave violation. All these matters were brought to the attention of the Indian Embassy.

The act was merely to intimidate me to sign the document. Six months have passed and I am without a job. My family is here and my daughter goes to school. I am living by begging and borrowing. Many institutes have come forward to hire my services. They all do have valid work permits and are willing to change my sponsorship. The major impediment, I need permission to work. When I approach the Labour Ministry with this request, they have directed me to the Ministry of Justice and on approaching the Ministry of Justice, I am directed to the Labour Ministry. So between these ministries I am being sandwiched for no fault of mine. I will be more than happy to leave the island if my dues are settled in full according to the labour laws for the private sector.

I strongly feel that only the press can play a role in bringing my plight to the attention of concerned authorities. Signed, Jacob Samuel[6]

Jacob's dilemma points to the vulnerabilities even well-placed individuals face in the difficult working environment of contemporary Bahrain. If we take his calculations at face value, his employer had accumulated a debt to Jacob of nearly $80,000. After resisting his employer's attempts to erase this debt, he appealed to the bureaucratic institutions of the state. My informants on the island were clear about the Indian embassy's inability or unwillingness to negotiate these sorts of dilemmas with the Bahraini government, and like several of my informants, Jacob found himself "sandwiched" between the Ministry of Labor and the Ministry of Justice. Although a handful of my informants had carried cases through the Ministry of Labor and Social Affairs to the courts, none had found success in this venture.[7] As one Indian individual told me, "nobody I know has ever received a good judgment from the court." Longva, who spent many hours of her fieldwork in the courthouses of Kuwait, concluded that "non-Kuwaitis, finally, had no absolute legal autonomy. They were all subordinate to their Kuwait employers/sponsors in what was to them one of the most important aspects of their lives, namely, work" (1997, 129). This conclusion matches the perception of the Indian community I encountered in Bahrain, and it is this perception—as much as the reality of the situation—that keeps noncitizens from engaging the extant legal framework on the island.

In his letter, Jacob also mentions that "many other institutes have come forward to hire my services." As this statement suggests, the kafala structures a labor market that is not free. Transmigrants are bound to particular jobs, and their ability to switch jobs depends on the goodwill and acquiescence of their kafeel. In essence, the foreign workers, whether laborers or professionals, are bonded labor, and the structural arrangement of the kafala fetters their ability to act as free agents on the labor market or, put another way, to escape the dominion and exploitation of particular sponsors.

The power of the sponsor to prevent foreign workers from departing the exploitative conditions of a particular job, however, is only one facet of the systemic control the diasporic elite face. Many of the professionals arrive alone—in the parlance of the diaspora, they are "in front" of families whose members await the necessary paperwork and visas in order to join them in Bahrain. Individuals seeking a "family visa" must, again, work through their kafeel to obtain such permission, and several of my informants reported this requirement as another fulcrum of abuse. They must prove that they earn over 250 dinars ($664) per month, the state-mandated minimum for those wishing to bring their families to Bahrain, and a figure barely large enough to cover the expenses of maintaining a family there, which typically includes the cost of the Indian diasporic community's private schools. They also need the sponsor to sign off on the paperwork that will allow their families to reside on the island.

Wives, sons, and daughters also face numerous difficulties in obtaining employment on the island. As another letter to the *Gulf Daily News* described the situation:

> My wife has both an NOC [no-objection certificate] from my sponsor as well as a job offer from a company who is providing sponsorship. We do not have any children. But unfortunately after dozens of visits to Immigration by the company's [representative] the transfer from my family visa to my wife's potential employer's visa is rejected. The reason specified was "Transfer from family to work is only possible if position in work permit is teacher, executive secretary or nurse." My wife's occupation does not fall in either of these categories. I would like to have GDNPR [General Directorate of Nationality, Passports and Residence] opinion on above as this is a crucial phase of life for

my wife. She has excellent qualifications and experience and the law saying she cannot work even if she gets a job and sponsorship will shatter her dreams. I would like to know if this is really a law?

The GDNPR spokesperson replied as follows: "We thank the reader for his complimentary comments. We would like to confirm that transfers from a family visa to a work visa are only possible through GDNPR if the job category is teacher, nurse or executive secretary. The only possible alternative for the reader's wife is for her prospective employer to approach the Ministry of Labour for a Local Transfer as it may be possible for her to transfer directly from one sponsor to another on a local transfer."[8] Although it is of interest that the opportunities for transmigrants' wives and daughters reveal the gendered aspects of the foreign workforce on the island, the key issue here is that obtaining the family visa, as well as obtaining a "local transfer," is contingent upon the goodwill of the sponsor (successful in this case). Hence the power invested in the kafala extends beyond the labor of an individual foreigner: the kafeel also has power over the very presence of a foreigner's spouse and children.

Both the diasporic elite and the transnational proletariat face similar, systemic vulnerabilities under the kafala. Because the transnational proletariat cannot bring family members to the island, however, the vectors of vulnerability surrounding foreign workers' families are unique to the diasporic elite. Yet these are not the only vulnerabilities unique to this class of foreign workers: members of the diasporic elite, and particularly merchants and business owners, face another distinct set of risks unique to their economic position. Bahraini law requires that all business ventures have at least one Bahraini owner. This rule has resulted in the formation of a class of "silent" or "sleeping" partners among the Bahraini citizenry—individuals who lend their name to the business registrations of foreign-born entrepreneurs. Leonard, working with the Indian population in Kuwait and the Emirates, says that "these working relationships are typically quite nominal, with sponsors taking commissions from many foreigners annually but not participating in the business" (2003, 138). In my discussions with the professional and entrepreneurial community, the established rate for this relationship was BD100 ($265) per month. Unlike the conditions reported by Leonard in the United Arab Emirates, however, in Bahrain these relationships are prone to abuse, and many Indian entrepreneurs I met related stories of financial disaster resulting from the silent partner relationship. Ahmed, an Indian Muslim, briefly described his own experience with a

Bahraini partner: "I started a business here a few years back, but it collapsed. Once it became successful, the sleeping partner stole it out from under me. Once he saw that the money was being made through my efforts, he took it from me." As these comments suggest, the relationship is inherently fraught with complications wrought by the citizen/noncitizen polarity, and the vulnerability foreign entrepreneurs face is reinforced by the difficulty they encounter in both accessing and utilizing the legal system.

A small number of individuals in the diaspora escape some portion of these vulnerabilities through gaining citizenship, which makes Bahrain exceptional in relation to the rest of the Gulf, where generally transmigrants (and particularly non-Arab transmigrants) can never become citizens (see Falzon 2003, 675; Leonard 2003, 139).[9] Bahrain has recently opened channels to allow applications for citizenship, and a small number of prominent foreign businessmen with long-standing ties in the kingdom have successfully applied. The explicit requirements include twenty-five years of residence (or fifteen years for those of Arab descent), although many of my contacts in the Indian community noted that some of the prominent businessmen who had achieved citizenship did not meet this requirement.[10] The application itself is followed by a series of interviews in which applicants are expected to demonstrate a facility with Arabic. Individuals also reported that large fees are involved, although the amounts described to me varied from BD20,000 ($53,000) to upward of BD70,000 ($186,000). Long delays are also the norm. As one individual stated, "I began the application process three years ago. They called me for interviews—they've interviewed me twice. The last one was a year ago, and they said they'd call me again. They haven't called since, so I'm just waiting." Another prosperous Indian merchant described his experience: after beginning the application process, they requested his passport. With a business that required constant travel back and forth to India, he rescinded his application after three months, as he needed his passport to travel.

Although Bahraini citizenship decreases the vulnerability of foreigner-born entrepreneurs and merchants to the kafala, it is a path only available to the wealthy. Moreover, it does little to address the lived experience of the diasporic elite on the island, a fact intricately related to the ethnocratic underpinnings of the concept of citizenship prevalent in the Gulf region. As one Indian merchant observed, "For the Muslims, maybe citizenship is a possibility, but for the rest of us, it's a different ballgame. . . . If I go to the market, to the souk and I see you [the author], I know you're a Westerner. If somebody sees me, he says, okay, an Indian. If I take a Bahraini passport, my face says that I'm an Indian. The people will still not take me as a Bahraini. They will treat me as an Indian."

My well-placed informants among the Indian community reported that the number of Indian nationals who successfully obtained citizenship could be counted on one hand. Although the number of Bahraini citizens of Indian origin is very small, many of the older families on the island possess a certificate of residence. Obtained before the 1950s, these permanent residence permits allow members of the Indian diaspora to be "self-sponsored" and thereby escape the power-laden relationship with a citizen-kafeel. For the remaining great majority, however, negotiating the complexities of residence permits, work permits, permits for family members, and contract renewals is a constant struggle.

In this section I have attempted to illuminate the Indian diasporic elite's experience with the kafala. I have focused specifically on the visa regulations, residence permits, business licenses, and other bureaucratic requirements that, en suite, channel power to the citizen-kafeel. Unlike the working-class Indians described in the previous chapter, members of the diasporic elite face less comprehensive risks in coming to Bahrain. Although the actual amount of debt involved may be much larger than that incurred by members of the transnational proletariat, few members of the diasporic elite incur debts of the relative magnitude of the working class. The vulnerabilities of the diasporic elite are typically confined to the businesses they have built on the island and the financial well-being of their nuclear family. As I illustrated in earlier chapters, the vulnerabilities of the Indian transnational proletariat encompass the productive assets of the extended family and, in a more poignant sense, their basic ability to survive.

Nonetheless, members of the Indian diasporic elite in Bahrain are susceptible to the power and inequities of a foreign system, a fact directly tied to their trans-status. Although they may bring a variety of strategies to the table, none overcomes the subjectification wrought by the citizenry's habitus—the set of learned dispositions that exert the citizen's dominance over foreigners, that reinforce the logic of race, ethnicity, nationality, religion, and culture over that of class; a habitus that continually asserts the dominance of citizens in a nation heavily dependent on the contribution of educated and professional foreigners. The fettered agency the diasporic elite brings to bear against the vulnerabilities of this system is often insufficient, and insecurity about the future in Bahrain is a common trope in their conversation. As a result, members of the diasporic elite commonly forge contingency plans as a response to the uncertain future. In the next section, I explore these contingency plans—themselves another form of agency—in depth.

Strategic Transnationalism

In one sense, the kafala can be conceived as a system for managing and controlling the flow of labor to the petroleum-rich states of the Arabian Peninsula. Through an examination of the practical and everyday experience of this system, I have sought to portray the kafala in terms of the power it channels and codifies—a system that not only manages the flow of transmigrants to the island, but also one that seeks to manage and control these foreign workers during their time on the island. I have argued that we can see these power relations in the everyday interactions between foreign workers and citizen-hosts, conceived in terms of habitus, and in the structural, bureaucratic practices and policies that underpin those interactions. In this section, I portray the agency deployed by Indian diasporic elite in reaction to the dominance they face in Bahrain.

In part, this agency may be viewed as a response to the difficult conditions and problematic, everyday relations codified by the kafala. This agency, however, can also be seen as a response to more general conditions—conditions outside the bounds of the everyday interactions I have described. Those conditions include a chronic uncertainty about the future. As noncitizens, the great majority of the diasporic elite live by the whims of the state and the citizenry: their tenure on the island is always under threat of revocation; the positions they hold are subject to their individual sponsors and to the Ministry of Labor and Social Affairs, which can, as its purview, revoke or fail to renew residence and work permits. Together, these more general vulnerabilities coalesce under the concept of Bahrainization.

In its simplest reading, Bahrainization is the nomenclature of the kingdom's efforts to replace foreign workers with citizens. The rudiments of this collection of policies were in place in the early 1970s. At the same time, Bahrainization is an ever-evolving set of policies and directives, often contradictory, that mandate particular ratios of citizen employees to transmigrants, often in particular sectors of the economy. For example, in the mid-1990s the state mandated that all taxi drivers on the island must be Bahraini nationals. During my fieldwork on the island, business owners reported that in many sectors one must hire one citizen for every transmigrant employed; hotels track their citizen-to-noncitizen employee ratios, and those with the largest proportion of citizen employees receive awards from the government. New Bahrainization policies are frequently announced in the newspapers of the island, and although infrequently codified in law or comprehensively enforced, they nonetheless destabilize the livelihoods of foreign workers on the island. Foreign entrepreneurs and business owners are never sure if the laws will allow them to continue working on the island; capital reinvested in the business is always at risk, for a single edict can close the door to particular sectors of the economy for foreign workers. During my time on the island (2002–3), for example, the new minister of labor and social affairs announced a directive of 100 percent Bahrainization for the ministry itself, which included the Bahrain Training Institute, my sponsor institution and home to a large staff of expatriate instructors on multiyear contracts. Similarly, a year after my departure, the minister of labor and social affairs announced the kingdom's plans to fully "Bahrainize" car sales showrooms, supermarkets, travel agencies, and furniture stores by 2006.

With the future of the transnational presence in the Bahraini workforce always uncertain, the active transnational connections established and maintained by members of the Indian diaspora are more than an attempt to keep in touch with the culture of their homeland; these connections are essential components of their livelihood strategies—active networks sought to balance the uncertainties of life outside the Indian state and, more specifically, the vulnerabilities unique to the nations of the Arabian Gulf. Although many of the families I spoke with maintain a presence in India, most have also extended their networks westward. Frequently these networks are an extension of historic, transnational familial and social networks established in the colonial and postcolonial era—rebuilding, for example, connections with portions of the family that found their way to colonial Africa under British rule or, alternatively, to England itself, where many of the former Indian colonial bureaucrats obtained citizenship.

Many of the family histories and migration narratives I collected illustrate these points, but in the sections that follow I present vignettes describing the particular circumstances and histories of two different members of the Indian diasporic elite in Bahrain.

Mariam's Story

Mariam's family is from Goa, the former Portuguese colony on India's western coast. Her father worked for the British colonial administration, a post that eventually carried him to colonial Uganda, where Mariam and three of her siblings were born. Her father retired from that position and moved back to India but was unable to secure sufficient employment to feed the family, so he returned to Africa. The three youngest children, including Mariam, remained in Goa with their mother to finish their schooling. When Idi Amin came to power in Uganda, her siblings, sensing trouble, began to move their money to Canada; at that time, Mariam noted, "Canada was still raw—they wanted people." One brother stayed behind in Africa and lost everything, and later went to Canada as a refugee.

Mariam married in Goa and planned a life in India. She and her husband moved about India in search of better work, but after the untimely death of her husband she returned to Goa to work as a teacher. Goa is a conservative city, she said, and the life of a widow is not an easy one. As related in the preceding chapter, Mariam stated that "a widow is never looked on in the same fashion as a normal person." With her family spread around the globe, Mariam began to consider other options. Her sister suggested she come to Bahrain. Although she had never been to Bahrain, it was like a homecoming: "we're a big family," she described, "and we're all separated. We're all out, some in Canada, wherever else, in Africa. My sister was here [in Bahrain], so coming to Bahrain, I felt like I was returning to my family, you know?" Her sister helped arrange employment for Mariam at one of the large embassies on the island.

After some years in Bahrain, Mariam remarried a Goan transmigrant she met on the island. They are uncertain about how long they will remain in Bahrain. Her daughter is in school at the American University in Dubai but intends to continue her studies in the United States. Her parents and siblings are naturalized British citizens. Three of her siblings are "out"—a term she used to describe their presence in Canada, and the remainder are "here," meaning in Bahrain or India. When I noted that she used "here" to refer to both Bahrain and India, she replied, "I know, I know! It's because we're so close to Bahrain—Bahrain is so close to India, we feel we are there. It's just like India here!" Her brothers in Canada have children now, most of whom have married Canadians. They still maintain a house in Goa—"we have our own place—you have to have one! In case you're thrown out of Bahrain, you have to have a roof over your head"—a common enough practice, but one not shared by all members of the diasporic elite.

For Mariam, Bahrain represents one juncture in her family's long transnational history. Through her familial relations, she maintains contact with her home city in India, with the United Kingdom, fleetingly with Africa, and most strongly with Canada. Her daughter, while at the time in the United Arab Emirates, plans on relocating to the United States, thereby establishing a new beachhead in the extended family's geographical distribution. Mariam's job in Bahrain is a good one—her position at a Western embassy provides an additional buffer against the tides of Bahrainization. At the same time, her husband's position at an advertising firm is more precarious, for it is the very sort of position that the government is seeking to Bahrainize. The network of family and friends, established over a lifetime, provides Mariam and her nuclear family with the opportunity to weigh the vulnerabilities of life in Bahrain against the costs of relocation to one of the other nodes in her global network.

Farid's Story

In the final decade of the nineteenth century, Farid's great grandfather, a Bohri Muslim from the westernmost Indian state of Gujarat, embarked on a pilgrimage to Mecca. The journey by ship and land took the better part of three months each way; including a two-month stay in Mecca, his sojourn lasted nearly eight months. After a stop at Muscat at the entrance to the Gulf and passage through the Strait of Hormuz, the ship anchored in the shallow bay between Muharraq and Manama, the two principal islands of Bahrain. There, before journeying onward to Mecca, Farid's great grandfather encountered a busy port and market, and a British/Indian colonial bureaucracy actively seeking merchants and traders from points east.

Returning from his pilgrimage, Farid's great grandfather began to plan for the move to Bahrain, and after ten years of preparation, he arrived in 1902. His brother eventually joined him, and the two—shuttling back and forth between Bombay and Bahrain—profited as merchant traders of various goods. Eventually, Farid's great-grandfather's three sons took over the business. Like the family's first generation of transmigrant merchants, the three brothers shuttled back and forth between Bombay and Bahrain every two or three years. One brother managed the business, the second, either in transit or in Bahrain, was brought up to speed, and the third cared for the families and properties in Bombay. One of the three brothers, a reckless spendthrift who, when alone in Bahrain, would inevitably purchase the latest model Mercedes or an American-made Harley Davidson motorcycle, was eventually pushed out of the business and permanently relocated to Bombay, where he was given a small piece of property to manage.

The two remaining brothers now controlled the business in Bahrain. In the years that followed, one brother's son fell in love with the other brother's daughter, and subsequently they married against the wishes of their parents. Farid was the new couple's firstborn son, and within a year of his birth (in the mid-1960s) the couple moved to Bahrain. Initially they lived with their parents in the "joint family" tradition of India, in a flat in the historic central souk of downtown Manama. Farid's father opened a haberdashery on one of the narrow thoroughfares of the souk, all under a business license acquired before regulations required a Bahraini partner. This arrangement means that he and his family are "self-sponsored." Today, Farid and his wife run the same store his father built decades ago, and he has several warehouses and a small office, all of which are located near the original business.

The business is profitable, but Farid remains insecure in Bahrain. Additional businesses he has opened over the years require a Bahraini "sleeping partner," and although the initial agreement is often for BD100 ($265) a month, these partners often increase their demands once a business shows a profit. As Farid noted, "He [the sleeping partner] comes and tells you he wants BD500 [$1,326], and you have no choice. You have to give it to him. Otherwise he'll just pack you off. Your whole existence in Bahrain depends on him." It is a constant threat, and he has avoided sleeping partners' attempted takeovers by loading threatened businesses with debt. Although he has the license for the haberdashery, he is not a permanent resident. He still has to renew his residence permit every two years.

Farid considered getting a Bahraini passport. Through a well-placed local contact, he weighed the option of paying BD20,000 ($53,056) for a Bahraini passport, calculating that he would then be able to save hundreds of dinars per month on the businesses by avoiding the need for sleeping partners. Instead, however, he began moving his resources to Canada. As he described the process, "it wasn't easy. I had to do a lot of running around, but I got my [Canadian] passport. So if I get kicked out of here—and that could happen, because there really aren't any laws here—if they did revoke my residence permit, there are no courts I could go to or anything like that. It would just be done.... But now I know I can go to Canada, and I'm relatively comfortable there. I could start a business, do something, get a job.... It's a safety net. At least in the back of my mind, that part is safe. I mean, it was a big thing for me. You might not understand."

As a fourth-generation Indian transmigrant, Farid has a significant connection to Bahrain. His businesses represent a considerable financial resource built over several generations. Moreover, the business license he inherited provides his cornerstone business—the haberdashery—with a degree of insulation against the vulnerability wrought by the kafala and sleeping-partner system. Nonetheless, the tenuousness of his existence in

Bahrain, illustrated by his inability to use the legal system and his distrust of the mercurial Central Population Register (which issues the residence permits), led him to procure citizenship in Canada.[11]

Aihwa Ong uses the term *flexible citizenship* "to refer especially to the strategies and effects of mobile managers, technocrats, and professionals seeking to both circumvent *and* benefit from different nation-state regimes by selecting different sites for investments, work, and family relocation" (1999, 112). Although both Farid and Mariam generally fit this model, I use the term *strategic transnationalism* as a means of downplaying the importance of citizenship in the diasporic elite's strategic geographical calculations. Although citizenship remains one important variable in their strategic planning, only a small handful of the Indian diasporic elite are citizens of Bahrain. Instead, like Farid, with citizenship in Canada, or Mariam, with citizenship in the United Kingdom and India, members of the Indian diasporic elite build transnational networks to mitigate the vulnerability that noncitizens face in Bahrain. In this calculus, the diasporic elite seeks to benefit from opportunities in Bahrain: as a primary regional nexus in the global financescape, Bahrain is dotted with transnational corporations that serve the more conservative surrounding nations. These opportunities, combined with the generally higher remuneration than that paid to those holding similar positions in India, make work in the Gulf a lucrative, if risky, venture for the Indian diasporic elite. In responding to the vulnerabilities wrought by the structure of dominance that constrains and controls the foreign population in Bahrain, the Indian elite build on historic networks forged in the colonial and postcolonial era—transnational networks that connect them to multiple continents. They also forge new networks that engage global capitalism in multiple territories and venues. Together, these historic and new networks—the essential fabric of this strategic transnationalism—are at once a reaction to the vulnerabilities particular to the Gulf states and a sophisticated and strategic adjustment to the mobility inherent to the demands of the neoliberal financescape.

Transnationals Unbound

The great majority of case studies in transnationalism focus on migration to the West, and particularly to the United States. The structure of dominance that Indian transmigrants face in Bahrain is composed of a significantly different set of vulnerabilities than those typically portrayed in these case studies. In this chapter I focus on the diasporic Indian elite, and through my analysis I challenge the fundamental bipolarity not only of these typical transnational models (in the sense of people with social fields spanning two nation-states), but also of diasporic models (in the sense of people with a particular relationship to a territorial homeland). Like a handful of other scholars concerned with contemporary transnationalism, I seek to illuminate the transnational lives of populations moving outside "the West," widely conceived.

Using the basic bifurcation suggested by Mahler and already used by Leonard, I compared the lives of the Indian diasporic elite in Bahrain with those of the Indian transnational proletariat on the island. My analysis suggests that, on the one hand, the diasporic elite face a variety of vulnerabilities unique to their socioeconomic position: the presence of their families on the island, for example, renders them vulnerable to particular forms of abuse under the sponsorship system. Similarly, the businesses they own and manage open them to another venue of vulnerability. On the other hand, the ethnocratic underpinnings of the structure of dominance in place on the island reject the class-based logic of the neoliberal system, and generally subject members of the diasporic elite to the same forms of everyday structural violence that their impoverished countrymen—the transnational proletariat—face. The color of their skin, their language, religion, and culture, their nationality: these vectors all come in to play in the subjectification of the diasporic elite as servants to the Bahraini national project.

Unlike their impoverished countrymen at work on the island, however, members of the Indian diasporic elite build and maintain a set of global networks to mitigate the vulnerabilities rendered by this structure of dominance. The insecurities of life in Bahrain, including the violent undercurrents of their everyday encounters with the citizenry, but also encompassing their structural inability to assert their rights in the bureaucratic machinery of the state, push them to a strategic transnationalism. Their lives are, in some sense, untethered from both the local milieu of Bahrain and the diasporic, ancestral homeland of India: their allegiance is to what Appadurai has called the "nonterritorial transnation" (1996, 173).

5 THE PUBLIC SPHERE

Social Clubs and Voluntary Associations
in the Indian Community

Typical portrayals of social relations in the Gulf states describe a nearly insurmountable divide between citizens and foreigners. The preceding chapters of this book certainly contribute to that portrait: the social divide between citizens and foreign workers in Bahrain is formidable, and although others have directed their attention to the many and interesting "exceptional" spaces—in marriage between citizen and foreigner, through the intimate and everyday contact between employer and domestic servant, or through the ongoing interactions between the elite classes of the different communities on the island—these arenas of interaction remain exceptions to the norm (see Nagy 2008). At the same time, one can delineate a public sphere whose boundaries encompass citizen and foreigner. In this chapter and the next, I examine two facets of this encompassing public sphere. In this chapter I explore the diasporic social clubs and a handful of other voluntary associations on the island. Those clubs and associations include long-standing regional clubs, such as the Kerala Club, as well as voluntary associations like the Toastmasters and Lions clubs that oftentimes convene citizens with foreigners of many different nationalities. In the next chapter, I describe another facet of this public sphere through an examination of the English-language newspapers on the island.

The theoretical foundations of the concept of the public sphere trace their genealogy to the work of Jürgen Habermas. In its most basic rendition, the public sphere represents an inclusive conceptual space where meanings are publicly articulated, produced, and negotiated (Habermas 1989). At the same time, the activity of this public sphere is more than a reflection or window to the public: it is a generative process by which the public is constituted. Habermas (1989) envisioned this public sphere as overlapping—and strategically between—the private sphere and the state. In that public space, individuals develop a collective identity and a set of interests distinct from those of both the private sphere and the state. Although this conception of the public sphere remains foundational, more recent work has pointed to particular problems with Habermas's formulation. More specifically, scholars have argued that the notion of an all-inclusive public sphere fails to grasp the nuances of social power: group formation is as much about who is excluded as included. Analyses often focus on the formation of "counterpublics" that challenge the hegemony of the dominant public sphere (Fraser 1992; Warner 2002). Overall, many contemporary scholars suggest that the public sphere is better understood by its frictions, divisions, and omissions than by its cohesion.[1]

Habermas's notion of a public sphere has been reinvigorated by the attention directed to the diasporic and transnational movement of peoples around the world. Ethnographers and other scholars attentive to these populations on the move have relied on his concept to delineate the cultural space where people distant from their homeland, and oftentimes distant from one another, forge some common communal identity (Appadurai 1996; Werbner 1998). Victoria Bernal's work, for example, reveals how the Internet serves not only as "an arena of nonviolent conflict in a violent world but also as a multiplier of outrage and as a vehicle for mobilizing action in situations of conflict" (2005, 662). Generally speaking, these scholars agree that there is more going on within these public spheres than the "rational discussion" proposed by Habermas: these public spheres are the sites at which culture is produced.

This model suggests that the task before me is to examine the contours of the Indian diasporic public sphere—to investigate how Indians in Bahrain engage in a communal diasporic public discourse with Indians from Canada, India itself, the other Gulf states, Singapore, and the countless other locations where members of this long-standing diaspora now make their home. This model also suggests that the business of unpacking the other public spheres in the cosmopolitan Gulf states—say, the Pakistani diasporic public sphere, the Filipino diasporic public sphere, or the Bahraini public sphere—is the purview of other ethnographers and scholars. Rather than pursuing this model, I am interested in delineating the contours of the public sphere that overlaps the many communities present on the island—a public sphere where Indians talk with other Indians, but also with Bahrainis, Pakistanis, Bangladeshis, Sri Lankans, Britishers, Americans, and the many other peoples who make a home on the island. The idea that Indians become and perform their "Indian-ness" in discussion with one another (and across the transnational divide) is certainly true. Yet they also become and perform that "Indian-ness" through discussion and debate with the many peoples who also make their home on the island. An examination of this overarching public sphere tells us something about the experiences of each group, about the way they perceive themselves, about the relations among these groups in Bahrain, and about the ideas that underpin the structural forces described in previous chapters.

Diasporic Social Clubs and Voluntary Associations

The Bab al-Bahrain, or "door to Bahrain," is a colonial-era edifice on the maritime front of the old souk in central Manama. Although infill and construction have pushed the actual shoreline well beyond the former wharf and customs house described by the oldest individuals with whom I spoke, the Bab al-Bahrain remains an important reference point in the contemporary city. From that central hub, the narrow roads crowded with pedestrians and slow-moving vehicles reach back into the heart of the market. Small hotels, mosques, countless stores, and restaurants line the close-quartered streets. By following these streets back from the waterfront, one eventually emerges into a dense residential neighborhood where residual members of the citizenry's most impoverished classes live side by side with the burgeoning population of transnational laborers.[2] Unlike their more fortunate brethren in labor camps or company-arranged apartment buildings, many of the transnational laborers in this beleaguered neighborhood are illegal workers. Through the confluence of circumstances described in previous chapters, the men in this neighborhood largely work on the black market, selling their labor to whomever they can find for a few dinars a day. In buildings rented from Bahraini owners, transmigrant laborers crowd into the small rooms. In some of the apartments men sleep in shifts.

On a hot summer night in 2003, one of these buildings caught fire. Sanjay, a South Indian laborer, had returned home some two hours earlier from a party at the company for which he currently works. He fell fast asleep. Shortly before midnight, he was abruptly awakened by the Pakistani men who roomed down the hall. Smoke had already filled the building. Together the men made their way to the roof. Finding a small ladder in the debris scattered on the rooftop, they laid it across the span between buildings and slowly crossed. With smoke billowing all around them, they thought that the building next door might also be on fire. They made a second crossing and were finally able to descend to the street. Outside their former home they gathered with the other workers, most of whom wore nothing more than their undergarments, and watched the building burn. Miraculously, all of the building's occupants survived. Sanjay lamented his own personal loss—80 dinars ($210) in savings, the air conditioner that he and his roommates had recently purchased, and the DVD player and television that he himself had purchased. Sanjay had been away from India for over ten years, and these last two items were his and his alone—the product of those many years of hard work, and items of significant symbolic as well as monetary value. Unlike the papers of many of his flatmates, his Central Population Register card and other valuable documents were with his current employer—part of his effort to again legalize his status on the island—and were hence spared from the flames.

For several nights the men slept on the sidewalk or in the beds of pickup trucks parked on the street. The owner of the building initially refused to provide any assistance, and few of the men had a responsible kafeel to which they might turn.[3] Within a few days, several groups materialized to provide assistance. The Pakistani Club provided air conditioners and assorted items to the Pakistani men in the building. A group called Helping Hands and another called the Art of Living contributed various essentials to the building's inhabitants regardless of nationality. Six days after the fire I received a call from my friend Santosh. He invited me to come down to Tamil Social and Cultural Association (TASCA), the principal social club for the Tamil contingent of the Indian community, and help with the allocation of essentials to the men displaced by the fire.[4] Twenty or thirty of the now-homeless Indian laborers waited in front of the club, and over the course of several hours we distributed bananas, rice, fruit drinks, work boots, lunch boxes, small cooking stoves (or "cookers" in the Indian iteration), and a variety of other items. Some of the men were from Tamil Nadu, but many came from other Indian states. Later, Sanjay and his former roommate came to my flat for a light dinner, after which we talked about the fire, their experiences in Bahrain, and the role that the various institutions of the Indian community had played in assisting them with their ongoing plight.

Over the course of a year in Bahrain I spent many of my evenings at TASCA, the Indian Club, and many of the other social clubs and voluntary associations in the diasporic community. The constellation of diasporic social institutions in Bahrain is unparalleled elsewhere in the Gulf, and it is around dramatic events like the one described here that many of them spring to action. My understanding of these clubs and associations began with an interest in how these social forms provided help and assistance to those transnational laborers most exploited by the system of relations in place on the island. In a sense, I remain tied to that analysis, for these clubs and associations provide the primary response to the periodic crises—both collective and individual—faced by members of the Indian community. As I came to know these clubs and associations better, however, I began to understand that these venues also constituted the primary social foundation for foreign workers' participation in the complex public sphere of contemporary Bahrain. In the remainder of this chapter, I move from looking at these clubs as a counterbalance to the structural violence of contemporary relations on the island to an understanding of how members of the Indian community position themselves in the public sphere through their participation in these clubs and associations.

Six Social Clubs

The constellation of social clubs and voluntary associations one encounters in Bahrain is unique in the Gulf context. In several of the other Gulf states—Oman, for example—the state allows only a single umbrella organization to serve each national contingent. In Bahrain, however, the government has allowed the florescence of these clubs to proceed with only occasional hindrance. As Fuad Khuri (1980) described, Bahraini social and political clubs have a long and important history in the political landscape of the island as the principal site of the citizenry's political activity under the authoritarian regime. Diasporic social clubs predate these indigenous clubs on the island, but today they also build on the legacy of those strong indigenous social clubs. The proliferation of these social clubs also marks Bahrain as more liberal and open than its neighbors, an identity that remains key to the state's vision of its ongoing role as a service hub to the conservative neighboring nations. Many of the transmigrants with whom I spoke noted that these social clubs are one of the particular attractions of diasporic life in Bahrain—a social luxury unavailable across the causeway in Saudi Arabia, for example. At the same time, the analysis presented here demonstrates that these social clubs package diasporic culture behind villa walls—effectively moving the practice of foreign culture out of the public sphere and, in many cases, beyond the direct concern of a citizenry that continues to struggle with the ramifications of the transnational presence on the island.

No simple accounting of these social clubs is possible, for the constellation of active clubs on the island includes not only those formal groups registered with the Ministry of Social Development, but also those informal groups active around the island. From the government's perspective, all these groups are classified as nongovernmental organizations. Prospective clubs must provide the ministry with an abundance of information, including minutes from the meeting of the founding general assembly, the names and signatures of founding members, copies of their identity cards, and the club's constitution. Registered groups also consent to regular monitoring by the state. As of 2008, the Ministry of Social Development recorded a total of 423 registered nongovernmental organizations. This number includes 46 diasporic social clubs and 19 religious organizations. The remaining clubs are predominately citizen-based organizations. I present brief snapshots of six different diasporic associations, which yields a fairly representative cross-section of the institutions that together make up much of the social fabric of diasporic life on the island.

The Indian Club

My first visit to the Indian Club occurred on one of the few rainy nights of my stay in Bahrain. Several weeks after my arrival on the island, an Indian professor and colleague from my institutional sponsor in Bahrain suggested we meet at the Indian Club for a drink and discussion. My gracious host had found himself on the tail end of a long career in academia, and so with a few years left in which to amass enough savings to retire comfortably, he and his wife had relocated from India to Bahrain for the opportunities it provided. The professor arrived at the club shortly after I did, and meeting at the entrance we moved from the densely urban streets of central Manama, bustling with South Asian workers, through the security checkpoint that ascertains one's membership or, in my case, guest status, and onto the grounds of the club. Children played cricket on the twin tennis courts, shouting to each other in English as their parents sat around the tables between the courts and the bar.

Founded in 1915, the Indian Club is the oldest of the Indian expatriate social clubs on the island (Franklin 1985, 488). It has the largest membership (estimated to me at 1,200 families), and that membership is regionally and religiously mixed. Although a handful of Bahrainis and other non-Indians hold memberships, Indians—and particularly South

Indians—predominate. The club relocated to its current premises in the mid-1940s, and those premises, including tennis courts, meeting halls, and other open spaces, are the largest among the South Asian expatriate clubs. Along with the sizable auditorium at the Indian School, the premises of the Indian Club often serve the community's need of accommodations for large meetings, celebrations, and other activities. The club's reading room contains a wide variety newspapers and periodicals from India. Two bars serve as meeting points for the diverse membership, and in the smaller adjoining meeting rooms I observed various performances and activities during my occasional visits.

The Indian Club principally serves the diasporic elite. In his close examination of the Indian Club two decades ago, Franklin found that a long waiting list for membership, combined with a vetting process that focuses on "prestige, occupation, and influence," serves to maintain a membership that, although from a diversity of regions within India, is fairly homogenous in terms of social class (1985, 490). Add to this calculus the fact that high membership dues screen the lower middle class from the membership rolls and we are left with a contemporary portrait similar to what Franklin described in the 1980s: the Indian Club remains a venue for the diasporic elite and their families.

Although its members may come from the middle and upper classes of the Indian diaspora, the club nonetheless includes individuals from across the categorical divisions—be they ethnic, regional, or religious—of the Indian community. As one of the former presidents of the club remarked, in many ways the trans-Indian identity fostered by the club is a vestige of social relations constructed in decades past: "In 1915 . . . it wasn't called the Indian Club, for there were very few Indians here [in Bahrain] . . . at the time it was the only club, and the population here were Indians. Not Keralite, not Karnataka, but Indians. So there was no need for these other clubs. It was only in recent years that they started forming these other clubs." In contrast to the florescence of regionally and religiously specific clubs, the Indian Club continues to represent itself as a venue specifically aligned with a particular vision of India—one aligned with both the Indian School and the Indian embassy, which are seen as representative of the whole of India. Beneath the surface, however, regional frictions and other lines of tension continue to be exerted and performed in the context of the club. The former president, continuing his comments from above, added that "the Indian Club now has become very political. You have the north and the south—you have different groups. . . . These are ethnic divisions that are played out in the context of the club, and geographical too, because you have the South Indian group—the Malayalee group, and you have the north Indian group. And I guess at the Indian Club, there is also the Sindhi group."

Although the Indian Club, like the Indian School and a handful of other institutions on the island, is configured around the idea of a singular national Indian identity, these venues nonetheless provide space for the expression of regional, ethnic, religious, and class-based identities within the larger domain of a single Indian national identity. Unlike the smaller regional clubs, which, individually, can be conceived of as locations for transmigrants to reconnect with particularistic Indian identities, the Indian Club serves as a domain for the iteration or performance of those identities in relation to one another. It is a venue in which the diasporic elite can challenge, articulate, or support the idea of a singular national identity that transcends the regional, linguistic, cultural, and religious differences attributed to the Indian homeland.

The Tamil Social and Cultural Association

For nearly twenty years, transmigrants from the state of Tamil Nadu met together unofficially. The once-small diasporic constituency organized meetings in each other's flats or borrowed larger spaces from existing clubs to produce the events and shows they planned together. At the turn of the millennium, the group finally secured premises in central Manama and registered with the Ministry of Social Development. The formalization of the Tamil Social and Cultural Association (TASCA) coincided with two decades of demographic expansion of the transmigrant networks between Tamil Nadu and Bahrain. Although the official numbers are not released by the Bahraini government, the Tamil community now claims to be second in size only to that of Kerala among the Indian communities on the island. Like many of the other regional social clubs, TASCA's membership is composed of a cross-section of the Tamil population that extends lower into the economic strata of the transmigrant population than does the Indian Club. Reasonable membership fees ensure that even the diasporic lower middle class can join, and although the poorest transmigrant laborers are still unable to participate in the routine club activities, much of the club's programming includes outreach activities to the labor camps and apartment buildings in which the poorest Tamil laborers dwell (see fig. 5.1).

Like many of the Indian social clubs, TASCA occupies a villa in one of the city's central neighborhoods. A low wall separates the premises from the street, and the front porch typically contains various pieces of furniture or

Figure 5.1. South Asian laborers displaced by the building fire await assistance from the TASCA outreach committee. Photograph by Andrew Gardner.

boxed items either on their way in or out of the club. Inside, what was once a former residence has been converted to a busy and crowded social club. The *majlis,* or greeting room, where the former residents once entertained visitors, is now one of the main meeting rooms for the members. Upstairs is a small bar—the principal source of income for the club—a game room, and offices. Like all the regional clubs, foot traffic in the club surges in the evening hours as men and women finish their workday.

Like most of the Indian social clubs, TASCA organizes a wide variety of events for its membership. Committees plan for celebrations of Chithirai Thirunaal, or the Tamil New Year, as well as for Diwali (the Pan-Indian/Hindu festival of lights) and Pongal (a four-day celebration, originally linked to bountiful crops, and particularly popular among Tamils). Like most of the Indian social clubs on the island, TASCA also plans a celebration for the Bahraini Eid holiday. The club's Ladies Wing demonstrates cooking techniques and spreads beauty tips among the interested members. There are dance classes for children, and the club maintains a library stocked with a variety of Tamil periodicals and literature. TASCA also fields sports teams in intramural competitions on the island. The Social Service Subcommittee of TASCA was particularly active during my time in Bahrain. Through that committee's efforts, the club provided food, free clothing, and advice to impoverished men in some of the Tamil labor camps. The committee also conducted medical-training and health education seminars in the camps, including various programs concerning good hygiene and the benefits of both yoga and meditation to the physiological well-being of day laborers.

TASCA is representative of the vast majority of the diasporic clubs in Bahrain. A handful of other clubs—the Pakistan Club, the Indian Club, and the now-defunct Indian Association—explicitly address their diasporic constituents at a national level. Conversely, numerous clubs are even more specific in their constituencies than TASCA: the Kerala Catholic Club, for example, draws individuals through the categories of both region and religion. TASCA, based on regional (and, in some senses, linguistic) affiliation, occupies the crowded middle ground between more specific and more general venues of affiliation on the island. That middle ground is perhaps best exemplified by the executive committee at the time of my research: the president, a Tamil Muslim, presided over an executive committee that included Hindu, Muslim, and Christian individuals.

Toastmasters

The Toastmasters Club was founded in the United States by Ralph C. Smedley, whose name was honored in the introductory remarks of every Toastmasters meeting I attended in Bahrain. Established in Santa Ana, California, in 1924, the club expanded rapidly during the mid-twentieth century and now includes 230,000 members worldwide. The club's introduction to the Gulf occurred through a direct American connection. In the 1950s, Bahrain constructed a small enclave by the name of Awali for American workers, most of whom were associated with the oil industry. The Bahrain chapter of the Toastmasters formed in Awali in 1964, and although the initial members were for the most part American, a few Indian engineers and technicians also participated. As the active American members departed the island, Indian participants continued to fuel the club's activity. Through the interest and dedication of this original diasporic cohort, the Toastmasters persevered and eventually flourished on the island. At the time of my fieldwork, there were twenty active chapters in greater Manama, and additional chapters have formed in the other Gulf states.[5] The chapter I joined was the current manifestation of that original chapter from Awali, and my first meeting was the group's 1,900th gathering.

Originally designed as a forum to "afford practice and training in the art of public speaking and in presiding over meetings, and to promote sociability and good fellowship among its members," the chapters in Bahrain serve that purpose and more.[6] For the diasporic elite, the Toastmasters meetings provide an opportunity to practice and engage the discursive terrain of the global financescape—to, as the Toastmasters Web site suggests, give better sales presentations, hone management skills, effectively develop and present ideas, and offer constructive criticism. In other chapters, the activities of a typical meeting serve a much more practical purpose: the speeches and presentations provide an ideal opportunity to practice English, the lingua franca of the higher echelons of the global economy, which brought many of the men and women to Bahrain.

The Manama chapter's membership dues ensure that only the elite can join this particular group. Meetings are held weekly at one of the nicest hotels on the island; men and women are expected to wear business attire. Although the majority of the members of this chapter were from the Indian diaspora, the membership also included individuals from Bahrain, Sri Lanka, Pakistan, the Philippines, and Bangladesh. Other chapters are regionally specific: TASCA, for example, has its own chapter of Toastmasters that draws from its Tamil membership, as do the chapters at many of the other regionally, linguistically, or ethnically homogeneous social clubs on the island. I attended meetings held by three different chapters, and at all three sets of meetings women were well represented in both the membership and the leadership.

In general terms, the topics presented and discussed during meetings centered on personal development and the tribulations of configuring a successful path through the cosmopolitan workplace in Bahrain. Members seemed to be reproducing, rehearsing, and reflecting upon the discourse they deploy daily in offices around the island. The Manama Toastmasters—the chapter I joined, and the most ethnically and nationally diverse chapter on the island—maintained an informal policy of omitting politically oriented topics (such as the policies of the Bahraini state, the Indian/Pakistani conflict, or the U.S. incursion in Iraq) from the presentations, perhaps because of the heterogeneous membership of the chapter. That there was no place for politics in their discussions is perhaps a reflection of the conditions and circumstances the members face in their everyday lives: politics, ethnicity, nationality, and religion confound the logic of the cosmopolitan and neoliberal workplace on the island.

The Lions Club

The original Lions Club in Bahrain, formed some twenty years ago, was the first of its kind in the Gulf. The Bahrain chapter grew rapidly, and the Lions Club of Riffa was formed in 1995 as an offshoot of the oversized original club. The Riffa chapter also met with success: it had 75 members at its high point in the late 1990s, but Bahrainization and the subsequent departures depleted membership to approximately 40 members. Although all are welcome, the Lions Club of Riffa is predominately Muslim and includes successful merchants, businessmen, and professionals from both the Indian and Pakistani communities. Many of these individuals are also leaders or former leaders of other social clubs and associations on the island. Like the Manama Toastmasters, the Lions Club of Riffa has no quarters of its own but instead gathers regularly at upscale hotels. Attendees are expected to wear business attire, and meetings typically included a dozen or so individuals. Three women also regularly participated during my interaction with the club.

The Riffa chapter's activities are largely oriented toward outreach. As the president stated, "we engage in social service regardless of caste, creed and color." Over a single year (2002), the club provided food to the poor during Ramadan, donated sewing machines and computers to the needy, funded a life-saving operation for a Bahraini child, took blind children on a beach picnic, took mentally disabled Bahraini children to a dolphin marine park, cleaned beaches, greeted sick children during the Eid holiday, sponsored a Bahraini youth's trip to a leadership training program in the United States, led a drug awareness campaign, conducted an essay contest for children, organized free dental hygiene and checkups for mentally disabled Bahraini children, and conducted a wide variety of other service and outreach activities. In pulling these activities together, members draw on the significant resources they command through their businesses and contacts; money, food, and a variety of other items are donated from their businesses to these ends.

Unlike many of the other diasporic associations on the island, the Lions Club of Riffa directs its outreach efforts primarily toward Bahraini citizens rather than toward the transmigrant underclass. In my discussions with the members of the club, several pointed to the history of the British presence on the island, whose legacy is now remembered by many as one of a group who "never gave anything back to the local community," to quote one of the club's members. The Lions Club of Riffa certainly will not suffer the same fate. Its coordinated efforts reach the lower classes of the Bahraini community, and the members are careful to always call photographers from the island's newspapers to document these events. The club also hosts several fancy dinners and events during the year at which luminaries from the Bahraini government, the business community, and the various embassies serve as guest speakers or honorable attendees. These activities not only reinforce the club's status among the diasporic classes but also counteract the popular perception of the diasporic communities as parasites on the Bahraini economy. Careful not to articulate a message critical of the systemic inequities within the Bahraini social structure, the elite members of the Riffa Lions Club envision their activities as returning something to the society in which they have prospered.

Ecumenical Council of Charity

Bahrain is somewhat unique in the context of the Gulf in terms of the proliferation of non-Muslim religious spaces on the island. Noteworthy is the large Hindu temple located in the center of the city's old market district. Invisible from the streets of the busy souk, the temple is entered through a long passageway, whose access is on a street crowded with Indian-owned businesses. This particular venue was established and is still controlled by the Bhatia segment of the Indian diaspora and mainly serves Hindus from Gujarat, Maharati, and Punjab;[7] two other temples in other locations (both in large villas) serve other Hindu constituencies.

The Christian community in Bahrain uses the large Catholic church (with a school), the historic Anglican church, and several other compounds scattered in the central districts of the city. The Anglican church grounds include the church itself, along with several wings. The spaces in those wings are loaned to a number of non-Anglican denominations and various associated groups. After several months on the island, I began attending meetings of the Ecumenical Council of Charity (ECC), held monthly in one of the rooms on the Anglican compound. The ECC is a nondenominational Christian voluntary organization specifically configured to reach out to individuals in crisis. Monthly meetings are informal and begin with a prayer. The remainder of the meeting consists of reporting on outreach activities currently under way and planning future efforts.

In the several meetings that I attended, discussion largely focused on the hospital visits conducted by a team of ECC members. Although their primary goal was to console individuals amid difficulties—and to pray for those individuals—the hospital visits also allowed the ECC to identify particular scenarios in which they might provide monetary or other forms of assistance to individuals in need. Examples from one of those meetings included the following:

- A Sri Lankan domestic worker had been diagnosed with breast cancer, but her sponsor refused to release her passport until she paid him 300 dinars [$850]. She was languishing in the hospital and did not have the money to pay for her release. The council decided to contribute 100 dinars [$265] to this end.

• A thirty-eight-year-old Indian male was injured by an automobile while riding his bicycle. He had a heart attack and suffered brain damage. The man needed to be repatriated to India, and although the sponsor was willing to pay for three seats (so he could lie down), two more seats were needed for a nurse and an assistant. The council decided to refer this case to the Indian embassy and to the Indian Community Relief Fund, as they have funds dedicated to this purpose.

• An Indian laborer suffered a heart attack on a construction site and was languishing in the hospital. His sponsor was unconcerned with the laborer's welfare. The ECC had successfully contacted his family to let them know that he was now in the hospital in Bahrain. Plans to repatriate him were under way, but details remained scarce. The council concluded that they would continue to evaluate the situation.

Overall, the ECC's efforts typically focused on contacting other agencies and institutions, thereby engaging the disparate and apolitical diasporic networks that take responsibility for the various transmigrant constituencies. Often this task is as simple as contacting the various embassies on the island. In many situations, however, the ECC also provided monetary support, particularly when injured, ill, or dead transmigrant laborers faced unresponsive sponsors. This assistance, while often framed in terms of a Christian ethos, was provided to individuals regardless of religion, ethnicity, or nationality.

Indian Ladies Association

As the former president and longtime member of the Indian Ladies Association stated, "we are a high-profile organization." Formed in 1956 by a group of wealthy women from Bahrain's Indian diaspora, the Indian Ladies Association (ILA) draws its membership from the Indian diasporic elite. Originally a forum for women to "hold a monthly tea and meet weekly to sew, make handicrafts, and socialize" (Franklin 1985, 487), the ILA in the intervening years has taken on a variety of more ambitious projects and goals, many of which are directly aimed at serving both the diasporic and indigenous populations on the island. The Kitchen Craft Committee and the Beauty and Fashion Committee of many years' standing have been joined by a Community Service Committee and its Workers' Subcommittee. Membership in the ILA fluctuated between 150 and 200 members over the decade prior to my fieldwork, and together the members, which included both professional women and the wives of businessmen and merchants, represented the social apex of the Indian community. The ILA also has a structural arrangement with the Indian embassy: the wife of the Indian ambassador is the honorary president of the association.

During 2002 and 2003, much of the ILA's energies were devoted to the ongoing support and maintenance of SNEHA, a center for mentally disabled youth from the diasporic communities on the island.[8] The seed for this project was planted by a former ILA member. She and her husband brought their mentally disabled child on their professional sojourn to the Gulf, and because the government-organized centers for such children on the island were for citizens only, they found no institutional support for the care of their child. Together the women of the ILA founded the SNEHA center, whose headquarters were located in a large office building in central Manama. The center was fully funded and partially staffed by the members of the association. In granting a charter for the center, the Bahraini government imposed a limit of twenty children, and the center was operating at full capacity in 2003. The budget for the center was approximately BD10,000 ($26,500), derived through a combination of donations and fund-raising. The SNEHA premises were also used for other purposes, including a low-cost English course aimed at the transmigrant working class.[9]

During my time in Bahrain, the ILA also conducted a wide variety of programs aimed at the men in the labor camps scattered about the island. Once a month the women, working closely with a set of labor camp supervisors, arranged for a home-cooked Indian meal to be delivered to a particular camp on Friday, typically the day of rest for most laborers. The members' contacts in the labor camps proved useful for planning the annual workers' talent show, held on the grounds of the Indian Club in 2003 (see fig. 5.2). This large event drew 1,600 laborers (along with a variety of luminaries from the diasporic community, all of whom sat in the reserved section in front of the stage). Laborers performed skits and songs for a variety of prizes, including a round-trip ticket to India on Air India. Performers from the Indian diasporic community and a few imported from India sang songs and danced, and food was provided to all the men. As the chairwoman of the Workers' Subcommittee observed: "[The workers] are talented, and they have the capacity, but unfortunately the way they live...they have no chance to show these talents. You see, you have to become a member of a club to show these kinds of talents, but where will they

Figure 5.2. Indian men dancing and celebrating at the 2003 workers' talent show, hosted by the Indian Ladies Association at the Indian Club. Photograph by Kristin Giordano.

get the kind of money to become a member? So we do this for them. They sing, they enjoy, they are quite happy."

Among its many other annual activities, the ILA also arranges a show for the Bahraini emir's wife and a variety of her female relatives and friends. As many of the women in the royal family have a minimal public presence, the event is relished by both parties.[10] The ILA arranges for the event to be held in a five-star hotel, and, as a former president of the ILA described, "we put on a colorful dance or fashion show for them, arrange raffle prizes for them—it's an evening just for them. It's only ladies—about 400 or 500." The ILA's interaction with the royal family also includes visits to the emir's wife's *majlis,* where, often, the association receives substantial donations that fund its projects. The interaction between the ILA and the royal family is unusual in comparison to the activities of other social clubs and associations on the island, and is a symbol of the status maintained by the members of the ILA.

As the tenor of the chairwoman's comments about the workers' talent show indicates, reaching out to the poorest members of the transmigrant class is an act that provides the men with a welcome and rare break from the difficult conditions they face in the camp and, at the same time, affirms the class distinctions within the diasporic community. The activities of the ILA—from its outreach activities with the labor camps to the private meetings with the women of the royal family—assert a parity between the elite members of Bahraini society and the elite members of the Indian diaspora. In other words, many of these activities highlight social class as the primary logic of the culturally plural space of Bahrain and, in doing so, push religion, ethnicity, and nationality into the shadows.

Social Clubs in Context

The social clubs and voluntary associations on the island take many forms, but they all share a set of challenges specific to the transnational milieu of contemporary Bahrain. Perhaps the foremost of these challenges revolves around the cyclical and itinerant nature of the transmigrants' stay in the Gulf. The nature of the transnational environment—where individuals are moving back and forth between India or moving onward from Bahrain to other locations—makes the retention of a core set of members difficult. Those with ample free time to organize, manage, and lead clubs or committees within clubs are commonly individuals in well-paid positions who observe typical work hours, either seven o'clock to three or nine o'clock to five. It is these very positions, however, that the collection of government policies known as Bahrainization seeks to replace with citizen-workers. Hence many of these social clubs must constantly cope with member attrition—and particularly the members most capable of devoting the time and energy to the club or association's activities. As the president of the Riffa chapter of the Lions Club described, "We started with 75 members, and eventually came down to less than 40 members. The main reason for the loss of members is departures related to the Bahrainization scheme. I don't blame the Bahrainis—this is their home, their place. But that's certainly the biggest cause. Like my brother—he left the island and is in the States, and he's started a new Lions Club in Chicago. But yes, departure is a problem. Last year we lost ten members. The year before that we lost even more."

By the end of my fieldwork in Bahrain, the president of the Riffa chapter had finalized his own plans for emigration to the United States. Vaishali, a longtime member of the Indian Ladies Association, painted a similar portrait: "Our membership fluctuates. This year, for example, I'll have a set of members that withdraw, but I'll have other new members that come.... Over the last few years, many have either retired and gone back—gone on to Canada or gone back to India because their husbands have lost their jobs. But the association is steady—we do the work! There are at least twenty members like me who've been constantly active since 1985. But with the others, you cannot say from year to year."

While clear about the challenges presented by the transnational milieu, Vaishali is also clear about the important role played by the social clubs and voluntary associations. Together, these social institutions comprise the basic social fabric of diasporic culture and society in Bahrain—the only diasporic institutions with some degree of permanence in the transnational milieu. For Durkheim, institutions such as these were the basis of society in that they transcend the individual's temporal existence; in the transnational milieu of contemporary Bahrain, it is not just the lifespan of the men and women that pales next to the permanence of these institutions—it is the transmigrants' temporary existence in the conduits of transnational migration that makes the relative permanence of these institutions so important.

The social clubs and other voluntary organizations face additional challenges in the context of contemporary Bahrain. The Bahraini Ministry of Social Affairs licenses and registers all social clubs. As one former club president commented: "The ministry must approve all these new clubs, and to get a license for a fresh club is not very easy. There are already more than 200 clubs here in Bahrain, and it's difficult to regulate. They want everybody to merge and form larger clubs. There are sports clubs, professional clubs, social clubs... and the government thinks this is a problem." In recent years, the Ministry of Social Development has monitored, disciplined, and closed several active clubs on the island. Oftentimes these events are in response to complaints from citizens about drinking and "mixing," the term generally used for open and public interaction between genders.[11] Vaishali also reported that the ministry curtailed the transnational movement of funds collected by clubs: "Initially, and even through 1991, we [the ILA] used to send money to India. We collect money, and we have a fund, so our members used to bring all kinds of applications. Suppose in my village there is a fund, an orphanage that needs a little money. So I can probably suggest my center, and maybe the name of somebody involved, but anyway, in 1991 the Ministry of Bahrain stopped that. There is no need to send it [money] to India, they said—why don't you spend it here?"

Relations between the diasporic social clubs and the government reveal another aspect of governance of the transnational populations on the island. The social clubs, while providing an important venue for sharing information and participating in the diasporic culture, nonetheless do not provide a platform for challenging the hegemony of the state, for asserting some semblance of basic rights for noncitizens, or for challenging the systemic aspects of the structural violence many foreign workers endure.[12] Some of the clubs and associations seek to assist laborers in particularly dire circumstances—the Ecumenical Council of Charity was engaged in a variety of outreach activities to the most impoverished laborers, and a dedicated TASCA subcommittee dealt weekly with delivering various forms of assistance to the most marginalized members of the Tamil community. Generally speaking, however, these activities posed no challenge to the structure of relations underlying the violence and exploitation many of these impoverished foreign workers endured. In paying off sponsors, providing food and shelter to workers abandoned by their kafeel, or raising funds to help sick or deceased foreign workers return to India, these clubs and associations sought to redress the detritus of this system without confronting its underlying cause. In short, the clubs and associations' activities were to be cultural, not political, in nature.

Indian Culture behind Walls

These social clubs and voluntary associations provide a constellation of options for performing "Indian-ness," although, as many of the men and women stated, outside their homes and social clubs they were simply treated as South Asians. In essence, the markers of more specific identities—class, region, religion, and so forth—were elided in the public sphere of Bahrain. In their descriptions, these homogenizing experiences in the public spaces and workplaces on the island took many forms. Newspapers refer to the nationality of foreigners, reporting them as Indian, Pakistani, Bangladeshi, and so forth. Even those Indians who were born and raised in Bahrain observed that having a Bahraini passport would do little to change the nature of their interactions with the citizenry: they are Indians and foreign to the genealogical conceptions of citizenship that shape relations between individuals and the state. In the world of Bahrain, Indian workers are constantly racialized. Faced with a system that reinforces this singular identity, social clubs and voluntary organizations provide a key venue for reinvesting in the specificities lurking beneath the transcendent Indian identity. It is in those venues that one can perform being a Keralite, or a Christian, or a

Tamil Catholic. In these clubs and associations individuals reconnect with the particularistic identities that make them Indian, that make them something more than just foreign workers. As the former president of one of the largest social clubs on the island described,

> [For Indians] away from those clubs, their life in the general world of Bahrain is a second class life. They have to obey someone, they have to do unpleasureable things to please someone. There's a kind of humiliation, frustration in their work. When they come from that world to the club, or to the Indian embassy, which is their own world, then there they remember that I'm an Indian citizen, and I have a right to complain about the table being dirty, or the bathroom stinking. They write a letter. It's the action of a person that's not satisfied with life in the outside world of Bahrain. He goes to his own, he's got no family here, he can't shout at his wife that his tea isn't ready. So such people, they take it out on someone somewhere. And the only people that will listen to them are their own people at the Indian School, Indian embassy, or Indian Club. If they did the same thing at their job, they would say pack up and leave the country.

Sheba George (2000) observed, in her analysis of the husbands of Keralite nurses within a community in the United States, that the men who accompany the nurses are disenfranchised and disempowered in the American workforce. Voluntary associations—and particularly churches—offer "a unique setting for men to restore their lost identity and their self esteem. To compensate for demotion in the labor market and family, they use the church in three significant ways: to assert their leadership, to develop a sense of belonging, and to secure their exclusiveness" (George 2000, 163). Voluntary associations in Bahrain serve a similar function: as spaces beyond the direct purview of citizens and state, social clubs and voluntary organizations provide key venues for the performance of "Indian-ness" and, at the same time, for the expression of the fissures in that identity.

For members of the Indian diaspora, social clubs and voluntary associations provide one of the principal venues for the articulation and, alternatively, the rejection of class. At one level, Indian social clubs provide a closed system, outside the purview of citizenry and state, and beyond the habitus of everyday interactions between citizen and foreigner. The social clubs and associations are spaces where the statuses native to India can be deployed and utilized. Alternatively, some of the voluntary clubs provide venues in which citizens and noncitizens mix, and, occasionally, locations where the class logic of the global capitalist system can be affirmed rather than rejected. At one Toastmasters meeting, for example, I watched a club secretary of Indian descent browbeat a Bahraini member for his suggestion on the format for an upcoming award ceremony. The Indian member's loud and angry tone was unusual—I had never observed any interaction like this outside the context of these social clubs and other voluntary organizations. Clubs like this chapter of the Toastmasters, designed for cosmopolitan English speakers from all the various communities on the island, provide not only venues in which middle-class and elite diasporic community members practice English. They also provide venues in which the discourse of the professional class is practiced and, simultaneously, in which statuses achieved under the logic of the global capitalist system are deployed and affirmed. Unlike other spaces on the island, at this meeting the Bahraini and Indian were on equal footing.

At other junctures, however, voluntary associations and social clubs provide a venue for rejecting class hierarchies of the global, capitalist political economy, for these social clubs also provide a venue for reaffirming the statuses and identities of the homeland. Although an individual's caste or status in India may hold little sway with his or her sponsor or, alternatively, in the larger context of Bahraini culture, those categories may find traction in the arena of the social club. Performing "Indian-ness" can take the form of reinvesting in the social and cultural aspects of Indian life that find no traction in the larger public sphere in Bahrain.

Social Clubs, Voluntary Organizations, and the Public Sphere

At first glance, these social clubs and voluntary associations might best be understood as another component of the stark social and cultural divisions that characterize the Gulf states. Amid the strikingly plural context of the contemporary Gulf, the proliferation of these clubs and associations in Bahrain moves the collective performance of Indian culture behind club walls and into conference rooms of the large hotels on the island. Although these spaces provide an arena for the construction of meaning—for the articulation of what it means to be an Indian, a Catholic Keralite Indian, or an elite cosmopolitan Indian—the generation of these identities seemingly occurs in enclaves beyond the view of the Bahraini public. If that separateness is as absolute as this analysis suggests, perhaps these clubs are best understood as nodes or venues in the Indian diasporic public sphere rather than as components of an all-encompassing public sphere located in Bahrain. Put another way, are these clubs and associations part of a heterogeneous Bahraini public sphere?

Several points can be brought to bear against this perspective. First, it seems obvious that as cloistered as much of this cultural performance is, nonetheless it is in constant dialogue with the experiences these men and women have outside those walls. The iteration of particularistic Indian identities is an act intricately intertwined with the world in which many of these men and women work and live. In the habitus of everyday interactions on the island, these men and women are homogeneously framed as South Asian labor; hence the act of seeking and performing more particularlistic identities occurs against that backdrop. In other words, the meanings and identities they construct behind club walls are a response to their experiences and frustrations outside those walls: the Lions Club's outreach activities to poor and disenfranchised Bahrainis is an assertion of the diasporic elite's status, of the elite's complicity with the vision of modernity promoted by the state, and, in the largest sense, with the neoliberal logic of a system that favors class over ethnicity, nationalism, religion, and culture. Or, in another sense, the intra-Indian political machinations of the Indian Club provide an opportunity to be political in ways that one cannot be beyond the walls of the club. As both of these examples suggest, the activities of these clubs are directly related to the experiences these men and women encounter in the larger public sphere in Bahrain.

Rather than think of these clubs and associations as components of discrete diasporic public spheres, I suggest we think of them as active participants in this plural and more comprehensive Bahraini public sphere. In this chapter, I have focused on how participation in that public sphere is filtered, constrained, and truncated by the social relations on the island. At times that governance seems external in nature. One can easily see, for example, how clubs and associations must avoid the ire of the state and citizenry, and therefore move their activities behind walls. At other times, however, it becomes apparent that these groups internalize the terms of this governance and collectively negotiate their representation to fit the public they imagine. These forces and tensions are threads we can continue to trace in an examination of the English-language newspapers.

6 CONTESTED IDENTITIES, CONTESTED POSITIONS

English-Language Newspapers and the Public Sphere

Several years ago in Bahrain a young married couple joined friends for a seaside walk. The young man, twenty-four years of age and a foreign worker from Nepal, worked as an air conditioner repairman on the island—a valuable technical trade in the sweltering kingdom. His young wife, aged twenty-one and also from Nepal, worked as a waitress somewhere on the island. Together, the group of friends spent the afternoon on the Causeway, the 26-kilometer collection of jetties and bridges that since 1986 has connected the small island kingdom with Saudi Arabia. At some point the young Nepalese couple diverged from their friends, clambered over the rocks along the shoreline, found a secluded spot and, by their own account, began kissing and cuddling.

High above them in the Causeway observation tower, a coastguard officer on routine patrol spotted the young couple below. To quote the officer, "I was on my routine duty in the King Fahad Causeway restaurant tower and I observed a man and a woman lying on the rocks on the embankment of the causeway bridge and performing sex openly.... I was surprised at witnessing this scene and decided to go down and stop this act. I caught them red-handed and then handed them over to the causeway police." It was further alleged that when arrested, the couple were naked from the waist down. The young man and his wife denied these allegations. In the young man's words, "We were simply sitting on the rocks and my wife was sitting on my legs and then this policeman arrived and arrested us and took us to the police station.... We were fully dressed and my wife was on my lap and we were only hugging each other and kissing." His wife delivered a similar version of the events to police: "I went with my husband near the sea and sat on the rocks on the embankment and then we started to exchange kisses with each other for about five minutes. Then suddenly this policeman appeared and arrested us." The fate of the young Nepalese couple remains a mystery to me, for I came to know about this particular sequence of events through the *Gulf Daily News,* the predominant English-language newspaper on the island.[1]

At one level, this newspaper has provided a tapestry of events, stories, and reports that continues to situate the ethnographic data I personally collected in 2002 and 2003. This particular story, for example, provides another glimpse of the governance of foreign workers on the island: their bodies, their behavior, and their relations can easily become the purview of both sponsors and the state. Perhaps more important, however, is that stories like this one are active agents of that governance, for stories broadcast through the newspapers, then told and retold in the many foreign communities on the island, delineate the powers of the state and reinforce the vulnerability that individual foreigners face. In the telling and retelling, these stories describe the parameters of appropriate and inappropriate behavior, and the risks foreigners face in an unfamiliar land.

More and more, however, I have also come to understand the role of this English-language newspaper as a central junction in the public discourse of the small island kingdom, a discourse that reveals the interests of the state, the topography of Bahraini nationalism, and the intricate friction between citizen and foreigner. Although newspapers have been of occasional interest to anthropologists, the connection between newspapers and national identity is well established in the broader literature (Anderson 1983; Hall 2005). In this chapter, I adopt Gupta's perspective that newspapers also provide the "raw material necessary for a thick description" of translocal phenomena such as the state—particularly, I argue, in the context of Bahrain and the neighboring Gulf states (Gupta 2006, 222). To make a long story short, events like the one I just described—in their occurrence, in the public discussions they engender, and in the parameters those public discussions take—reveal the tectonic frictions underlying the extraordinarily transnational environs of the contemporary Gulf. Also, they provide us with a second glimpse at the public sphere I began describing in the previous chapter.

ENGLISH-LANGUAGE NEWSPAPERS IN BAHRAIN

The *Gulf Daily News* is the older of the two primary English-language newspapers on the island. Both newspapers—the *Gulf Daily News* and the

Bahrain Tribune—have Arabic sister papers with which they share content. Founded in 1978, the *Gulf Daily News* was for many years the only English-language newspaper on the island. The newspaper's journalistic staff includes Indians, Bahrainis, Filipinos, and Britishers, many of whom provide a direct link between the newspaper and issues in their respective diasporic or local communities. Although primarily staffed by foreigners for much of its history, the *Gulf Daily News* was long regarded as pro-government. Over the last decade, however, it has established a much more nuanced and complex position relative to the state.

Because Arabic is the national language in Bahrain, one might assume that the *Gulf Daily News* and other English-language newspapers primarily serve the expatriate community and hence are peripheral to the overarching public sphere this (and the previous) chapter seeks to chart. To the contrary, however, English has emerged as the primary and common language that bridges the many national communities at work on the island. Although not all Indians speak (or read) English, and not all Bahrainis speak (or read) English, it is the primary language of the private sector, and it is the only language that significant portions of all the various national communities on the island speak. As a widely distributed cultural text, the *Gulf Daily News* probably reaches a more diverse and broader audience than any other medium on the island.[2]

The contention that the *Gulf Daily News* plays a central role in the intercommunity public space in Bahrain should not obscure the fact that all newspapers on the island exist under heavy censorship. Much of that censorship occurs as direct state intervention. In 2008, for example, the International Press Institute began its report on media freedom in Bahrain with these sentences: "State authorities have carried out a systematic attack on all forms of free expression in Bahrain this year, severely limiting the ease with which human rights activists, civil society representatives and journalists can carry out their work. Through intensified censorship of the Internet and an increased number of legal cases against journalists, the state's attempts to silent dissent have been far reaching" (IPI 2008). In particular, intense state censorship surrounded "Bandargate," the nomenclature for the events and public reactions following the actions of Sudanese-born British adviser Salah al-Bandar after he released a report and supporting documents contending that high-level government officials and representatives of the royal family were tampering with elections and working on a variety of other fronts to ensure the continuing dominance of the Sunni minority of the citizenry. Journalists writing about the report were prosecuted, and the courts issued a permanent ban on reportage concerning the Bandar report. State-based censorship encompasses a variety of other issues as well, including women's rights in Bahrain, the state's security apparatus, and high-level financial corruption on the island. Journalists and editors are typically sued for defamation and face significant fines and six-month to five-year prison sentences for "press offences."[3]

Explicit state-based censorship, however, is only one aspect of how the power of the state is exerted in this public discourse. The threat of censorship (with the accompanying fines, prison time, and deportation) is internalized by the various participants in this public sphere, albeit to varying degrees. As one self-described blogger/insider wrote,

> I agree... that the censorship policies of the editor-in-chiefs of papers in magical Arabia strangle and dilute a lot of stories and even perhaps portray an incorrect picture to readers. However, the issue is more complicated when you take into consideration that we (journalists/editors/columnists) are self-censored to begin with, especially when it comes to touchy issues.
>
> Allow me, as an insider, if you may, to run by you a common scenario, in our papers: As a journalist, I would tone down my story and add a twist to it, which will make it more acceptable to the news editor, who would be the first person to read the article. The news editor, in turn, would dilute the potentially damaging story, cutting out anything the self-censored journalist may have slipped into the copy to suit the paper's policies and the whims of the editor-in-chief. Then the "sensitive" story goes to the editor-in-chief's desk, who may use his own judgement to either publish or kill the story.
>
> If the story is to be published, the top-notch editor would be risking a show down with authorities the next morning but would be scoring brownie points with his journalists and news editor. It is important for any editor-in-chief to appear strong and in charge of his own decisions. Secretly and away from prying eyes, he may seek "advice" on whether to carry the story or not even after agreeing to run it and may then hold it for a day or two, depending on what else is going on. If he decides to kill the story, then our enterprising editorial team may challenge his decision, take back the story, rewrite and re-edit it, until it looks and sounds nothing like it originally was.
>
> Only once all and each of our strictly abided to self-censorship criteria are fulfilled, does the story make the headlines. Not surprisingly

enough and despite all this care and sensitivity in handling the story, all hell breaks loose once it is finally published. The authorities are angry, the source is mad, everyone calls for beheading everyone else and life continues as normal as we write and rewrite the truth as we see it and as we think the authorities would like to see it... regardless of what it really is... for in reality the truth is merely a matter of perception.[4]

As this purported insider's description makes clear, the internalization of the interests of the state yields a self-censorship that operates at many different levels of the journalistic enterprise. Editors perhaps reflect the interests of the state in the stories they choose to run or not run, but the feedback from this process ensures that journalists and columnists also conform to the perceived norms. By this argument, these columnists and journalists envision, write, and submit stories that avoid a host of sensitive topics. This portrayal suggests an almost panoptic state-based regime that shapes the "reality" purveyed in the public sphere of Bahrain.

My analysis of the *Gulf Daily News* suggests a more nuanced scenario. As the story with which this chapter began suggests, some of the recurring themes in the *Gulf Daily News* directly reflect the power and interests of the state. Stories like the one concerning the Nepalese couple directly convey the power of the state and the parameters of vulnerability that foreign workers face during their sojourn on the island. In the remainder of this chapter, I consider five other recurring themes in the *Gulf Daily News,* and although this list is not exhaustive, these five threads displace the notion of the state's omnipotence in this public discourse. Specifically, these themes paint a more complex portrait of the interests and the stakeholders' contributions to this public discourse. Certainly the interests of the state, and its power to censor, remain a central factor in this public sphere. But the conversations, discussions, and announcements these themes distill typically triangulate among citizens, the state, and the foreign communities on the island, and the alignments of those various groups shift at different times and contexts.

Envisioning the Modernity of Bahrain's Near Future

The *Gulf Daily News,* and for that matter all the newspapers on the island, adeptly promotes a particular vision of Bahrain's path to the future. This portrayal typically focuses on the island nation's numerous infrastructural modernization projects and real estate developments, from those imagined, envisioned, or proposed to those under way or nearing completion. Supporting those announcements of material projects is a steady stream of proclamations concerning the financial and economic well-being of the island kingdom—messages fine-tuned to affirm Bahrain's central role in the region's global financescape. The articulation of these interrelated themes is a veritable constant in the island's newspapers. A recent headline, for example, announced "Bahrain on Right Track," from an article heralding the fact that "one of the world's top financial ratings agencies yesterday issued a glowing report on Bahrain's economic prospects."[5] Other headlines report that Bahrain's "Future Glitters," that Bahrain was experiencing "Growth in the Fast Lane!" that Bahrain was in a "Banking Boom!" and that a "$3BN Sea City" would soon begin construction. As these examples suggest, the newspaper provides an important forum for announcing new projects and key milestones in the economic development of the kingdom. Collectively these portrayals lodge Bahrain as an active and successful participant in the global political economy and simultaneously buttress the idea of the royal family's benevolent stewardship of a nation during a period of dramatic change.

These articles also mine an aesthetic vein. Artists' computer-generated renditions of the skyscrapers and real estate developments to be built are centrally featured in the newspaper. These images, ubiquitous not just in Bahrain but in all of the Gulf states, portray a clean, manicured, organized, and architecturally inventive near future. The bird's-eye views digitally generated by architects, designers, and artists contain only vaguely sketched humans or, more commonly, no people at all. These images are often accompanied by photographs of Bahrain's leaders convened with European or North American CEOs and their architectural models, reinforcing the role of the Bahraini leadership as stewards of modernity and development (see Dresch 2005, 6). The portraits of Bahrain's near future and the architectural models around which these men convene draw on a stock of imagery that aligns the national vision with a global and cosmopolitan future. In doing so, these images marginalize the particular and local, for as a genre they present a modernity without place—a vision of Bahrain that is both vague and generic, and one that is palatable in the sociocultural context of the contemporary island.

In both image and word this neoliberal vision of Bahrain's future is portrayed as frictionless and indisputably good. It meshes the interests of the ethnocratic state and its Sunni leadership with that of the foreign, cosmopolitan elite residents of the island. At the same time, this vision masks the heavy dependence on foreign labor and foreign ingenuity: with

Figure 6.1. Newspaper headline from the *Gulf Daily News*.

the private sector predominantly composed of foreign workers, the humans missing from these artistic renditions are not Bahrainis. This vision of modernity also masks the inequities of distribution on the island, in that the Shi'ite underclass stands to benefit little from this growth. This underclass's critiques—and, in fact, all critiques—of the inequities of distribution on the island are muted in the symbolic and discursive presentation of Bahrain's glorious path to the future.

All of this suggests several things about the newspaper and the public sphere in Bahrain. Gupta argues that the newspaper is not simply the arm of the state but rather exists at the confluence of folk, regional, and national

Figure 6.2. The Bahrain Financial Harbour project in an artist's rendition. http://www.bfharbour.com.

ideologies "competing with each other and with *transnational* flows of information, tastes, and styles" (2006, 213). Although that competition is apparent in some of the other themes described, the monolithic portrayal of Bahrain's near future seems uncontested in the pages of the *Gulf Daily News*. In both symbolic and discursive terms, the modernity promoted in the newspaper should be seen not as a window to a collective and homogeneous idea of Bahraini nationhood, but as an assertion of a particular vision of Bahraini nationhood—one aligned with the cosmopolitan interests of those classes that most directly benefit from the neoliberal flow of capital.

Mapping the Bureaucracy and Critiquing the System

The Letters to the Editor section of the *Gulf Daily News* burgeons with contributions concerning the many challenges foreigners face in navigating the Bahraini system. In earlier chapters, I used the ethnographic data I collected in Bahrain to portray the lives of the Indian foreigners on the island; it should be clear that many of them are isolated, that their primary contact was a labor broker in now-distant India, and that only their kafeel is there to officially represent them once they are in Bahrain. Although this structure of dominance isolates foreigners and prevents them from accessing the bureaucratic conduits of power through which they are governed, the newspaper—and particularly the Letters to the Editor section—functions as a public forum for solving the day-to-day problems foreign workers typically encounter on the island.

Consider, for example, this question from the Letters section of the *Gulf Daily News:* "My visa expired more than six months ago and I have given notice to my sponsor that I am going to change my visa and my new sponsor has got the labour permit. But my sponsor is not returning my passport (and my family's). Now he has promised me that since he is abroad he will return it on arrival. How can I have a new visa?"[6] In reply, the *GDN* editor directed the author to a series of Web pages that might help him navigate the state bureaucracy. Dozens of questions of this sort appear in the Letters to the Editor section every month. Their writers ask for advice, guidance, or clarification, and typically focus on the Byzantine processes that govern the flow of human capital to the island kingdom.

At other junctures, the desire for advice, guidance, or clarification gives way to complaints and open critique. For example, the following letter addresses a previous letter in the *Gulf Daily News,* as well as the published response (by a government representative) to that letter: "A letter clearly asked for information about 'Housemaid visas for expats' (*GDN* October 9). The response to it just states that there are specific rules for it and to contact the Labour Ministry. Why haven't these specific rules been published? We would all like them to be published. The answer was not specific. Why do government departments always give vague answers and not specific information? Why this red tapism?"[7] The accusation of "red tapism" from this anonymous letter writer is part of a broader critique levied by foreign writers in this section of the newspaper. Collectively they accuse the government of bureaucratic ineptitude; they posit themselves and other foreigners like them as disempowered but rational agents of modernity.

The ideological parameters of this position are more clearly visible in this long retort responding to recent changes and a host of broader systemic problems the anonymous author encountered in Bahrain:

> Recently we have been inundated with comments concerning the rights of Bahrainis, and only Bahrainis, to determine the future of this

country and to influence legislators in making change. But, who will listen to my voice? And why should I have a voice? As a businessman I am contributing to the country and the government in many ways, which are quite often ignored or forgotten by our MPs [members of Parliament] and the ordinary people.

I pay municipal taxes on both my residence and my place of business (nearly BD100 per month); I pay Commercial Registration fees, Chamber of Commerce levy, LMRA fees, residence visa and other government charges. In addition I am paying rents into the pockets of citizens and wages that go into circulation through my employees' rents and shopping etc; I am also regularly asked to sponsor local charity events, the proceeds of which go to many local worthy causes. In total, I am probably paying indirect "taxation" amounting to BD20,000 per year to Bahraini economy. And in exchange for that, I have absolutely no representation.

Young women at the LMRA regularly berate me for not employing more Bahrainis, or not filling in forms, or not changing the way I do business to suit their demands. These very same women insist I use a Bahraini to interact with their desks as I am not considered capable. This forces me to visit them several times on each matter, as the Bahraini doesn't understand my business or its needs.

And now, the MPs, whose salaries I am indirectly contributing to, are starting to introduce laws that will restrict my freedom and limit my lifestyle. Fortunately, I can conduct my business from anywhere in the region; maybe it's time to consider changing my base—Muscat is very appealing. Have our esteemed legislators heard the story of the goose that laid the golden egg—but of course, they wouldn't as that is another decadent folly from the West. A little like the fairy tale of Business-Friendly Bahrain.

Signed, A Frustrated Businessman.[8]

This letter and many others like it clearly illustrate the ideological positioning that goes on in the Letters to the Editor section of the newspaper. The author—"Frustrated Businessman"—maps his contributions to the Bahraini economy, positioning himself as an ideal entrepreneur directly contributing to Bahrain's national interests. At the same time, Bahrainis are portrayed as incompetent stewards of the system they host: they fail to give him the rights he sees as appropriate to his economic contribution, they fail to recognize and respect that contribution, they fail to efficiently assist him with the management of his business, and they seemingly wish to build a culturally uncomfortable environment for the author and his foreign employees. Many of the letters to the editor contribute to this overarching theme, and the rhetorical path that "Frustrated Businessman" follows is a common one: specific criticisms escalate into broad denunciations of Bahraini incompetence and contradiction.

A few points merit further discussion. Although much of my analysis of the activity in this facet of the public sphere is focused on the cultural and ideological negotiation of the various collective identities present on the island, we ought not lose sight of the mundane functions this venue also serves. For foreign workers isolated in an unfamiliar system and bound to a sponsor who may not have their interests at heart, the Letters to the Editor sections of the English-language newspapers provide an important clearinghouse for information on how to navigate the system in which they find themselves enmeshed. This venue disseminates information and strategies integral to the foreign workers under this comprehensive governance, and, as the second and third letters exemplify, it provides a rare space for foreigners to publicly critique the state. Certainly there are limitations to this facet of the public sphere, for this venue is open only to those foreigners and citizens with a mastery of English. Nonetheless, the anonymity of the letters to the editor encourages discussions and critiques that one would rarely hear in other public spaces on the island.

The Global Appeal

In his book about the emergence of a unified and global indigenous identity, Ronald Niezen portrays indigenous peoples' increasingly sophisticated use of the global media to publicize the conflicts with the states under which they oftentimes suffer. In particular, he focuses on the "politics of shame," or the process by which small and marginalized indigenous groups garner global attention and occasionally repulse their more powerful foes (Niezen 2003, 28). By pursuing this strategy, these groups seek more than a witness to their oppression: the threat of attention to their dilemmas and tribulations is a weapon in and of itself. Its successful use is an increasingly common aspect of numerous studies in political ecology and related fields (Brosius 1999; Hornborg 2005).

That same stratagem can be delineated in the *Gulf Daily News*. Occasional travesties or state-generated actions perceived as particularly egregious become the focus of attention in the newspapers. In August 2006, for example, a fire in the decrepit accommodations of a large group of South

Asian laborers took the lives of sixteen men. In the weeks that followed the fire, a series of headlines in the *Gulf Daily News* reported that "Officials 'Must Quit over Fire Tragedy,'" that the "Camp Horror Could Have Been Averted," and that "Bodies [of the deceased workers were] 'Stuffed into Drawers.'"[9] These articles were daily accompanied by irate letters to the editor lamenting the conditions in which the laborers were forced to dwell, as well as the response of both the state and the men's sponsor to the tragedy. Similar collective responses followed what is commonly referred to in Bahrain as the "dhow tragedy" (in which a large and overfilled party dhow capsized in the bay, leaving fifty-eight dead), as well as the state's effort to block access to Mahmood's Den, one of the first and most widely read blogs in Bahrain and staunchly focused on civil rights issues.

In this sense, the *Gulf Daily News* functions as a conduit that allows the foreign and disenfranchised communities to challenge—and potentially circumvent—the governance of the state. Journalists, editors, and letter writers, by focusing on the injustices, violence, and exploitation levied against foreign workers (or, in the case of Mahmood's Den, against vociferous citizens), attempt to bring global attention to these events through a politics of shame. As these examples suggest, oftentimes these stories and letters provide noncitizens and the predominantly foreign journalists of the *Gulf Daily News* with an opportunity to directly accuse citizens—and occasionally the state itself—of injustice. By illuminating the causes and conditions of these events, members of the various communities on the island seek to push back against the injustices they perceive. Although this sort of journalistic discourse is more common in western Europe and the United States, in the context of Bahrain—where foreign workers have little recourse within the legal system, are bound to their kafeel/sponsors, and are marginalized by the state—the attention garnered by these articles and letters provides a significant source of collective power in the absence of other options.

Cultural Friction and Open Debate

Bahrain, as we have seen in previous chapters, is marked by significant social divides. Although individuals from different communities may mingle with citizens in the workplace, generally there is a dearth of interaction between citizens and foreigners—a noteworthy state of affairs in both Bahrain and its neighbors (e.g., see Vora 2008). As I have argued, there are good reasons for this segregation. From the perspective of foreign workers, citizens are a potentially threatening force capable of interfering with their tenuous status on the island, and hence a potential threat to the significant resources most of these foreigners have committed to secure employment on the island. Against the backdrop of these social divisions and the truncated public presence of foreign communities on the island, the Letters to the Editor section of the *Gulf Daily News* stands in stark contrast. Things that never would be uttered in a public setting make frequent appearances in this section of the paper, and open debates are waged over the course of weeks or months. Certainly the anonymity of this section plays an instrumental role in forging the freedoms of this space, but that ought not eclipse the fact that this venue is of extraordinary interest, for it is one of the only venues where countless individuals, both foreign and native, engage in extensive debate.

Although my interest in this section of the newspaper was piqued almost immediately upon arrival on the island, perhaps the most demonstrative example of the scope and terrain of these debates occurred several years after my departure. In the summer of 2006 a Budweiser Battle of the Bands competition was held in Manama. As the various letters to the editor that followed the event indicate, the top prize was taken by a Filipino/Filipina group named Bahrain Chili Band.[10] The debate kicked off with the comments from an anonymous writer who suggested that their performance was "nothing short of a strip show, just like the ones you see in Pat Pong, Thailand." These sentiments were confirmed by a writer named Lizy, who noted that their performance was "simply a strip show...[that] brings down the name of Filipinas in Bahrain." She further wondered why the organizers couldn't impose a dress code on the competition.

This open debate then turned on the comments of an author writing under the moniker of Fatami. She argued that nakedness is natural—we're all born that way. Continuing, she implored others to "look at the beaches in Europe. There are clothing optional beaches which allow women the option of going without their tops and hardly anyone looks at them except the Americans who go wild over female breasts because of their puritan upbringing." These comments ignited the debate, and in the days that followed a slew of letters reproached Fatami. "Concerned Filipina" stated that the women in Bahrain Chili Band were not at the beach, but rather at a hotel, and that Fatami should try to practice what she preaches on the streets of Manama and see how it goes. Mohammed, speaking in the plural, sought to pierce the anonymity of this dialogue with a series of questions: "Who are you? Where do you stand? Which point do you speak from? And are you Muslim?" He concluded with the suggestion that "if you are Arabic and Muslim we recommend you to read the Holy Quran and review it carefully. You might have missed some very important explanation." Two days later, Oamir concurs with Mohammed and further accuses Fatami of thinking only of her body, not her mind.

Fatami's reply, printed a few days later, contends that the laws that Oamir cites were "established 1,500 years ago and have not been updated since.... You and a lot of people living in the Middle East have archaic ideal about women.... Women are now equal to men in all parts of the world except some areas of the Middle East where they are still being held back. A woman has a brain and can use it, so free her and let her make her own decisions." Another anonymous writer joined the debate, contending that only in the liberal West can "man marry man and women can marry women. Please keep your broad minds and so-called freedom in the west only. It is not applicable here. Women are not equal in any part of the world...the reality is that women can never be equal to men." This argument concluded with a final letter from Fatami in which she remarked that women now only need men for sperm, which is easily attainable at sperm banks. "As I said before," she continued, "you guys in the Middle East are way behind the times. Just look at the traffic, parking problems in Bahrain that you cannot solve."[11]

Readily visible in this debate are the complex positions of the various communities on the island. The two Filipina contributors, for example, avoid express support for their countrywomen's performance: instead, they scold the women—and Fatami—for degrading the collective image of Filipinos on the island. This stance echoes the work of others who have tracked how members of these foreign communities both in the Gulf and other places internalize the terms of their own oppression (Constable 1997; Nagy 2008). It is equally interesting how the debate steadily ascends to the topics of gender, Islam, and Western culture. One can read much into Mohammed's use of the plural (for Bahrainis? Arabs? Muslims?), in comparison with the singular deployed by the other writers, as well as his attempt to discern Fatami's positionality from behind the curtain of anonymity afforded by the newspaper.

For the purposes of this chapter, what is of interest is not just the content of the debate but the fact that the everyday conditions in which transmigrants live in the Gulf rarely allow for discussion and debate across ethnic and national divides. Foreign workers, typically caught in extraordinarily unequal relationships with their sponsors and citizens as a whole, would never purvey these opinions in public venues. The anonymity of the Letters to the Editor section—an anonymity challenged at one point by Mohammed's interest in discerning Fatima's background—provides a public space for citizens and foreigners to engage one another on equal footing.

Demonstrating Compliance

Arriving on the island as a lone anthropologist without significant contacts, I quickly sought any engagement with the South Asian community I hoped to study. The various social clubs and voluntary associations of the South Asian community allowed me to quickly begin to engage that community. Indeed, those clubs and associations emerged as central to my analysis of this diasporic community. The Lions Club of Riffa in particular provided me with a network of friends and contacts that connected me with many of the luminaries of the South Asian community, and as both a member and participant-observer in this club I was allowed to deeply engage and participate in the club's activities and the processes by which its activities were guided. Those activities included trips to the Dolphin Park for mentally disabled Bahraini children, events for sick Bahraini children during the Eid holiday, a beach picnic for blind Bahraini children, and much more. For a club whose membership was almost entirely composed of wealthy Muslim South Asian businessmen, it is noteworthy that nearly all of their outreach activities were aimed at segments of the Bahraini community.

At most of the public activities and events I attended that were held by the Lions and the other clubs, photographers and reporters from the newspapers were present. Indeed, after a few weeks of attending these meetings, I spent a substantial portion of my monthly budget on a pair of new suits, for it seemed as if most of these photographs appeared in the newspapers the next day. Both the *Gulf Daily News* and the *Bahrain Tribune* devote significant space—often an entire page—to photographs taken at the conclusion of meetings and official gatherings.

Consider the coincidence of the two facts. First, like many of the other elite diasporic voluntary associations on the island, the Lions Club of Riffa channeled its international call to service toward disadvantaged Bahrainis. Second, all of these sorts of clubs and associations are careful to report and photograph their activities in the English-language newspapers on the island. Through my interviews with members of these clubs, I came to understand that their service, while completed with the best of intentions, also served to promote their ethnic and national communities on the island, and to demonstrate their compliance and affiliation with the predominant

Figure 6.3. The author and fellow members of the Riffa chapter of the Lions Club. Photographer unknown.

national vision promoted by the state. In essence, the men and women of these clubs were arguing—against the tides of Bahrainization, and against the problematic daily interactions with citizens—that they were valuable assets to the state and its citizenry, that they were fine and upstanding (non)citizens, and that they posed no cultural threat to Bahraini society. Like the Filipina women who supported the criticisms levied against the Bahrain Chili Band, and like the "Frustrated Businessman" who complained about the conditions of entrepreneurship in Bahrain, members of the diasporic elite use this public forum to position themselves in support and compliance with the vision promoted by the state. Put another way, the public space managed by the newspaper functions not just as a venue for that national vision to be deployed: it is also a venue for various communities to resist, accommodate, or in this case promote their compliance with that vision.

Contradictions, Modernity, and Strife

At the outset of the previous chapter, I sought to delineate a public sphere that encompassed some portion of the many and diverse cultures and communities on the island. To that end, I have described two venues in which the generation and activity of this public sphere seem particularly acute. In the social clubs and other voluntary associations, foreigners often find spaces where they can interact with citizens as relative equals. Moreover, the identities they collectively establish in those clubs and associations, even when constrained from active participation in this public sphere, deeply reflect the social conditions they face on the island. The English-language newspapers, meanwhile, provide one of the primary stages on which collective identities are articulated, rehearsed, and negotiated in relation to one another, to the state, and to a global cosmopolitan audience.

The bulk of my analysis has been devoted to demarcating the spaces, both virtual and real, where this public sphere is generated. But what about the content of this public sphere? In other words, what can we say about what is being said and written? Certainly interpretations could lead in many different directions. To my mind, however, there is one theme—or, better, bifurcation—that encapsulates many of these public discussions, arguments, and performances. In many of the junctures and arenas described in the previous two chapters, foreigners in the Gulf reinforce their position as integral and docile instruments of the prevalent national vision. In the case of the debate concerning the Budweiser Band competition, the Filipina writers scold their countrywomen for their cultural transgressions; in many junctures, foreigners portray themselves as dedicated workers; and as the evidence from the Lions Club suggests, they publicly marry their efforts to the articulated interests of the state. They assert, sometimes vociferously, the need for a more transparent state and for an efficient and accommodative bureaucracy. I understand this perspective as an essentially neoliberal one, for in their contentions they seek to extend the economic vision of the nation that predominates on the island to the social and cultural realm. They seek a more meritocratic workplace, a more transparent state bureaucracy, the implementation of a universal set of rights that inhere to the individual rather than the social collective, and a sociocultural context that respects and accommodates the diversity of its workforce.

What, then, are the citizens of Bahrain saying in this public sphere? In the most general sense, the discursive terrain of these public interactions with South Asian workers often frames foreigners as a potential source of pollution, disorder, and danger. Whether we are talking about the police monitoring and regulating the behavior of the young Nepalese couple whose story began this chapter, or about the response to Fatima concerning her knowledge and understanding of the Quranic tradition, or about the public consternation concerning "mixing" at the social clubs, these debates and interactions shift the discussion away from the cosmopolitan and neoliberal terms that predominate in the national vision and toward a set of terms grounded in cultural difference. That said, in these two chapters the voices of the citizenry in this public sphere are faint. In the final chapter of this book, I focus on the citizenry and state, and map the culturally framed frictions described here over the social and political realities of contemporary Bahrain.

7 THE INVIGORATED STATE

Transnationalism, Citizen, and State

The multifaceted system that governs foreign laborers in Bahrain—a system of arrangements, norms, laws, ideas, and beliefs—has been the center of attention in my analysis. The danger in focusing so closely on the structural violence this system produces, however, rests in the portrayal of Bahraini citizens as what Anthony Giddens called "structural dopes" (1979, 52)—as nothing more than the empty vessels through which foreigners are governed or, in the vocabulary of my analysis, as the faceless agents of the structural violence endured by the foreign laboring class. In this chapter my primary task is to remedy that shallow portrayal. By turning the analytic lens on the Bahraini citizenry, I illuminate their experiences, both complicate and humanize their portrayal in this book, and better contextualize the structural violence that foreign labor endures.

With the abundance of attention paid to transnational communities and their relationship to the states from which they come, the impact of transnational movement on host nations is often eclipsed—hence Mahler's call to examine "the role transmigrants play in transforming those communities that they occupy which are not their communities of origin" (1998, 93; see also Reitz 2003). In illuminating the Bahraini perspective, I also investigate the considerable role the large transmigrant communities have played in shaping the experience, identity, and social relations of the Bahraini people.

The argument at the foundation of this chapter can be summarized as follows: the system by which foreigners are governed, as described in previous chapters and rooted in the institutions and policies of the state, is a strategic response to the challenges and pressures of the contemporary global order. Decades of dependence on inexpensive, educated, and trained transnational laborers who, together, remain integral to the construction and maintenance of the Gulf-wide vision of modernity has left much of the citizenry poorly positioned to compete in the private sector. Instead, the state itself emerges as the locus of their power in the global system. The habitus of everyday interactions with foreigners and the institutional governance of transmigrants on the island become two facets of an increasingly invigorated state. The state is the tool through which the citizens negotiate the impacts of the transnational flows of people, capital, ideas, and culture. The state, however, is also the tool through which citizens insulate themselves from the logic of those transnational flows. Potential resistance to the inequalities codified by the Bahraini state is trumped by the state's ongoing role as the nexus of the citizens' collective resistance to the neoliberal calculus of the global political economy.

The Nation as Host

One afternoon during my fieldwork a Bahraini friend, Abdullah, suggested I accompany him to the house he had occupied as a child. His father, and his father's father, had been prosperous merchants in the city of Manama, and the significant dwelling was only a ten-minute walk—through winding alleys, down a few long boulevards, and then back again into a few winding alleys—from my small flat in the neighborhood of Hoora. Like many others in the middle class, his family had long ago abandoned the city center for the suburbs. Indeed, this house had been rented to a large contingent of South Asian laborers, and the detritus of their impoverished existence could still be seen in the now-empty rooms of the decrepit villa.

The house itself fit squarely within one aspect of the island's historic architectural vernacular. The interior was impervious to the eyes on the street—yielding only a few doorways and high windows to pedestrians. This description hints at an old trope in the literature concerning the prominence of the public/private divide in the spatial arrangement of life in the Middle East, and without straying too far down that path I add that the house was arranged around a central courtyard. Like both historic and contemporary homes on the island, it included a *majlis*, or reception room near the front of the house, in which members of the family hosted guests. These greeting rooms represent a liminal space that bridges the divide between public spaces outside the home and the private space of the home's interior.

What was perhaps most interesting about this house, however, was that it also included a small and separate living quarters located at one corner of the home. The single doorway to this apartment led to the street, so that no passage was possible between the main house and the guest apartment. My host was in the midst of a long narrative about his childhood—describing, for example, how he used to sit in the room upstairs listening to the Beatles—but I eventually asked him about this separate apartment and its purpose. He said that the small apartment was constructed to accommodate the foreign merchants with whom his father and grandfather traded. I later confirmed that this feature was common enough among merchants' houses from that era, and the episode I describe here sank into the recesses of the field notes I maintained while on the island.

I eventually returned to this field note with particular interest, for over the intervening years I have come to think of the layout of this traditional merchant's home as a spatial metaphor that speaks to the transnationality of the island and, more specifically, to the way that the Bahraini citizenry and state have configured their relationship to the peoples and cultures they host on the island. Consider the house that Abdullah's grandfather constructed and its small apartment in which traveling merchants might stay: this guest apartment was at once part of the house, but also clearly distinct and separate from it. His grandfather, like many others on the island, constructed a home in this manner to accommodate the presence of foreigners while, at the same time, insulating the private sphere from foreign incursion. This spatial relationship within the merchant's home helps us understand a key aspect of the Bahraini national imaginary that congeals around the idea of hospitality and the roles of host and guest.

The conceptualization of the nation-as-host is certainly a product of Bahrain's particular historical circumstances. With its rich pearl beds and capable port, the island emerged as a regional entrepôt in the larger trade circuits of the Indian Ocean world. This trade brought much of that world to the island's shores and produced centuries of conditions whereby the indigenous Bahrainis and other early arrivals negotiated their identity against the heterogeneous cast of foreigners, who included merchants, traders, slaves, conquerors, and many others who passed through the bustling port. Moreover, in the last centuries Bahrain functioned as the seat of the British colonial presence in the region, a situation and set of relations that produced an even more complex form of hospitality as the peoples of the island negotiated the legal and political mechanisms for sharing power. Decades of struggle over which peoples on the island were subject to indigenous

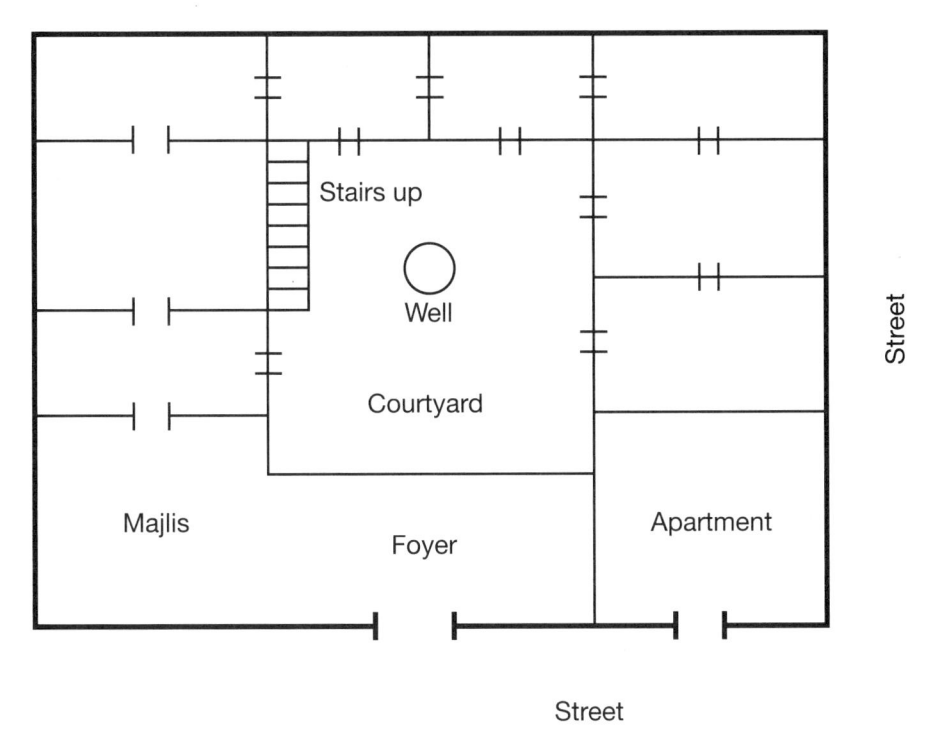

Figure 7.1. Diagram of the merchant's home. Drawing courtesy of Hammad Iqbal.

Bahraini law and which were subject to British jurisdiction, for example, can be seen as a renegotiation of that line dividing the foreign from the local.

This idea of the nation-as-host takes more practical form in the kafala itself. As described in earlier chapters, transmigrants are tied to particular sponsors: adult Bahrainis often "host" numerous transmigrants, both in the workplace and in the home. From the Bahraini perspective, this relationship entails a responsibility for the behavior of these individuals: foreign laborers are conceived as a type of guest, potentially unruly and incursive, but also potentially a source of profit. Perhaps more illuminating is the sleeping-partner arrangement (described at length in chap. 4) whereby Bahraini citizens sell their right to own and operate a business to foreign entrepreneurs. In a sense, then, the Bahraini partners host the activities of a private sector, and in doing so they establish a profitable relationship to those entrepreneurial activities without subjecting themselves to the logic and, more specifically, the risks associated with the private sphere.

The essential argument I make here is that the notion of hospitality distills a key aspect of the Bahraini experience and helps explain the topography of the contemporary arrangements on the island. The modernization that occurred during the second half of the twentieth century brought rapid and wholesale changes to Bahrain. Both the notion of hospitality and the arrangement of the kafala have deep historic roots in the culture of Bahrain (Beaugé 1985; Longva 1997), but this notion of hospitality reveals more than the architecture of relations between individual citizens and foreigners. It also provides us with an understanding of Bahraini national identity, the Bahrainis' concept of themselves as individual members of that society, and their collective concept of their relationship with the diverse communities and cultures that stream to the small island. Succinctly, then, I see hospitality as window to Bahraini national imaginary.

Space and the City

As the example of the merchant family's house suggests, a traditional spatial discourse is part of the relationship Bahrainis established with foreigners on the island. That spatial relationship, illustrated best by the wall between the merchant family's guest room (as a space for the foreign) and the home itself (as the space for the local), can be projected onto the city as a whole, for Manama and all the many booming cities of the Gulf can be conceived as complex amalgamations of enclaves and discrete cultural spaces. In that amalgamation one can perceive the ongoing tension produced by Bahraini society's attempt to accommodate what Paul Dresch (2006) has called "foreign matter."[1]

At the most macroscopic level, the singular urban agglomeration on the island is a growing mosaic of exceptional legal and economic zones. Like many of the other Gulf nations, Bahrain has declared and constructed numerous exceptional zones and spaces as part of its effort to attract foreign investment. Investment parks and freeholder zones are rapidly proliferating on the island. The Bahrain Logistic Zone (BLZ), for example, was recently described in a Bahraini newspaper as "the Middle East's first boutique multimodal logistics hub focusing on re-export and value-adding logistics activities. With zero tax, goods can be imported and re-exported without incurring customs duties and 100 per cent foreign ownership is permitted."[2] The key aspect to the BLZ, like many of these exceptional spaces, is the possibility of full ownership of property by foreign companies. This policy is, of course, in stark contrast to the regulations in place for the surrounding spaces on the island. In effect, these policies seek to consign and compartmentalize the industry and culture of the neoliberal global system to discrete and particular spaces on the island.

The spatial consignment of foreign matter is perhaps most apparent in the location of people in the city. As noted previously, the central portions of the city, once dense Bahraini neighborhoods, have been largely abandoned to the foreign workforce. Middle-class foreigners often find homes in compounds, or in the conglomeration of homes and apartments separated from public spaces by high walls and security guards (essentially what one would call a gated community in the United States). Even more striking, however, is the plan for increased numbers of "bachelor cities"—massive master-planned spaces meant to house and contain large numbers of foreign laborers. Proponents of these plans typically describe the pollutive threat of the largely male workforce, and the bachelor cities are seen as a mechanism for protecting Bahraini culture from this foreign presence.

As the domiciles of many foreigners are cordoned off from public space, so too the social and cultural activities of those populations are also subject to this spatial governance. The restaurants, bars, and beaches that serve the cosmopolitan elite—or better, are funded, designed, and marketed to that foreign elite—are themselves cloistered, exceptional zones in the larger tapestry of the city. Non-Islamic religious activity, while tolerated on the island, is similarly consigned to a few key locations. And the many social clubs that serve the various diasporas on the island are, almost without exception, located in walled villas out of view from the street. Unruly, potentially pollutive, and essentially foreign cultural practices are spatially segregated in the larger arena of the city.

What I chart here is not the successful and comprehensive division of that foreign matter from the local or indigenous space. In fact, the tension and friction generated by these exceptional spaces is a constant: "foreign matter" bleeds beyond its confines, public consternation and occasionally violence ensue, and often the state steps in to negotiate a solution.[3] Rather, my interests are in delineating the forces and ideas behind the compulsion to maintain these exceptional spaces and their distinction. State and citizenry attempt to confine the economic activity of global capitalism, the bodies of the foreign laboring class, and the performance of the many and diverse cultures present on the island to discrete and exceptional spaces. This confinement echoes the spatial relations of the merchant's house and illuminates the underlying logic of this system: "foreign matter," as Dresch

(2006) calls it, must be accommodated, for it is inextricably interwoven and, indeed, essential to the national vision widely promoted on the island. Simultaneously, however, the boundaries that distinguish that foreign matter from the local and indigenous must be policed and maintained.

THE WELFARE STATE

In late spring 2003 a group of road haulage and construction companies called for a formal protest at the Ministry of Labor and Social Affairs.[4] In 2001, the ministry had passed a ban on foreign drivers as part of a set of policies that furthered Bahrainization in both the public and private sectors. The haulage and construction companies protested the impact of this particular directive, and their complaints were specific: the new citizen-drivers were inexperienced and damaged the trucks; the citizen-employees drove at high speeds and endangered others on the road; the citizen-drivers frequently called in sick, to the point where one business owner contended that half of his workforce was often absent; and the citizen-drivers typically moved on to other jobs within a few months, particularly to positions in the government. As a result, insurance rates charged to the companies had risen, Saudi transportation companies (which employ inexpensive foreign drivers) were beginning to compete for business on the island, and the Bahraini companies were unable to meet their delivery obligations. Although the Ministry of Labor lifted its ban on expatriate drivers in March 2003 for situations in which "suitable Bahrainis" could not be found, permits for foreign workers were still not forthcoming. As the ministry argued, suitable Bahrainis were available.

The haulage and construction companies scheduled the rally at the Ministry of Labor and Social Affairs for the morning of May 4, 2003. At the last minute, however, it was postponed indefinitely in lieu of a second rally planned for the same morning. A sit-in of unemployed citizens, co-organized by the Wefaq National Islamic Society, the National Democratic Action Society, the National Grouping Democratic Society, and the Islamic Action Society asked all of Bahrain's "unemployed and those without benefits to join this peaceful sit-in along with their families, to bring attention to their plight." The road haulage and construction companies issued a statement indicating their solidarity with the unemployed workers. As the spokesman for the haulage and construction companies stated, "Attention should be given to the unemployed and the step to temporarily suspend our protest is part of our support for 100 percent Bahrainization and the demand that the Labor and Social Affairs Ministry take more active steps to ensure a real solution for the problem."

That morning some two hundred jobless citizens gathered in front of the prime minister's office. Many in the crowd waved flatbread above their heads, symbolizing their inability to feed their families. One protester spread his numerous diplomas about on the sidewalk, arguing that his state-approved education as a computing trainee left him unable to find a job. Another sat with his small child and, describing his situation, said he had been unemployed for a year. Ironically, his last job had been as a driver. Along with 60 other workers, he had signed a petition demanding BD150 ($398) per month (a raise of BD30/$80). The company had countered with an offer of BD10 per month. At that point he had quit in protest.

The irony, of course, rests in the coincidence of these two planned events: the first, a set of companies protesting their inability to find and keep skilled citizen-drivers; and the second, planned for exactly the same morning, the former truck driver, along with hundreds of others, protesting his inability to find a job. One imagines that if both rallies had occurred as planned, many of the unemployed men may have found jobs with the trucking companies, and unemployment on the island, estimated to be well above 15 percent over the past decade, would have dropped a decimal point or two. Yet the logic of this imagined scenario depends on a particular set of neoliberal ideas—on the idea of a free and open labor market, as well as the primacy of competitiveness, and on the notion of a government constructed to facilitate a thriving private sector (see Farmer 2003, 5–6). In Bahrain, however, the logic of these ideas has little traction, even among the most disenfranchised citizenry.

In all the states of the GCC, the bonanza of petroleum wealth has yielded governments in which the leadership distributes some portion of the wealth to its citizen-subjects. The content and quantity of this support have varied over time and region; analysis typically focuses on free or low-cost utilities, free or low-cost housing, free education, and free health care (Kapiszewski 2001; Nagy 2004).[5] In Bahrain, widely recognized as one of the poorest of the Gulf states, these benefits have diminished over time. At present the government heavily subsidizes fuel, electricity, water, and some food on the island. Education and health care remain free for citizens. The state also provides low-cost housing to citizens, although the long delays involved in the distribution of that housing are a source of strife for the disenfranchised class of the citizenry.

Perhaps the most significant component of the redistribution of petroleum wealth rests in public-sector employment.[6] Although consolidated data about the public sector are not available, an undersecretary at the Ministry of Labor and Social Affairs recently stated that 92 percent of the national (as opposed to foreign) workforce is employed in the public sector—"the highest percentage in the world" (Horton 2004).[7] In Bahrain the public sector continues to dominate many activities in the economy, for that public sector encompasses much of the petroleum industry, the aluminum industry, and telecommunications. Employment in those (and many other) sectors is distributed by the Sunni-controlled government. The "tacit guarantee" of public-sector employment for all male nationals remains the bedrock of the state's relationship to the citizenry (Louër 2008).

In Bahrain and the other Gulf states, the significant entitlements that accompany citizenship are often portrayed as the primary mechanism by which the state and its leadership build and maintain legitimacy (Khalaf 1992; Longva 2000). It is, however, important to distinguish between the benefits available equally to all citizens (such as free health care, government-subsidized utilities, and free education) and those that are distributed unequally to the citizenry (such as jobs in the public sector). In the latter case, the inequalities of this distribution forge economic classes out of sectarian divisions. It was the Shi'ite citizen-participants in this research who pointed out the realities of the situation to me. As they observed, many of the government ministries are predominantly, if not exclusively, Sunni—particularly the ministries of Interior and Defense, both of which are at the center of the state's repressive apparatus.[8] The unequal distribution of state-controlled wealth complicates theories of the welfare state, for it reveals the sectarian, tribal, and essentially personal logic of patronage at work in the apparatus of the Bahraini state.

The royal *majlis*, particularly popular with the formal ruler, provided a spatial venue for these personal appeals. One of my informants recalled his experience at the royal *majlis*:

> I went to the emir's court—this was during the current king's father's rule—and back then they gave away all kinds of money. The government here—no secret—it was corrupt. And at the court, people were there asking for money for all kinds of reasons. All kinds of people. I was there to ask for money to help me with my education in the states, because my dad couldn't help me for the entire stay. So I was there to ask for some money and do the paperwork. Next to me was

this fat-cat royal family member, and I knew his son, so I asked him if he was Ahmed's dad. He looked at me, but didn't say anything. He looked like he didn't want to be there... and then I overheard his conversation at the desk, and it ends up he was there to get money for his whole family's tour around Europe that summer. He was getting the royal court to pay for it! He was a Khalifa, and he didn't want to pay for it out of pocket, and he wanted himself and his wives to have a free ride around Europe that summer. And then there was this old Shi'i man, with a long white beard, and he had holes all over his thobe [the long-sleeved ankle length garment typically worn by Arab men in the Gulf], and he was walking around with his son who was on a crutch, and he was trying to get money for his son's medication. He was anguished, walking from office to office. I was just trying to get money for college. I could have gone to the University of Bahrain, but if the royal family can help me, great. But I felt guilty—I felt it was such a shady society, a shady government that doesn't really care. And I just wanted to get up and leave the country right there. I can remember both their faces. And yeah, the Shi'a are really on the bottom of the pile.

With the new leadership, these distributions more commonly take the form of royal decrees or orders (a new housing complex for the poor, loans from the state to be forgiven, and so forth). This patron-client model, overlaid upon the relationship between citizen and the state, suggests that the Bahraini state has accommodated rather than replaced the tribal tradition (Nakhleh 1976, 176), and that in both its embodied personal form and as a standard structural bureaucracy the state forges inequality and divisions among the citizenry.

The Bahraini state, then, faces a difficult and seemingly contradictory set of tasks. While it structures difference among its citizenry, it also seeks to build a cohesive and unified sense of nationalism. This latter goal is aided by the presence of the large expatriate workforce of noncitizens against which unified national identity can be asserted. More important, however, the legitimacy of the leadership and the cohesion of Bahraini nationalism both rest on the promise of public-sector employment.[9] The rallies and marches that were an almost weekly occurrence during my fieldwork in Bahrain never challenged the idea of the state as controlling of industry and jobs; instead, invectives emphasized the inequities of the distribution of those jobs, or the inability of the state to provide enough jobs for the burgeoning population of unemployed and underemployed. Through this process the more fundamental question of the state's legitimacy is masked.

Again one can perceive the pattern first portrayed in my description of the merchant family's house. Jobs in the public sector are distributed through a complex fusion of a meritocratic logic—that is, who is properly qualified for the job—and a familial, sectarian, and tribally focused logic. The many disenfranchised citizens I came to know do not consider an occupation in the private sector a viable option: they don't protest the lack of jobs in the private sector but rather the inability of the state to provide them with public-sector jobs. Macroscopically, the relationship between this burgeoning public sector and the private sector resembles the distinction that threads through this chapter, for the state itself is configured as an institution for managing—or hosting—the foreign matter of the private sector, while simultaneously insulating citizens from its logic.

BAHRAINIZATION AND THE FUNCTIONS OF THE STATE

The collection of policies and directives known as Bahrainization is a complex and ever-evolving mix of components, all of which are central functions of the state and important elements in the experiences of both citizens and noncitizens on the island. In its most distilled form, Bahrainization is best represented by those policies that require a certain percentage of citizen-employees in particular types of companies. Edicts are often issued by "sector," although the sectors often vary in scale: where one edict might be aimed at the private sector as a whole, another might address a specific "sector" such as the hospitality sector, the travel sector, and so forth. Edicts pertaining to sectors are complemented by an ever-changing system of monetary incentives that encourages companies to meet or exceed particular citizen-to-noncitizen ratios within a sectoral workforce. As one of the most active arenas of state activity, updates and alterations to these policies are a constant source of news in the local and international media. For example: "Firms are requested to increase employment of nationals by 5 percent a year until one-half of the labor force is Bahraini. New establishments employing 10 or more workers are required to have 20 percent Bahrainis in their workforce, with further annual increase of 5 percent until 50 percent is reached. Firms of less than 10 employees must employ at least one Bahraini other than the owner" (Fasano and Goyal 2004, 28).

Particular regulations like the one just quoted are singular components of Bahrainization. Although many of these policies are aimed at the private sector in general, the micro-sectoral approach is particularly active. The taxi "sector" was fully localized in the 1990s; today in Bahrain, unlike most of the other nations of the Gulf, taxi drivers must be Bahraini citizens. Similar results have been achieved in other sectors. In a shift that predated my arrival on the island by only a few years, employees at petrol stations were required to be citizens. One of my informants said that the guards at shopping malls are now all Bahraini. Another informant conveyed his impressions of Bahrainization with a story: "My wife and I had a broken washing machine in our flat, and we called for someone to pick it up and repair it. When the repairmen arrived to take the machine away, they were all Bahraini. This too you would not have seen four years ago." Shortly after my departure, the government announced plans to "Bahrainize" the travel sector, much to the consternation of the legion of foreign travel agents who serve the various transmigrant communities on the island.

Sectoral edicts and mandates governing the ratio of citizens to noncitizens in the workforce constitute the most visible facet of Bahrainization on the island. If, however, we define Bahrainization as those policies and practices that discourage foreign labor from finding and keeping employment on the island, we can include in that category many of those described in earlier chapters, including all those policies and practices that indirectly achieve this same end by preventing or dissuading foreign labor from successfully competing with citizens in the job market. Recently, for example, the government announced its intentions to impose a five-year limit on residence permits, thereby effectively limiting transmigrants' ability to derive profit from a sojourn on the island. Similarly, policies that prevent individuals from interacting directly with the government, visa regulations that make it difficult to move back and forth between India and Bahrain, a sponsorship system that locks transmigrants into a structured and often-problematic relationship with a citizen-sponsor—all of these policies and practices handicap foreign participation in the job market and thereby encourage businesses to hire Bahraini citizens. Put another way, then, the expanded definition I have delineated here suggests that Bahrainization includes all the edicts, policies, and practices that forge structural differences and impediments for noncitizens in the workplace. And this definition tells us something about the function of the Bahraini state: not only does the state directly deliver wealth to the citizenry (in the form of low-cost utilities, free education, and public-sector employment), but through

Bahrainization it also structures the private sector in ways that are beneficial to citizens and detrimental to noncitizens.

Building on this essential function, the state has emerged as the principal nexus for managing and indeed harnessing "foreign matter," of which the entrepreneurial activities of the private sector are only one part. In other words, the legitimacy of the state in the eyes of the citizenry is tied not only to its ability to distribute wealth, and not only to its ability to manage the private sector, but also to its role in governing foreign influences on the island. In 2003 and 2004, citizen groups and municipal councils moved against the display of "scantily clad mannequins," against the pork discreetly served in many Asian restaurants on the island, and against "indecent imagery" in advertisements.[10] Often the social clubs become targets. A Manama Municipal Council member recently declared the intent of the Segaiya neighborhood's Bahraini population to burn down a building occupied by Asian laborers. In public discussions the issues of sewage and overcrowding gave way to what Councilor Ibrahim Hassan Ismail called the "moral aspect" of the problem: "The tenants, who are usually Asian, roam around in their underwear with disregard to the social and Islamic laws of the country."[11]

These moral issues are also factors in the relations between the state and the Indian social clubs. The Young Goans Club, formed in 1952 and now one of the oldest of the Indian community's social clubs, recently boasted of over six hundred members. After complaints from neighbors (who were largely concerned with the proximity of an Iranian school and the possibility of schoolchildren witnessing men and women "mixing"), the club relocated from its central site near the souk, its home for fifty years, to the busy-with-nightlife neighborhood of Hoora. Again, however, the club faced complaints from neighbors. Those complaints eventually percolated from the municipality to the Ministry of Labor and Social Affairs, the arm of the government that issues permits and oversees the diasporic social clubs. At this juncture, objections to the club focused on its location near a mosque and the presence of a bar on the premises. The ministry revoked the club's license to serve alcohol, thereby removing the club's principal source of income. Unable to make rent, the club faced legal action from the landlord and the ministry ordered it closed. Numerous other social clubs have faced similar issues.

As this example suggests, the citizenry's expectations of the state surpass the simple disbursement of wealth. Although the orchestration of relations with the foreign population remains a central concern of the state, citizens' expectations have accumulated around this core function. Over time, expectations of the state have come to include the more vague responsibility of safeguarding citizens from the potentially detrimental impacts of global capitalism and, specifically, from the social and cultural worlds of the foreign populations at work on the island. It is here that the contradictions wrought by these circumstances are most apparent: while the vision of a modern, developed, and cosmopolitan nation is actively promoted by the state, much of the baggage that accompanies these activities is less welcome. As the state acts to staunch the spread of particular foreign practices, customs, and behavior, it simultaneously shores up its relationship with its citizenry by reinforcing its role as the principal tool by which citizens mitigate their relationship to the culturally heterogeneous flows that continue to arrive on their shores.

Resistance in the Workplace

Many of the small- and medium-sized businesses in Bahrain are actively managed—and often partially owned—by Indian expatriates. Ask one of these Indian entrepreneurs what happens when a young, unemployed Bahraini drops in to apply for a job and they will tell some version of the same story: the Bahraini will demand to work a single shift, ending his day at two in the afternoon or thereabouts. This stance is often the first point of negotiation. Should the Bahraini yield to the employer's demand to work the regular two shifts with a midday break, or should the employer find a way to accommodate the request for a single shift, the Bahraini will move on to a brief discussion of pay, set somewhere at or above the government-mandated minimum for nationals (nearly twice that of the going market rate for labor). If an agreement is reached, more problems are likely to ensue. The Bahraini will drift into work late. He will stand about, talking with the other Bahraini workers, and rarely help out unless under direct supervision. Even if extra pay is offered, he is unlikely to show up on weekends or holidays to assist with, say, an urgent shipment. In the end, he won't stay at the job long—perhaps a year, perhaps less.

Although there are exceptions to this scenario, the basic thread of the story was repeated in numerous interviews I conducted with Indian business owners on the island. When asked about the reasons for this problem, business owners pointed to a culturally inherent trait of laziness or lethargy among the indigenous citizenry. As one business owner described the frustrations he and other business owners face with the requirement to employ Bahrainis, he observed that because of the incentives and directives comprising the government's Bahrainization policy, Indian-owned businesses are desperate to hire Bahrainis. Indian business owners and managers, however, are "going to be so restricted with what they've got, in terms of the kind of people, how qualified they are. The effort that they [Bahrainis] would normally put in is half as much as an expatriate. When you think about wanting to put a Bahraini in, well, they're so lazy. They just don't do as much." Another merchant who employs dozens of Bahraini citizens stated, "I think the basic problem is with their attitude. They're just not used to working—especially hard work. They've taken it very easy all these years, and that has passed on to the younger generation. And that's one of the basic reasons that you can't rely on them." Or, as a Bahraini acquaintance related:

> The things people say about the Bahraini work ethic—well, I agree with it in general. They feel like they're entitled to more than what they're getting, and they feel like they shouldn't be doing as much as they are for it. A lot of people criticize Bahrainis for not performing as well as Indian workers.... You can see it firsthand. Just go into any place. Go to Jasmis [a fast-food restaurant that has begun to employ Bahrainis] or any retail place. See how the Bahraini man or lady behind the counter treats you. They'll be talking to a co-worker or on the mobile, or they'll yell to the person behind you.

Although the popular comprehension of Bahrainis in the workforce focuses on an inherent laziness and proclivity toward leisure, even my informants place these behaviors within the historical context of Bahrain. In remarking that "they've taken it easy all these years" or in arguing that Bahrainis "feel like they're entitled to more than what they're getting," the men quoted here echo scholarly analyses of the structural issues operating in the petroleum states' workforces. In his analysis of Saudi Arabia, Champion calls the pervasive reticence to work the "mudir syndrome," using the Arabic word for "director" as a gloss for the common attitude that "nothing less than a position of authority, status, and respect is honorable" (Champion 1999, 5; see also al-Moosa and McLachlan 1985). In general, these analyses focus on the great wealth derived from petroleum reserves and the small indigenous population, a combination of historical coincidences yielding a scenario in which states forge a social contract based on the "legitimacy of largesse," largely through public-sector employment (Champion 1999, 16). Others have traced the mudir syndrome to the traditional Bedouin contempt for agrarian work (see Champion 1999, n. 34; Detzner 2003, 48) or to the legacy of slavery in the region (Wilson and Graham 1994, 256). All of these explanations see the citizenry's contemporary contempt for the workplace, and for menial labor in particular, as a vestige of former social, political, and economic configurations on the island.

The details in this chapter challenge the premises of these analyses and suggest that there are rational and contemporary reasons for these attitudes. First, the large public sector, as the principal form of employment for Bahrainis in recent times, continues to exert its influence on the private sector. In the scenario described by the Indian business owners, for example, the ubiquitous wish to end the workday at 2:00 p.m. reflects the hours typical of the public sector, where the workweek is 34, rather than 48+ hours, and ends at 2:00 p.m. Similarly, the extremely high rates of turnover in private-sector jobs reflect the robust public sector, for many of the young men seeking jobs as menial laborers are merely biding their time awaiting an opening in the public sector. Menial and other entry-level positions in the private sector typically lack benefit packages, unlike their counterparts in the public sector. And whereas the private-sector workplaces function primarily in English, Malayalam, or other languages of the diasporas, government workplaces function in Arabic.

From the perspective of the expatriate business owners, the formidable role of the public sector in shaping the citizenry's expectations of the private sector causes many problems, and they have configured unique solutions to the issue. Several of the business owners I spoke with were so frustrated by the situation that they simply paid Bahraini citizens to stay at home, thereby meeting the requirements of sectoral Bahrainization regulations without encountering the problems of dealing with citizens in the workplace. As another Indian merchant said, "Maybe out of ten Bahrainis, you can find two or three that work. But first of all, why should you go to the trouble of weeding out two guys out of ten? You have to go through twenty guys before you get three that can work. It's too much hassle and trouble. It's just better to pay that guy and tell him not to come."

I encountered a related scenario at the Bahrain Training Institute (BTI). Describing the chain of events to me, a foreign faculty member remarked that the institute's custodial staff had been recently "Bahrainized." Student nationals were hired from the BTI trainee pool at a rate of BD120 to BD130 [$320 to $340] per month, roughly twice the salary of the transmigrant custodial staff. The citizen-custodians, my informant said, "would show up for work in street clothes and would spend most of their time standing around talking to each other and the other trainees. As a result, the toilets were filthy, there was no soap, and there was no toilet paper in any of the bathrooms. Even the director noticed." A solution was subsequently devised: the Bahraini day crew was followed by an Indian night crew. The night crew had to do all the work left undone by the day crew. In my interview with one of the members of this Indian work crew, he said that the new schedule means that they—the Indian crew—now have to do twice as much work.

Notions of citizenship and the appropriateness of particular forms of employment also reveal how conceptions of citizenship mingle with ethnic and racial hierarchies in Bahrain. In one of my interviews, I spoke with an Indian restaurant owner about the problems he faced with his Bahraini employees. He said that recently the young Bahraini men he employed informed him that they were unwilling to wait on Indian customers and that they would only wait on Bahrainis. Of course situations like these cause all sorts of difficulties in the contemporary workplace in Bahrain; simultaneously, they are symptomatic of the underlying racial construction of citizenship.

From the perspective of the Indian business owners and managers, the structure of the labor market in Bahrain creates significant impediments to the success of their entrepreneurial ventures. Businesses pay a variety of fees to import foreign laborers who they are then unable to fire (for the contracted period). Owners and managers must also take on a government-mandated workforce of citizen-employees, many of whom are unwilling to perform the basic duties associated with the position. The owners typically attribute the poor quality of Bahraini labor to a sense of entitlement of cultural, or even biological, origins. Yet from the perspective of Bahraini citizens, their decisions about employment and their behavior at work are extremely coherent. Forced by penury to enter the private-sector workforce, the unskilled citizen faces a losing proposition. He is often less educated than the foreign laborer with whom he competes. His English skills—vital to global commerce on the island— are less developed than those of the foreign workers. And his chances for advancement in the Indian-owned businesses of the island are negligible. That he applied for the job at all means he was unable to secure a position in the public sector, and the time spent moving boxes about the warehouse floor is time away from the activities that contribute and strengthen his social capital in the indigenous system—the reinforcement of social and familial connections, being seen with the right people in the right places, and all the other social activities that, under the Western model, would easily fit into conceptions of "leisure."

From the perspective of the unskilled citizen, the distended public sector represents the core component of an alternative occupational system. Because this sector continues to function, at least in part, by a genealogical logic, citizens are much better positioned to succeed in this alternative system. Whereas at the most basic level the public sector provides citizens with jobs, we can also conceive of the public sector as a form of resistance to a Western-derived meritocracy in whose calculus the unskilled Bahraini will most likely fail. The durability of this dual economy is certainly in doubt, for as the population grows and the petroleum revenues dwindle, maintenance of the large public sector will become an impossible burden for the state. The expectations of the citizenry, however, and the sense of entitlement constructed over decades in which this dual system flourished are slow to change. After all, there are few places in the world in which a son does not expect to have the same opportunities as his father.

WASTA AND THE LOGIC OF LEISURE

If the public sector operates by a distinct and alternative logic, how might one describe the basic parameters of that system? And what exactly do citizen and state seek to protect, or perhaps preserve, in maintaining this dual system? In this section, I examine the conduits through which citizens access the security and wealth controlled by the state. Along the way, the attributes associated with this citizenry, described by Indian businessmen as a penchant for leisure, an inherent laziness, and an overriding lack of commitment to work, become something more than individual acts of resistance to the neoliberal workplace: in combination with the institution of the public sector, these acts of resistance constitute a systemic effort to preserve an essentially ascribed system of relations configured around the relations of family, kinship, and tribe.

In describing the foundational role of family and kinship in Jeddah—the cosmopolitan hub of the Kingdom of Saudi Arabia and, in that sense, a setting similar to contemporary Bahrain—Soraya Altorki observes:

> The family constitutes a person's reservoir of economic security, political influence, social support, and psychological succor.... Kinship

and friendship links combine the functions that in Western countries are divided between distinct reference groups outside a person's family, such as neighbors, colleagues, business partners, professional associations, and clubs. In Saudi Arabia these links entail an elaborate system of reciprocal right-duty relationships. Many of these relationships are activated in casual contexts and informal visiting and in sporadic exchanges of favors. They are ritually expressed and reinforced on special occasions such as life-crisis events like birth, naming ceremonies, marriage, divorce, sickness, and death, where the participation of network members is mandatory. A person's failure to participate in these occasions without an acceptable excuse implies a rejection of his/her role in that network. (1985, 81)

Altorki describes the fundamental importance of casual and informal activity—glossed as leisure in the Western nomenclature—to the social relations of the contemporary Saudi citizenry. Using this model as a springboard for further analysis, I turn to the concept of *wasta* as a window into the mechanics of this system.

Wasta is a versatile notion with no immediate parallel in the English language. Generally, the term refers to mediation or intercession by a third party, although it can also refer to the influence possessed by an individual (Cunningham and Sarayrah 1993, 1994; Detzner 2003). Perhaps the closest analogy in English would be social capital, described by Bourdieu as "the sum of the resources, actual or virtual, that accrue to an individual or a group by virtue of possessing a durable network of more or less institutionalized relationships of mutual acquaintance or recognition" (Bourdieu and Wacquant 1992, 119). The versatility of the notion was well described by one of my informants:

> *Wasta* strictly translates into "intermediary" or "intermediary means." *Wasta* is a way to get there. When I say that I have a *wasta* in the Traffic Directorate, it means that I've got somebody there who can help me cut through the red tape. They can take care of my problem. But that term really evolved new meanings—now you can say, "oh, his dad is a real *wasta*," meaning he can get stuff done for you. So it refers to a person. But you can also think of it as a process: "*wasta* does its worth." You're not talking about a specific person anymore. Or "with *wasta* you can do anything." "You better get *wasta*" is a very common clause in speech. If you have *wasta*, you can get it done in

a day. It means you can get it done if you have a way—an intermediary way, a way to get in, or someone inside the system. People even talk about Vitamin W—that's *wasta*.

Wasta remains an essential feature of the social landscape on the island and has already been defined as the logic by which public-sector employment is obtained (Khuri 1980, 123; Louër 2008, 38). If the relationship between citizen and state is at least partly characterized by an enduring familial and tribal fabric, it is wasta that helps us understand how family and tribe function in a bureaucratic context—how individuals connect with the resources controlled by the government. My informants described many scenarios that might potentially require wasta: securing placement at the University of Bahrain, obtaining the appropriate papers for importing labor, or securing public housing or government loans, for example. Similarly, for both men and women seeking jobs in the public sector, familial, sectarian, and tribal connections—all essential components of wasta—are key factors (Pirzada and Puri 1998). The power of these relations is further magnified, one of my informants added, by the size of the city-state, where it is commonly believed that everyone knows everyone, at least in terms of their family and sect.

The connections between wasta and the public sector are particularly intricate. Unlike the private sector—which is composed of myriad businesses, including both global concerns with formalized hiring policies and local concerns managed or run by expatriates—the public sector is a direct extension of the state, an extension of the ruling family, and a manifestation of its hegemony over the island. Although private businesses are concerned with profit, and thereby at least nominally interested in finding the most capable and least expensive employee for a particular position, the public sector provides ample room for ulterior motives to be exercised in the hiring process. Because of the desirability of these public-sector jobs—both for the comforts of working in Arabic and the short working hours, but also because of the remuneration, and particularly the pensions, low-cost housing loans, and other programs—wasta functions as the mechanism for what Bourdieu called the transformation of capital (Bourdieu 1986; see also Kilankiewicz 1996). The public sector provides citizens with a venue in which their social capital can be transformed into economic capital.

Although an individual's wasta is constructed on the foundation of his or her location in the social fabric of tribe and family on the island, wasta is not static. Yet building and maintaining wasta are activities whose logic is difficult to pinpoint. When asked directly about the mechanisms for forging and maintaining social capital, the citizens I spoke with often appealed to generalities about knowing the right people, being seen in the right places, and more specifically, the combination of the two. As one young Bahraini described: "There's no denying that Bahrainis believe knowing the right people is essential to getting ahead in life. They believe that if they hang out with the right people, one day they're going to get the right job—that the friend is going to do them a favor. Whether it works out or not, they're going to hang on to that person... because those connections are so important. If you want to get your business registered, and you don't just want to sit on the list, you have to know someone. You have to have wasta."

Wasta is accumulated and deployed through networks that rely heavily on familial, tribal, and sectarian affiliation. The genealogical foundation of this system means that foreigners are marginalized in its calculus and that one citizen may have more wasta than the next. As Detzner described in her analysis of Saudi Arabia, "foreigners lack these important connections... and are disconnected from the myriad family, tribal and regional allegiances in the country" (2003, 50). Wasta, then, is a form of social capital that largely flows through the exclusive and endogamous social relations of the citizenry.

In systemic terms, wasta contradicts the logic of the global financescape and, in a larger sense, the neoliberalism codified in the rhetoric of Bahrain's national vision. Although many of the international agencies and states with which Bahrain deals clamor for open markets, good governance, transparency, and equality under the law, wasta provides an alternative set of avenues that inherently favor citizens over noncitizens and Sunni (who maintain stronger tribal allegiances) over Shi'a. In his analysis of the legal framework of Bahrain in the early 1980s, Franklin made a parallel point about the concept of justice: "A universal code of justice was—and is—antithetical to the categorical principle on which his authority and the plural order rested" (1985, 72).[12] That same plural order relies on categorical principles to organize the workforce. Where the neoliberal model lauds open, free, and meritocratic labor markets, wasta comprises the basis of a system that favors those with localized tribal and familial connections over those without. In this system, citizens have more power than noncitizens, and Sunnis have more power than Shi'ites.

As a social force with both deep historical roots and a pervasive presence in the contemporary milieu, wasta represents a key facet of the citizenry's resistance to the fundamental terms of the global financescape. Faced with a global and dominant neoliberal ideology that lauds open markets, a meritocratic labor force, and transparency in both public and private sectors, citizenry and state have configured an alternative system in the public sector. The individual acts of resistance charted in the previous sections are emblematic of a systemic rejection of the terms of neoliberal arena: for the middle and lower classes of the citizenry, the chances for success in the English-speaking, foreign-dominated workforce are negligible. Rather than directly compete for positions with well-trained and linguistically versatile foreign workers, citizen-laborers focus their energies on investing and maintaining the social capital, or wasta, that potentially leads to jobs in the public sector. What looks like laziness, leisure, and lassitude becomes something quite rational: an investment in a cohesive but separate system that coexists with Bahrain's private sector.

Tradition, Modernity and Social Change

Two decades ago, Soraya Altorki and Donald Cole (1989) published their fascinating ethnography of the Saudi Arabian city of 'Unayzah. In their concluding analysis, they argue concertedly against the idea that the Arabian urbanites they came to know were somehow bound to a traditionalism that was incompatible with modernity. In making their case, Altorki and Cole purvey an economic determinism against the Orientalist preoccupation with Middle Eastern traditionalism: the Saudi work ethic, they argue, is merely a reflection of the economic relations of contemporary 'Unayzah. The work ethic (or lack thereof) will "change according to economic imperatives" (Altorki and Cole 1989, 242).

The concept of change in this reasoning masks more than it reveals and simplifies a process that is complex. In Bahrain, the "economic imperatives" include a citizenry with a significant lower middle class now pushed to the margins of the welfare state. Their attitudes—that is, their work ethic, their expectations for employment, their idea of appropriate and inappropriate forms of labor—do not change overnight. Indeed, the fifteen years of episodic violence between members of the Shi'ite underclass and the Sunni-controlled state can be read as resistance to the "economic imperatives" of this period.

As Altorki and Cole suggested for 'Unayzah, the story of Bahrain is not a story of a people trapped in the gravity of their own traditions. It is, however, a story about how tradition—imagined, partial, revised, and contested—becomes a tool by which the citizenry and state seek to insulate themselves from the logic of the global and neoliberal system in which they are now enmeshed. To put this narrative into context, it's not that citizens in Bahrain don't want a booming and modern nation, or that they feel no allegiance to the hypermodern and cosmopolitan national vision promoted by the dominant elite; rather, it is that they don't want to submit themselves to the logic of a system in whose competitive, market-based calculus the great majority of the citizenry are poorly positioned to succeed. The divide between the public and private sectors, the social and ethnic distinctions that characterize the contemporary Gulf, and the mechanics of the kafala system all become part of the orchestration of this bifurcated system, and hence part of the process by which a distinctive and alternative socio-economic system is maintained. That alternative system provides citizens with a refuge from the grinding logic of the neoliberal system.

Hospitality, as a practice with a long tradition in Arab cultures, helps explain how the relationship between these two systems is locally conceptualized. In Bahrain, those ideas and practices were developed over centuries of coexistence with the foreign peoples who passed through the port of Manama. Beginning with a description of a merchant family's aging house, I have connected the layout of that house to the social, economic, and indeed, cultural structure of the contemporary island. Citizens host the foreigners integral to their collective national vision of modernity. They use the role of host to conceptualize and structure their relationship to the cultural aspects of that foreign matter. This role provides a culturally familiar mechanism for embracing the presence of global capitalism in the shared national vision of modernity without accepting the underlying values of that essentially neoliberal system.

8 CONCLUSION

Bahrain at the Vanguard of Change in the Gulf

A year before my first trip to the Arabian Peninsula I was part of a team of researchers and ethnographers exploring the impact of the offshore oil industry on the families and communities of southern Louisiana. In this large and multifaceted project, one of my principal assignments was to immerse myself in the world of the men at the bottom of the oil sector's occupational hierarchy—the roughnecks and roustabouts who work on the rigs, platforms, and yards scattered across southern Louisiana and its coastal waters. I made my home at a down-at-the-heels motel next to the highway in New Iberia, Louisiana, where these roughnecks and roustabouts would stay, drink, and spend much (and oftentimes all) of the money they had just earned from two weeks of work offshore. During my first few days at the motel I was surprised by the smell of Indian food wafting through the courtyard, and after some investigation I found and befriended a group of eight Indian men living in two of the rooms. Trained as welders in a renowned shipbuilding city in India, these men had paid exorbitant fees for the right to come weld in the shipyards of southern Louisiana for two years under the United States' H-visa system. Two months after their arrival, they were let go by the fabrication company that had brought them to the United States. They and their families continued to carry the astronomical debts held by the labor brokers back in India. Holed up in the motel and desperate for work, they had become "illegal" immigrants.

I bring up this episode to reinforce the point that although the cultures and societies described in this book are both distant and different from the American one, the problems, dilemmas, and exploitation generated by the transnational movement of labor are not consigned to Bahrain or the other Gulf states. Even the kafala has analogies in the American context: the men I met in southern Louisiana were, like the men I encountered in Bahrain, legally tied to a single employer and, simultaneously, burdened with a transnational debt. When framing the ethnographic study presented in this book, then, the reader should keep in mind that these problems, and the structural violence evident in these foreign workers' experiences in Bahrain, are not a unique product of Arabian culture or society. Rather, attempts to systematically control and govern the transnational movement of labor become particularized to the contexts in which those flows take place. The arrangement of inequality and the justification of exploitation are articulated through the particular experiences of the peoples and societies that deploy that governance. The Arab ideal of hospitality, the gender norms for the region, the historic kafala system, the relations of the tribe — these become the tools by which the Bahrainis grapple with and govern the transnational flow of labor to their island.

Structural violence is a versatile concept, and I recognize that its application here is a departure from the norm. A more standard use of the concept would focus on the considerable constellation of forces that push Indian men and women out of their homes to seek work in the Gulf states. Although the forces pushing the men out of India certainly merit more attention, I have kept my focus squarely on the arrangements in which these transmigrants become enmeshed once they arrive in the Gulf. In more theoretical terms, I use Eric Wolf's notion of structural power, and particularly his focus on the power exercised in the orchestration of settings and relations, to connect the seemingly disparate forces that shape foreign workers' experiences in Bahrain. I envision this path as one that reveals the mechanics of structural violence, and one that demonstrates how these structural arrangements produce the interpersonal violence that peppered the lives of the men and women I came to know.

What, then, ought to be done about this situation? One of the overarching purposes of this book is to better inform those directly concerned with the policies, laws, and practices that manage and govern the flow of transnational labor to the Gulf. For many anthropologists, and particularly for those with no penchant for brands of the discipline that operate under the banners of public anthropology and applied anthropology, further recommendations may seem audacious and misguided. I, however, do not count myself among them.

First, the kafala system ought to be dismantled or significantly altered so that workers can legally and swiftly leave the employ of abusive or otherwise problematic sponsors. This move is perhaps already under way in Bahrain. In early 2009, the minister of labor and social affairs announced plans to "scrap the sponsorship system" in August of that year. Details remain scarce, but reports suggest that the plan is much more tailored than a wholesale plan to scrap the sponsorship system: in essence, the state will now control the right of workers to switch employers. Before 2009, sponsors themselves had to accede to any change in sponsorship. Under the new plan, the Labor Market Regulatory Authority will hear petitions or otherwise govern the movement of workers between jobs. These proposed changes have been spearheaded by the progressive and occasionally combative minister of labor and social affairs, Dr. Majeed Mohsen al-Alawi. He has faced increasing resistance to the proposed changes from citizen groups, Parliament, and most directly, from the Bahrain Chamber of Commerce and Industry.

This resistance merits discussion, for in the debates surrounding the proposed and upcoming changes, the forces and parties who directly benefit from the exploitation of transnational labor have become apparent. In essence, for the first time the positions of the proponents of the status quo have been articulated in Bahrain's public sphere. Although these debates are both ongoing and evolving, several parameters can be identified from the initial arguments. Perhaps the most comprehensive contention of the opposition suggests that the proposed changes will significantly undermine the competitiveness of the Bahrain labor market. The changes will make Bahrain increasingly unattractive for business and therefore undermine the kingdom's position in the global political economy. In this argument, the ongoing exploitation of the foreign labor force is a necessity rendered by the neoliberal environment and Bahrain's ascendant position in that system. Within this larger contention, many more specific arguments about the potential impacts of the changes have been articulated. Business leaders, for example, have expressed grave concerns about the potential theft of confidential information as workers move between companies. As one group of fishermen argued, the proposed changes "will have a huge impact on fishermen's livelihoods. Fishermen waste a lot of time, money and effort to teach their laborers the craft. Now, they can just leave with all that knowledge and cause the fisherman big losses."[1] Business leaders also contend that the freedom to move between jobs will allow workers to "blackmail" employers—to, in essence, "impose their terms and conditions" on employers and, problematically, to "leave companies at their own will and according to their wishes."[2] Opponents have also argued that the impact of the proposed changes will largely be borne by small businesses and entrepreneurs, and will most certainly result in higher unemployment among the citizenry.[3]

These contentions represent a significant rhetorical shift in the defense of the sponsorship system. As Longva (1997) observed over a decade ago, the sponsorship system was conceived and defended as a cultural practice that bonded foreign outsiders to members of the indigenous social matrix. Citizens, in sponsoring foreigners, took on the obligation for their well-being and responsibility for their behavior and actions in local society. The recent debates over the proposed changes to the sponsorship system in Bahrain, however, abandon all pretense of traditional and cultural justifications for the sponsorship system. Instead, we are left with a purely economic argument: disrupting the status quo will empower workers, thereby mitigating employers' ability to exploit this foreign workforce and handicapping Bahrain's position in the regional and global economy. In making their case, opponents of the proposed changes also clearly articulate a perspective on basic labor rights substantially removed from that of the dominant Western discourse. The idea that laborers should have the freedom and right to depart a particular employer is portrayed as unique, as an undeserved "extra privilege," and as a disruptive and unbalanced change that heavily favors foreign workers.[4]

Opponents have forwarded a variety of options, alternative plans, and conditions intended to preserve the position of sponsors amid the proposed changes. The lower house of the Bahraini Parliament, for example, is seeking a clause requiring workers to complete one year of service before being allowed to switch employers.[5] Others have suggested that the sponsorship system should be managed by the private sector.[6] Much of the argument, however, centers on the criteria by which the Labor Market Regulatory Authority will adjudicate requests from foreign workers to switch jobs. Considering how the courts handled Vijay's predicament (described in chap. 4), or how recent quarrels between housemaids and their sponsors have been settled (Strobl 2009), it seems clear that establishing a legal process for laborers to petition the state for permission to switch employers is, at best, one small step toward abolishing the sponsorship system and the structural violence it produces.

Improving the conditions for foreign labor in Bahrain will also require that existing laws be comprehensively enforced. For example, it is against Bahraini law for sponsors to hold the passports of the laborers they sponsor, yet nearly every laborer I spoke with was without his passport. Similarly, nonpayment of wages was an extraordinarily widespread practice in the labor camps I visited in Bahrain. The enforcement of existing laws should encompass significant fines and other punishments, all of which should be deployed in a transparent and public manner. Finally, these changes and protections need to extend to those foreign workers in the household; a universal set of labor rights ought to cover all foreigners employed in Bahrain. Embarking on these recommendations would reinforce Bahrain's position at the vanguard of progressive change in the Gulf.

These recommendations closely resemble those now being promoted by the institutions and trans-state organizations concerned with labor and human rights in the GCC, but their implications ought to be fully considered. In the penultimate chapter of this book I argued that the kafala, the social segregation characteristic of all the Gulf states, and the arrangements that marry the private sector to the foreign labor force are all facets of the citizenry's and the state's strategic response to the global and neoliberal system to which their national aspirations are tied. The recommended changes to the labor market, combined with those already under way, would mark a significant step in the erosion of the forces and arrangements that insulate the citizenry from the logic of the system from which they seek to profit. The same forces and arrangements indicted by a rights-based perspective preserve an alternative and local social system with a distinct logic of its own. Altering the system by which "foreign matter" is governed and controlled will reverberate deeply in Bahraini society.

When I discuss my research, colleagues often point out to me that Bahrain is an exceptional place in the context of the GCC states. The implication behind these contentions is that the structural violence I describe is unique to Bahrain and attenuated or altogether absent in the neighboring countries. More research, and particularly more ethnographically grounded research, is needed before this contention can be properly addressed. And Bahrain is different in ways that play a role in the lives of the foreign laborers who toil on the island. Unlike the other states of the GCC, Bahrain has a Sunni leadership who rule over a Shi'ite majority composed of both the indigenous inhabitants of the island as well as the more recent Persian arrivals. The citizenry is ethnically heterogeneous, and definitely more fractious and divided than its neighbors. Moreover, Bahrain lacks the spectacular wealth of many of the other GCC states. Bahrain's public sector can no longer accommodate the majority of the working citizenry, and members of the middle class are increasingly pushed into direct competition with the foreigners in their midst. These shifting political and economic realities are one of the engines driving the structural violence described in this book, and together they distinguish Bahrain from its neighbors in the Gulf.

At the same time, however, Bahrain has much in common with its neighbors. The kafala remains ubiquitous in the Gulf states, for example, and it is the coincidence of this arrangement with the motive of profit that forges a space conducive to the violence I've described. And like the neighboring states, Bahrain and its citizenry continue to struggle with the ramifications of rapid development, the cultural heterogeneity of the many peoples at work on the island, and the preservation of a social and cultural identity amid an era of extraordinarily rapid change. Bahrain's exceptional qualities, and particularly the presence of a middle class increasingly marginalized from ethnocratic logic of the public sector, are better understood as a glimpse into the future of the wealthier neighboring states. While the populations of the Gulf states continue to grow at astonishing rates, petroleum remains a finite resource. The frictions of Bahrain are not unique or peripheral to the experiences of the other GCC states. Rather, contemporary Bahrain provides us with a portrait of the frictions that occur when the oil runs out.

NOTES

1. Introduction

1. Nor are accurate data available concerning the size or nationalities of these transmigrant populations, or even of the national populations (Kapiszewski 2001, 63). Scholars working in the Gulf point to several overlapping factors to explain this dearth of contextual data. Many of the sending countries lack the bureaucratic infrastructure to accurately gather data about the number of people departing for the Gulf (Nair 1999; Demery 1986, 19). Similarly, the coexistence of formal and informal migration conduits between South Asia and the Gulf would confound any simple calculations based on migration through formal channels even if such capacities did exist. Conversely, because undocumented migration is rare in most of the Gulf states, one suspects that at least basic demographic data describing the national components of the foreign worker populations must exist. All the foreign workers I encountered in Bahrain, for example, had at one point been "properly" registered with the Population Registration Ministry and received an identity card listing their nationality and other data. Bahrain and most of its neighbors, however, release only aggregate demographic data concerning the foreign populations: we know, for example, that the Bahraini government counted 205,626 Asians in the 2001 census, but we have no idea how many of those Asians are from Bangladesh, India, and so forth. It is often suggested that this obfuscation reflects the tenuous political and cultural climate of countries where these foreign populations often outnumber the citizenry (Kapiszewski 2001, 27; Leonard 2002, 215; 2003, 133). That only a handful of social scientists have had the opportunity or desire to explore these truly massive migratory conduits is compounded by the fact that the foreign populations in the Gulf states are uncharted territory in the larger ethnography of transnational migration, and the violence levied against these men and women is a reason for—and a product of—the silence concerning the lives of foreigners in the Gulf.

2. Anh Longva's pathbreaking book on relations between citizens and foreign workers in Kuwait grazes this topic, but in calling the relationship a "structure of dominance," she avoids directly engaging the violence produced in the lives of the men and women working in the Gulf states (Longva 1997). In effect, she focuses more on the inequalities in the distribution of power and less on the lived experiences of those dominated by that power.

3. This connection is perhaps most clearly distilled in Scheper-Hughes and Bourgois's definition of structural violence as "the violence of poverty, hunger, social exclusion and humiliation" (2004, 1).

4. Sadly, he was released from his position three days before my arrival on the island.

5. I build here upon my many conversations with Sharon Nagy.

6. The terms *financescapes* and *mediascapes* were coined by Arjun Appadurai (1996) and appear throughout this volume.

7. The Gulf Cooperation Council was formed in early 1981. Its membership comprises the heads of the six Gulf states: Kuwait, Saudi Arabia, Bahrain, Qatar, United Arab Emirates, and Oman (Zahlan 1989, 135).

8. The Bahrain government published the 2000 census in Arabic, English, and Malayalam. The newspapers expressed much consternation about the last of these: Indians claimed that Hindi is the national language of India, and hence Malayalam was a poor choice on the government's part. The official Bahraini response stated that the purpose behind the choice was simply to reach as many individuals as possible, and with the large Keralite community on the island, Malayalam was the logical choice.

9. Although most scholars report that citizenship in the Gulf states is not available to transmigrants (Leonard 2003, 139; Falzon 2003, 675), Bahrain and several other states allow foreigners to become citizens. Naturalization of Arab foreigners—and, particularly, Sunni Arab foreigners—is reportedly substantial (Wright 2008). For South Asians, however, naturalization is difficult and rare, particularly because a demonstration of facility with Arabic remains a key juncture in the application process.

10. These words appear on the Toastmasters Web page.

11. The name Santosh is a pseudonym. I use it because Santosh still lives and works in Bahrain, and I wish to protect him from repercussions for assisting me with this project.

12. "Bahrain Labour Minister Seeks Support for Scrapping Sponsorship System," *Gulf News* (Dubai, UAE), May 28, 2009; "Date with History," *Gulf Daily News* (Manama, Bahrain), May 14, 2009; "Bahrain to Halt Labour Sponsorship," *Al-Jazeera* (Doha, Qatar), May 7, 2009.

2. Pearls, Oil, and the British Empire

1. Vertovec notes that "transnationalism (as long-distance networks) certainly preceded 'the nation.' Yet today these systems of ties, interactions, exchanges and

mobility function intensively and in real time while being spread throughout the world. New technologies, especially involving telecommunications, serve to connect such networks with increasing speed and efficiency" (1999, 447).

2. Although this statement is generally true, it needs some qualification. In Bahrain, Oman, and several other GCC states, wealthy and established South Asian transmigrants, albeit in limited numbers, have received GCC passports. Naturalization has occurred more widely, if sporadically, among Arab and Middle Eastern transmigrant populations in the GCC states. In Bahrain, the racial policies of naturalization are explicit rather than implicit: the law mandates a period of fifteen years for Arab applicants, and twenty-five years for non-Arab applicants.

3. In 2006, Bahrain's crown prince and the Bahrain Defense Force's commander in chief declared that a new labor law, under development at the time, would eventually lead to the scrapping of the sponsorship system. The changes being deployed at the time of this writing suggest something less than the wholesale scrapping of the sponsorship system, an issue explored in more depth in the concluding chapter of this book.

4. As Longva notes, "Lack of legal protection, the predominance of women [in the domestic sector], and low educational background combined to make domestic workers the most vulnerable to exploitation and abuse, a situation of which the labor-sending countries were acutely aware" (1997, 70).

5. In Bahrain, that threshold was BD250 ($663) a month at the time this research was conducted. Foreign workers seeking visas for family members must also secure permission from their sponsor.

6. Although there is some uniformity to the transmigrant experience in all the Gulf states, the unique social, cultural, historical, economic, and demographic facets of the individual states connote that neither Bahrain nor any of the other GCC states can serve as an unadulterated proxy for its neighbors. This suggests that the experience of foreigners in each of these respective states, while similar, is not the same. For example, the petroleum wealth in Qatar, Kuwait, and portions of the United Arab Emirates far outpaces that of Bahrain and Oman—a fact that, in these wealthier states, results in more housemaids per house, different attitudes concerning the work appropriate for the citizenry, and an expanded welfare system. The ethnic patterns of both the citizenry and foreign communities also differ: Oman through both its proximity to the African continent and through its historical relations with Zanzibar, Saudi and its long accommodation of Yemeni transmigration, and Bahrain and its long-standing connections to Iran, are all factors in shaping the variable ethnic relations in these respective states. So in spite of the commonalities among the Gulf states—all have a citizenry composed predominately of Arabs, all discourage assimilation, all provide roughly the same sort of work for transmigrants, all are engaged in the process of trying to compel or persuade their burgeoning young population to take the sort of jobs now held by foreign workers—there is nonetheless significant variation among them. The experiences of the Indian transmigrants in Bahrain can only serve as a rough proxy for the experience of foreign workers in the Gulf as a whole.

7. I nonetheless continue to refer to this collection of islands in the singular, not only because this is common usage in Bahrain itself but also because through the continual infill in the bays near Manama, the many islands are seemingly merging into one.

8. The Persians controlled the island until 1718, when the Arabs of what is today Oman gained control of the island (Lorimer 1908b, 836–37). By the middle of the eighteenth century, the Hawala Arabs (Arabs from Persia) lived on the island in great numbers and are still represented today (837). In 1753, the Persians again moved on the island. They were driven from the islands by the 'Utub in 1783 (839). The Portuguese were ousted from Bahrain in 1602 (Khuri 1980, 17).

9. Writing in 1908, J. G. Lorimer of the Indian Civil Service described the following groups: the Baharinah, although not really a tribe, consisted of those Shi'a who, as families, predated the arrival of the Sunni al-Khalifas. The Sunni Hawala, mostly townsmen, were (and are) Arabs from Persia who claim an Arabian tribal genealogy. In addition to the 'Utub, two other Sunni tribes—the Dawasir and the Sadah—made their home on the island. As a mercantile hub for the region, the island also accommodated Persians, Basra Arabs, Hindus, and Jews.

10. Wallerstein originally posited the world-system framework in the social sciences, but it was Wolf's revision of this framework that most captured the attention of anthropologists, particularly for his contention that the "history" of the peoples who came into contact with colonial powers, and more importantly, the history of the cultural and mercantile interconnections between those peoples, predated European contact (Wallerstein 1974; Wolf 1982). The history of Bahrain provides rich support for this contention.

11. Buckingham (1971) notes that the pearls are called the *roomaan el-bahr*, or pomegranates of the sea.

12. Jenner cites evidence that the divers occasionally worked in depths as deep as twelve fathoms (seventy-two feet), although dives in depths of six fathoms (thirty-six feet) was more common (1984, 27).

13. Although he includes no page reference, Jenner (1984) refers to Sir Charles Belgrave's work throughout this section.

14. "Natural pearls attained unprecedented value around 1910, when elite upper classes vied with each other to buy them. The fact that a two-strand natural pearl necklace (128 pearls) was considered fair exchange for a six-story Renaissance mansion on Fifth Avenue in New York City clearly describes the zenith of the pearling trade. As both were valued at $1 million, it was a trade Mrs. Morton Plant confidently made with Jacques Cartier in 1917" (Misiorowski 1998).

15. These rulers later signed a more comprehensive treaty, known as the Maritime Truce or Trucial System, in which they gave up their right to wage maritime warfare against each other in return for British protection against the same. Bahrain was admitted to the Maritime Truce in 1861 (Onley 2004, 31–32, 53–54, 72–75).

16. By 1915, the indigenous leaders officially ceded jurisdiction over foreigners to the British Political Agent (Zahlan 1989, 49).

17. In describing the "indigenous" system of leadership, Khuri makes detailed note of the tribal councils (*majalis*) and the religious courts. These are not as hierarchical as Western systems of management. In the *majalis* meetings, "tribal chiefs took counsel with close relatives, consultants, intimates, supporters, or guests. They discussed a wide variety of subjects: tribal history, religion, law and justice, treaties with foreign powers, marriages that might have political significance, boat construction, pearl production, palm cultivation, date crops, trade, markets, prices, wages, weather, and any news items of the day" (Khuri 1980, 37).

18. The wealth generated by petroleum was not under the direct control of the Khalifa family. The concession for oil production on the island was originally held by Gulf Oil, the American oil company that had recently ridden the Spindletop boom in East Texas to its pinnacle and then beyond to the crash on the other side. When Gulf Oil became part of the American group in the Turkish Oil Company, however, it also became a signatory to the Red Line Agreement—a pact that precluded any of the oil companies active in the region, as signatories, from operating independently in areas specified on the agreement's map, of which Bahrain was one. Hence the Bahrain concession was passed to a Canadian subsidiary of SOCAL, or Standard Oil of California, which was not bound by the restriction, and it was SOCAL that established the Bahrain Petroleum Company, more frequently referred to in Bahrain as BAPCO (Yergin 1991, 282; Franklin 1985, 85). The fact that an American company came to control any portion of oil production in Bahrain was the result of the particularities of this historical juncture. The British were wary of the American presence in the region, and they had established agreements with local sheikhs that "oil development should be entrusted only to British concerns, and that the British government would be in charge of their foreign relations" (Yergin 1991, 283). In 1929, the British reconsidered their position and, in anticipation of the benefit of American capital to the development of oil in the region, capitulated (283).

19. As David Holden describes in condescending fashion, "the Indian rupee is still Bahrain's official currency, and in the influx of Indians and Pakistanis that came in the British wake nearly every shop seems to have been opened by a Jamshid or a Jahshanmall, and every clerk seems to be a Singh, or maybe Mukerjee" (1966, 176). The rupee was replaced by the Bahraini dinar (BD) in 1965.

20. Oman contains a significant Shi'ite population, although they are not a majority. The former Sunni powerholders in Iraq—a country that is neither a member of the Gulf Cooperation Council nor a monarchy—until recently wielded power over a Shi'ite majority. Although the Shi'ites are a minority in Saudi Arabia, they predominate in the eastern provinces of Saudi Arabia.

21. May Seikaly sees Bahrain as the most problematic of the Gulf states. She states that it is the poorest and least endowed, it is characterized by a general malaise resulting from high unemployment, and its social and political unrest have resulted in "violent, sustained uprising" on the island (Seikaly 2001, 180).

22. Bahrain serves as an offshore banking center to Saudi wealth, a position confirmed by important concessions from the Saudi Arabian Monetary Agency. Saudi has also helped Bahrain by maintaining high production on a shared oilfield, and by being instrumental in attracting GCC-sponsored projects to Bahrain (Zahlan 1989, 63).

3. Foreign Labor in Peril

1. "Youths 'Terrorize Labour Camp Men,'" *Gulf Daily News* (Manama, Bahrain), August 29, 2004.

2. In Bahrain, these amnesty periods occur infrequently. The last two occurred in 2002 and 2007. These amnesty periods are rarely accompanied by a state-organized roundup of undocumented workers. Although the state maintains the capacity to conduct such roundups, it has been reticent to deploy this capacity in recent years.

3. This scene is roughly reminiscent of the protest in rural India described by Akhil Gupta—an encirclement of those in power that is, in Gupta's words, "a common form of civil disobedience in India" (2006, 220).

4. Although this phrase accurately reflects the sentiments of the many older foreign workers I interviewed, Seccombe and Lawless state that the labor-recruiting system was, even in the early decades of the twentieth century, "widely abused by the recruiters for their personal profit" (1986, 100).

5. These issues have been explored by Seymour (1999, 2002) and others. Chopra's contribution (2005) is attentive to migration, birth order, and family dynamics. Her portrayal definitely reinforces the position that migrants are one component of household-level strategies.

6. Several of the illegal laborers I interviewed remarked that lawyers, manpower agency representatives, and other citizens had exploited the laborers' status by promising to regularize their visas for various fees. Many of these individuals simply disappeared after receiving some payment, whereas others returned regularly with reports of incremental progress and demands for more money. None of the men I spoke with had successfully resolved his status situation through these means.

7. In 2006, Bahrain moved its weekend to Friday/Saturday.

8. See Gamburd (2000) and Strobl (2009) for an in-depth discussion of the conditions housemaids face in the Gulf.

9. This description closely resembles Kearney's analysis of the U.S./Mexico border, where "bordering policies and practices result in a net transfer of value from the immigrant-migrant community into the greater U.S. economy" (Kearney 2004, 143).

4. Strategic Transnationalism

1. It is particularly difficult to gauge the size of the Indian diasporic elite because the Bahraini census aggregates all Asian transmigrants. The 2001 census reported a total of 205,626 Asian transmigrants on the island. This number includes individuals

from India, Pakistan, Bangladesh, Nepal, and several other nations. It is generally agreed that the Indian population is the largest component of the Asian community. The same census reports that 32,662 individuals of Asian descent reported their reason of residence on the island as "with family." This number, doubled to include spouses, serves as a basic proxy for the total size of the Asian diasporic elite, for only those with substantial incomes can afford to bring spouses and children to the island. Keeping in mind that this total (approximately 64,000) includes Indians, Pakistanis, Filipinos, Bangladeshis, and smaller communities from other South Asian nations, we can roughly estimate the size of the Indian diasporic elite to be in the tens of thousands.

2. Leichtman (2005) focuses on the fact that the U.S. scholars largely ignore the impact of colonialism. To that I add that they also do not consider the potential implications of nondemocratic environments and alternative structures of control.

3. Here I am building on the ideas presented in an American Anthropological Association session that I cochaired with Heather Hindman, titled "Movements Outside 'the West': Contemporary Issues and Current Dilemmas in Transnational Anthropology," November 2003.

4. These headlines appeared in the *Gulf Daily News* on May 29, 2003, July 11, 2003, and May 18, 2003, respectively.

5. Like Anhil earlier, this letter writer makes an explicit appeal to the neoliberal logic of the Bahraini national vision.

6. Jacob Samuel, letter to the editor, *Gulf Daily News,* September 10, 2004.

7. One wealthy merchant described a successful case waged against an Emirati business partner who attempted to take over the business. Although the Indian merchant received a successful verdict in his case, he stated that he still had not collected a single dirham (the Emirati currency) as a result of the judgment. Another merchant remarked that he has had some success collecting on the numerous bad checks he receives from Bahrainis, but the process typically takes five years.

8. Anonymous, letter to the editor, *Gulf Daily News,* November 19, 2004.

9. Anh Longva, in her ethnography of foreign workers and citizens in Kuwait, remarks on the periodic loopholes in naturalization policy through which foreigners have become citizens (2000, 185).

10. These requirements are spelled out in the Bahraini Nationality Law of September 16, 1963.

11. Farid described the process of procuring Canadian citizenship: "That just means money—it only means money. They don't care who you are. They just want money. Show us this much money, you get it. Don't have the money? You don't get it. Let's face it. Getting a visa to America or Europe, in the end of the day, at the end of the whole thing, the criteria is money. They are looking to see if this person is going to come back or not. So the criteria they use is—does he have a business here? Does he have money? Does he have a bank account? Does he have the ties to bring him back? And most of those ties are money."

5. The Public Sphere

1. In the context of the Gulf states, one may also question the Habermasian fetishization of European democracy, and particularly the era of French salons—issues that become particularly acute when seeking to apply these concepts in a complex, nondemocratic environment that includes both citizens and transmigrants.

2. Generally speaking, the disenfranchised citizens of whom I speak are principally Shi'ite, often referred to as al-Baharna. I describe this population at length in chapters 2 and 6.

3. Three weeks later, and to much public fanfare, the Bahraini landlord offered to pay one month's rent for the workers displaced by the fire.

4. As I describe in earlier chapters, the laboring class is largely composed of transmigrant men. Although a small number of women arrive to work under similar contracts, and even larger numbers arrive to work as housemaids, few of these women find their way to the central neighborhood described here.

5. According to one of my informants, there are over two thousand members in the Gulf region. The Toastmasters Web site reports 9 chapters in Kuwait, 37 in Saudi Arabia, 13 in Qatar, 28 in the UAE, and 14 in Oman as of 2005.

6. This quotation is from the Toastmasters Web site.

7. Unusually, they actually own the property upon which the temple stands.

8. Although SNEHA is always capitalized in print, it is not an acronym. Rather, as one of the members noted, the word is a play on the Sanskrit for "loving care."

9. The Indian Ladies Association asked me to coteach the English course in 2003. I met weekly with a group of approximately forty men and women who sought to improve their English conversational skills.

10. The current emir's wife, in a break with tradition, is outgoing and maintains a significant public profile on the island.

11. For a good example, see the letter to the editor titled "Segregation 'Helps Avert Moral Decay,'" *Gulf Daily News*, August 25, 2004.

12. In the 1990s the Indian community formed the Co-ordination Committee of Indian Associations as an overarching body meant to represent the interests of all the social clubs on the island. My informants reported the mixed success of this venture: most noted that the committee itself has become mired in the politics of the Indian community.

6. Contested Identities, Contested Positions

1. "'Sex in Public' Couple Jailed," *Gulf Daily News*, October 25, 2006.

2. Although there has been much attention paid to blogs and other Internet forums, lack of access to the Internet effectively screens out much of the lower segments of the population in Bahrain from participating in these forums.

3. International Press Institute, Bahrain Report, May 8, 2008, http://www.freemedia.at/index.php?id=227&tx_ttnews[tt_news]=2563&tx_ttnews[backPid]=334&cHash=7ce11dca09 (accessed June 19, 2009).

4. Comment on Jaddwilliam2 Blog, June 19, 2006, http://jaddwilliam2.blogspot.com.

5. "Bahrain on Right Track," *Gulf Daily News,* June 2, 2009.

6. Syed Ahmed Khan and Family, letter to the editor, *Gulf Daily News,* August 21, 2008.

7. Anonymous letter to the editor, *Gulf Daily News,* October 13, 2006.

8. Anonymous letter to the editor, *Gulf Daily News,* February 27, 2009.

9. "Officials 'Must Quit over Fire Tragedy,'" *Gulf Daily News,* August 1, 2006; "Camp Horror Could Have Been Averted," letter to the editor, *Gulf Daily News,* August 2, 2006; "Bodies Stuffed into Drawers," *Gulf Daily News,* July 31, 2006.

10. I encourage readers to view their performances on YouTube.

11. These quotations and summaries were drawn from letters published in the *Gulf Daily News,* August 23 and 31, September 4, 7, 14, 16, 21, 27, and 29, 2006, respectively.

7. The Invigorated State

1. Longva suggests that this foreign matter is best conceived as an "international" norm of Euro-American pedigree (Longva 2005; Dresch 2005, 5).

2. "Bahrain Logistic Zone to Be Pivotal Middle East Hub," newsletter, Office of the Economic Representative of Bahrain, July 21, 2008.

3. Should the state not effectively quell the consternation, citizens take it upon themselves to remedy the situation.

4. These events, and the quotations in this section, are documented in three sequential articles in the *Gulf Daily News:* "Bahrain Firms Hit by Shortage of Drivers," May 1, 2004; "Jobless to Stage Peaceful Protest," May 4, 2004; and "Jobs Demand by Protesters," May 5, 2004.

5. Four percent of Bahrain's annual budget is devoted to providing the citizenry with housing (*Bahrain Brief* 1, no. 7 [August 2000]).

6. Sulayman Khalaf noted the redistribution, and the implications of civic employment, in his analysis of Kuwait (1992, 65–66).

7. Other sources report different numbers. Hammouya (1999, 17) reports that 28.3 percent of the total workforce is employed in the public sector. As Hammouya states (1999, 8), the significant differences in the reported size of the public sector relate directly to the difficulty of defining the boundaries of the public sector. In Bahrain, many citizens are directly employed by government offices; others, however, are employed by state-owned industries, or by the police force or national guard, for example.

8. See Louër (2008) for a more in-depth discussion of the systemic exclusion of Shi'ite citizens from key components of the state apparatus.

9. Champion, describing Saudi Arabia, calls the social contract the "legitimacy of largesse" (1999, n. 23), where the welfare state is forged in return for political quiescence. He also argues that "more realistic socioeconomic expectations appear to be gradually gaining prevalence" (4). This form of authority also resembles what Weber called "patrimonial administration" (1947, 351–54). The role of the public sector in this calculus is explored at length by Laurence Louër (2008).

10. "Ban Mannequin Displays of Lingerie!" *Gulf Daily News,* November 18, 2004; *Gulf Daily News,* September 4, 2004.

11. "Vigilante Threat to Labour Camp," *Gulf Daily News,* November 9, 2004. These "social and Islamic laws of the country" are not codified.

12. "Saudis have never had a single unified legal code that is evenly applied or can be consulted.... They claim to operate according to Shari'a law, but [there is] no lasting consensus about its make-up.... A consequence of the lack of a uniform, enforceable legal code is what would be perceived in the West as widespread corruption and nepotism. However, in Saudi society the family is so central that it is considered dishonorable not to use any means at one's disposal, including, often, one's bureaucratic position, to get a relative a job, or make sure an unfavorable legal decision is reversed so as to protect their interests" (Detzner 2003, 50).

8. Conclusion

1. "Fishermen's Fury over Labour Law," *Gulf Daily News,* May 27, 2009.

2. "Bahrain Business Community Blasts Al Alawi over Scrapping Sponsorship System, *Gulf News* (Dubai), May 8, 2009.

3. "Chamber in Job Switch Rules Row," *Gulf Daily News,* May 26, 2009.

4. "Bahrain Business Community Blasts Al Alawi"; "Fishermen's Fury over Labour Law."

5. "Bahrain Labour Minister Seeks Support for Scrapping Sponsorship System," *Gulf News* (Dubai), May 27, 2009.

6. "Sponsorships 'Must Be Scrapped,'" *Gulf Daily News,* April 7, 2008.

REFERENCES

Abu-Lughod, Janet. 1987. "The Islamic City—Historic Myth, Islamic Essence, and Contemporary Relevance." *International Journal of Middle East Studies* 19: 155–76.
Ali, Jasim. 2009. "Bahrain's Budget Still Shows Oil Dependency." *Gulf News*. March 21.
Altorki, Soraya. 1985. "The Anthropologist in the Field: A Case of 'Indigenous Anthropology' from Saudi Arabia." In *Arab Society: Social Science Perspectives*, ed. Nicholas S. Hopkins and Saad Eddin Ibrahim, 76–83. Cairo: American University in Cairo Press.
Altorki, Soraya, and Donald Cole. 1989. *Arabian Oasis City: The Transformation of 'Unayzah*. Austin: University of Texas Press.
Anderson, Benedict. 1983. *Imagined Communities: Reflections on the Origin and Spread of Nationalism*. London: Verso.
Anthony, T. A. 1993. "Documentation of the Modern History of Bahrain from American Sources (1900–1938)." In *Bahrain through the Ages: The History*, ed. Abdullah bin Khalid al-Khalifa and Michael Rice, 62–77. London: Kegan Paul International.
Appadurai, Arjun. 1990. "Disjuncture and Difference in the Global Cultural Economy." *Public Culture* 2(2): 1–24.
———. 1996. *Modernity at Large: Cultural Dimensions of Globalization*. Minneapolis: University of Minnesota Press.
Azhar, Muhammad. 1999. "Indo-Bahrain Economic Relations in the Nineties." In *India, Bahrain and Qatar: Political, Economic and Strategic Dimensions*, ed. A. K. Pasha. Delhi: Gyan Sugar Publications.
Azzam, H., and C. Moujabber. 1985. "Women and Development in the Gulf States." In *Women, Employment and Development in the Arab World*, ed. Julinda Abu Nasr, Nabil F. Khoury, and Henry T. Azzam, 59–72. Berlin: Mouton Publishers.

Bales, Kevin. 2004. *Disposable People: New Slavery in the Global Economy.* Berkeley: University of California Press.

——. 2005. *Understanding Global Slavery: A Reader.* Berkeley: University of California Press.

Basch, Linda G., Nina Glick, and Cristina Szanton Blanc. 1994. *Nations Unbound: Transnational Projects, Postcolonial Predicaments, and Deterritorialized Nation-States.* Langhorne, PA: Gordon and Breach.

Beaugé, G. 1985. "Le rôle de l'état dans les migrations de travailleurs et la diversification économique des pays de la Péninsule Arabe." *Revue Tiers-Monde* 103 (special issue): 597–620.

——. 1986. La kafala: Un système de gestion transitoire de la main-d'oeuvre et du capital dans les pays du golfe. *Revue Européenne des Migrations Internationales* 2(1): 109–22.

Bernal, Victoria. 2005. "Eritrea On-Line: Diaspora, Cyberspace, and the Public Sphere." *American Ethnologist* 32(4): 660–75.

Blank, Jonah. 2001. *Mullahs on the Mainframe.* Chicago: University of Chicago Press.

Bourdieu, Pierre. 1986. "The Forms of Capital." In *Handbook of Theory and Research for the Sociology of Education,* ed. J. G. Richardson, 241–58. New York: Greenwood Press.

——. 1987. *Distinction: A Social Critique of the Judgment of Taste.* Trans. Richard Nice. Cambridge: Harvard University Press.

Bourdieu, Pierre, and Lois J. D. Wacquant. 1992. *An Invitation to Reflexive Sociology.* Chicago: University of Chicago Press.

Bourgois, Philippe. 1991. "Confronting the Ethics of Ethnography: Lessons from Fieldwork in Central America." In *Decolonizing Anthropology: Moving Further toward an Anthropology for Liberation,* ed. Faye V. Harrison, 110–26. Washington, DC: American Anthropological Association.

Brochmann, Grete. 1993. *Middle East Avenue: Female Migration from Sri Lanka to the Gulf.* Boulder, CO: Westview Press.

Brosius, Peter. 1999. "Green Dots, Pink Hearts: Displacing Politics From the Malaysian Rain Forest." *American Anthropologist* 101(1): 36–57.

Buckingham, J. S. 1971. *Travels in Assyria, Media, and Persia.* Westmead, UK: Gregg International Publishers. First published in 1829.

Carter, John. 2005. "The History and Prehistory of Pearling in the Persian Gulf." *Journal of the Economic and Social History of the Orient* 48(2): 139–209.

Champion, Daryl. 1999. "The Kingdom of Saudi Arabia: Elements of Instability within Stability." *Meria* 3(4): 1–23.

Chopra, Radhika. 2005. "Sisters and Brothers: Schooling, Family and Migration." In *Educational Regimes in Contemporary India,* ed. Radhika Chopra and Patricia Jeffery, 299–315. New Delhi: Sage Publications.

Clarke, Angela. 1981. *The Islands of Bahrain: An Illustrated Guide to Their Heritage.* Manama: Bahrain Historical and Archaeological Society.

Clifford, James. 1994. "Diasporas." *Cultural Anthropology* 9(3): 302–38.

Constable, Nicole. 1997. *Maid to Order in Hong Kong: Stories of Filipina Workers.* Ithaca: Cornell University Press.

Cunningham, Robert, and Yasin K. Sarayrah. 1993. *Wasta: The Hidden Force in Middle Eastern Society.* Westport, CT: Praeger.

———. 1994. "Taming Wasta to Achieve Development." *Arab Studies Quarterly* 16(3): 29–42.

De Genova, Nicholas. 2002. "Migrant 'Illegality' and Deportability in Everyday Life." *Annual Review of Anthropology* 31: 419–47.

Demery, Lionel. 1986. "Asian Labor Migration: An Empirical Assessment." In *Asian Labor Migration: Pipeline to the Middle East,* ed. Fred Arnold and Nasra M. Shah, 17–46. Boulder, CO: Westview Press.

Detzner, Sarah. 2003. "Now or Never: The Impact of Saudi Arabian Culture on Economic Development." *Journal of Political Science* 1 (Spring): 44–55.

Directorate of Statistics. 1999. Statistical abstract. Population and Social Statistic Section, Central Statistics Organization. Manama, Bahrain.

Douglas, Mary. 2002. *Purity and Danger: An Analysis of the Concept of Pollution and Taboo.* New York: Routledge. First published in 1966.

Dresch, Paul. 2005. Introduction to *Monarchies and Nations: Globalisation and Identity in the Arab States of the Gulf.* Ed. Paul Dresch and James Piscatori. London: I. B. Tauris.

———. 2006. "The Place of Strangers in Gulf Society." In *Globalization and the Gulf,* ed. John Fox, Nada Mourtada-Sabbah, and Mohammed al-Mutawa. London: Routledge.

Eelens, F., T. Schampers, and J. D. Speckman. 1992. *Labour Migration to the Middle East: From Sri Lanka to the Gulf.* London: Kegan Paul.

Falzon, Mark-Anthony. 2003. "'Bombay, Our Cultural Heart': Rethinking the Relation between Homeland and Diaspora." *Ethnic and Racial Studies* 26(4): 662–83.

Farah, Talal Toufic. 1985. *Protection and Politics in Bahrain, 1869–1915.* Beirut: American University of Beirut Press.

Farmer, Paul. 2003. *Pathologies of Power: Health, Human Rights, and the New War on the Poor.* Berkeley: University of California Press.

———. 2004. "An Anthropology of Structural Violence." *Current Anthropology* 45(3): 305–25.

Fasano, Ugo, and Richi Goyal. 2004. "Emerging Strains in GCC Labor Markets." IMF Working Paper No. WP/04/71. April.

Foucault, Michel. 1985. *The Foucault Reader.* Ed. Paul Rabinow. New York: Pantheon Books.

Franklin, Robert Lee. 1985. "The Indian Community in Bahrain: Labor Migration in a Plural Society." Ph.D. diss., Department of Anthropology, Harvard University.

Fraser, Nancy. 1992. "Rethinking the Public Sphere: A Contribution to the Critique of Actually Existing Democracy." In *Habermas and the Public Sphere,* ed. Craig Calhoun, 109–42. Cambridge, MA: MIT Press.

Fuccaro, Nelida. 2000. "Understanding the Urban History of Bahrain." *Critique* 17: 49–81.
Fuglerud, Øivind. 1999. *Life on the Outside: The Tamil Diaspora and Long-Distance Nationalism.* London: Pluto Press.
Galtung, Johan. 1969. "Violence, Peace and Peace Research." *Journal of Peace Research* 6(3): 167–91.
Gamburd, Michele Ruth. 2000. *The Kitchen Spoon's Handle: Transnationalism and Sri Lanka's Migrant Housemaids.* Ithaca: Cornell University Press.
Gardner, Andrew. 2004. "The Political Ecology of Bedouin Pastoralism in the Kingdom of Saudi Arabia." In *Political Ecology across Spaces, Scales and Social Groups,* ed. Lisa Gezon and Susan Paulson. New Brunswick, NJ: Rutgers University Press.
Gardner, Andrew, and Timothy Finan. 2004. "Navigating Modernization: Bedouin Pastoralism and Climate Information in the Kingdom of Saudi Arabia." *MIT Electronic Journal of Middle East Studies* 4 (Spring): 59–72.
George, Sheba. 2000. "'Dirty Nurses' and 'Men Who Play': Gender and Class in Transnational Migration." In *Global Ethnography: Forces, Connections, and Imaginations in a Postmodern World,* by Michael Burawoy et al., 144–74. Berkeley: University of California Press.
Giddens, Anthony. 1979. *Central Problems in Social Theory.* London: Macmillan.
Goldring, Luin. 1998. "The Power of Status in Transnational Social Fields." In *Transnationalism From Below,* ed. Michael Peter Smith and Luis Eduardo Guarnizo, 165–95. New Brunswick, NJ: Transaction Publishers.
Goldstein, Daniel M. 2004. *The Spectacular City: Violence and Performance in Urban Bolivia.* Durham, NC: Duke University Press.
Green, Linda. 1999. *Fear as a Way of Life: Mayan Widows in Rural Guatemala.* New York: Columbia University Press.
———. 2004. Written response to "An Anthropology of Structural Violence," by Paul Farmer. *Current Anthropology* 45(3): 319–20.
Gupta, Akhil. 2006. "Blurred Boundaries: The Discourse of Corruption, the Culture of Politics, and the Imagined State." In *The Anthropology of the State: A Reader,* ed. Aradhana Sharma and Akhil Gupta. Malden, MA: Blackwell.
Habermas, Jürgen. 1989. *The Structural Transformation of the Public Sphere: An Inquiry into a Category of Bourgeois Society.* Trans. T. Burger and F. Lawrence. Cambridge, MA: MIT Press. First published in 1962.
Hall, Stuart. 2005. "Popular Culture and the State." In *The Anthropology of the State,* ed. Aradhana Sharma and Akhil Gupta. Malden, MA: Blackwell.
Hammouya, Messaoud. 1999. "Statistics on Public Sector Employment: Methodology, Structures and Trends." Bureau of Statistics Working Paper, Sectoral Activities Programme. Geneva: International Labour Office.
Hannerz, Ulf. 1996. *Transnational Connections: Culture, People, Places.* London: Routledge.
Heyman, Josiah M., and Alan Smart. 1999. "States and Illegal Practices: An Overview." In *States and Illegal Practices,* ed. Josiah M. Heyman. New York: Berg.

Hobsbawm, E. J. 1990. *Nations and Nationalism since 1780*. Cambridge: Cambridge University Press.
Holden, David. 1966. *Farewell to Arabia*. New York: Walker.
Holloway, John. 1994. "Global Capital and the National State." *Capital and Class* 52 (Spring): 23–49.
Holmes, Seth. 2007. "'Oaxacans Like to Work Bent Over': The Naturalization of Social Suffering among Berry Farm Workers." *International Migration* 45(3): 39–68.
Hornborg, Alf. 2005. "Undermining Modernity: Protecting Landscapes and Meanings among the Mi'kmaq of Nova Scotia." In *Political Ecology across Spaces, Scales, and Social Groups*, ed. Susan Paulson and Lisa Gezon. New Brunswick, NJ: Rutgers University Press.
Horton, Sarah. 2004. "A Wake-up Call to Job-Seekers." *Gulf Daily News*. September 18.
IPI (International Press Institute). 2008. Bahrain. http://www.freemedia.at/publications/world-press-freedom-review/mena/singleview/bahrain/365d9be3fa/ (accessed November 1, 2009).
Isin, Engin F. 2002. *Being Political: Genealogies of Citizenship*. Minneapolis: University of Minnesota Press.
Jenner, Michael. 1984. *Bahrain: Gulf Heritage in Transition*. London: Longman.
Kapiszewski, Andrzej. 2001. *Nationals and Expatriates: Population and Labour Dilemmas of the Gulf Cooperation Council States*. Ithaca, NY: Ithaca Press.
———. 2006. "Arab versus Asian Migrant Workers in the GCC Countries." United Nations Expert Group Meeting on International Migration and Development in the Arab Region, Population Division, Department of Economic and Social Affairs. Beirut. May 22.
Kearney, Michael. 1991. "Borders and Boundaries of State and Self at the End of Empire." *Journal of Historical Sociology* 4(1): 52–74.
———. 2004. "The Classifying and Value-Filtering Missions of Borders." *Anthropological Theory* 4(2): 131–56.
Khalaf, Sulayman. 1992. "Gulf Societies and the Image of Unlimited Good." *Dialectical Anthropology* 17: 53–84.
Khalaf, Sulayman, and Saad Alkobaisi. 1999. "Migrants' Strategies of Coping and Patterns of Accommodation in the Oil-Rich Gulf Societies: Evidence from the UAE." *British Journal of Middle Eastern Studies* 26(2): 271–98.
Khuri, Fuad I. 1980. *Tribe and State in Bahrain*. Chicago: University of Chicago Press.
Kilankiewicz, G. 1996. "Social Capital and Social Change." *British Journal of Sociology* 47(3): 427–41.
King, Anthony, ed. 1991. *Culture, Globalization and the World-System: Contemporary Conditions for the Representation of Identity*. Binghamton: State University of New York Press.
Kurien, Prema. 2002. *Kaleidoscopic Ethnicity: International Migration and the Reconstruction of Community Identities in India*. New Brunswick, NJ: Rutgers University Press.

Landen, Robert G. 1967. *Oman since 1845: Disruptive Modernization in a Traditional Arab Society.* Princeton: Princeton University Press.

Leichtman, Mara. 2005. "The Legacy of Transnational Lives: Beyond the First Generation of Lebanese in Senegal." *Ethnic and Racial Studies* 28(4): 663–86.

Leonard, Karen. 1999. "Construction of Identity in Diaspora: Emigrants from Hyderabad, India." In *Expanding Landscapes: South Asians in Diaspora*, ed. Carla Petievich. Delhi: Manohar.

———. 2002. "South Asian Women in the Gulf: Families and Futures Reconfigured." In *Trans-status Subjects: Gender in the Globalization of South and Southeast Asia*, ed. Sonita Sarker and Esha Niyogi De, 213–31. Durham, NC: Duke University Press.

———. 2003. "South Asian Workers in the Gulf: Jockeying for Places." In *Globalization under Construction: Governmentality, Law and Identity*, ed. Richard Perry and William Maurer, 129–70. Minneapolis: University of Minnesota Press.

Longva, Anh. 1997. *Walls Built on Sand: Migration, Exclusion and Society in Kuwait.* Boulder, CO: Westview Press.

———. 1999. "Keeping Migrant Workers In Check: The *Kafala* System in the Gulf." *Middle East Report* 211 (Summer): 20–22.

———. 2000. "Citizenship in the Gulf States: Conceptualization and Practice." In *Citizenship and the State in the Middle East*, ed. N. A. Butenschon, U. Davis, and M. Hassassian, 179–97. Syracuse, NY: Syracuse University Press.

———. 2005. "Neither Autocracy nor Democracy but Ethnocracy: Citizens, Expatriates and the Socio-Political Regime in Kuwait." In *Monarchies and Nations: Globalization and Identity in the Arab States of the Gulf*, ed. Paul Dresch and James Piscatori, 114–35. London: I. B. Tauris.

Lorimer, J. G. 1908. *Gazetteer of the Persian Gulf, Oman and Central Arabia.* 3 vols. Calcutta: Superintendent Government Printing.

Louër, Laurence. 2008. "The Political Impact of Labor Migration in Bahrain." *City and Society* 20(1): 32–53.

Mahler, Sarah J. 1998. "Theoretical and Empirical Contributions Toward a Research Agenda for Transnationalism." In *Transnationalism from Below*, ed. Michael Peter Smith and Luis Eduardo Guarnizo, 64–102. New Brunswick, NJ: Transaction Publishers.

Malinowski, Bronislaw. 1922. *Argonauts of the Western Pacific.* New York: E. P. Dutton.

Matthei, Linda Miller, and David A. Smith. 1998. "'Belizean "Boyz 'n the 'Hood"?' Garifuna Labor Migration and Transnational Identity." In *Transnationalism from Below*, ed. Michael Peter Smith and Luis Eduardo Guarnizo, 270–90. New Brunswick, NJ: Transaction Publishers.

Mazzarella, William. 2003. *Shoveling Smoke: Advertising and Globalization in Contemporary India.* Durham, NC: Duke University Press.

Mintz, Sidney. 1985. *Sweetness and Power: The Place of Sugar in Modern History.* New York: Viking.

Misiorowski, Elise. 1998. "Pearls with a Past." *Professional Jeweler Magazine*, September.

Moosa, Abdulrasool al-, and Keith McLachlan. 1985. *Immigrant Labor in Kuwait*. London: Croom Helm.

Muraikhi, Khalil M. al-. 1991. *Glimpses of Bahrain from Its Past*. Manama, Bahrain: Government Press, Ministry of Information.

Nagy, Sharon. 1998. "'This Time I Think I'll Try a Filipina': Global and Local Influences on Relations between Foreign Household Workers and Their Employers in Doha, Qatar." *City and Society* (annual review), 83–103.

———. 2004. "Keeping Families Together: Housing Policy, Social Strategies and Family in Qatar." *MIT Electronic Journal of Middle East Studies* 4 (Spring): 42–58.

———. 2008. "The Search for Miss Philippines Bahrain—Possibilities for Representation in Expatriate Communities." *City and Society* 20(1): 79–104.

Nair, P. R. Gopinathan. 1999. "Return of Overseas Contract Workers and Their Rehabilitation and Development in Kerala (India): A Critical Account of Policies, Performance and Prospects." *International Migration* 37(1): 209–42.

Nakhleh, Emile A. 1976. *Bahrain*. Lexington, MA: Lexington Books.

Nambiar, A. C. K. 1995. "The Socio-Economic Conditions of Gulf Migrants." Report by the Malabar Institute for Development, Research and Action. New Delhi: Commonwealth Publishers.

Niezen, Ronald. 2003. *The Origins of Indigenism*. Berkeley: University of California Press.

Ong, Aihwa. 1999. *Flexible Citizenship: The Cultural Logics of Transnationality*. Durham, NC: Duke University Press.

Onley, James. 2004. "The Politics of Protection in the Gulf: Arab Rulers and the British Resident in the Nineteenth Century." *New Arabian Studies* 6:30–92.

———. 2007. *The Arabian Frontier Of the British Raj: Merchants, Rulers, and the British in the Nineteenth-Century Gulf*. Oxford: Oxford University Press.

Osella, Filippo, and Caroline Osella. 2000a. "Migration, Money and Masculinity in Kerala." *Journal of the Royal Anthropological Institute* 6(1): 117–33.

———. 2000b. *Social Mobility in Kerala: Modernity and Identity in Conflict*. London: Pluto Press.

Owen, Roderic. 1957. *The Golden Bubble: Arabian Gulf Documentary*. London: Collins.

Palgrave, William Gifford. 1982. *Narrative of a Year's Journey through Central and Eastern Arabia (1862–1863)*. Amersham, UK: Demand Reprints. First published in 1865.

Pertierra, Raul. 1994. "Lured Abroad: The Case of Ilocano Overseas Workers." *Sojourn* 9(1): 54–80.

Peutz, Nathalie. 2006. "Embarking on an Anthropology of Removal." *Current Anthropology* 47(2): 217–41.

Pirzada, Shaziae, and Anjali Puri. 1998. *Vignettes: The Women of Bahrain*. Bahrain: Dar Akhbar al-Khaleej Press.

Rasheed, Madawi al-. 2005. Introduction to *Transnational Connections and the Arab Gulf*, ed. Madawi al-Rasheed. London: Routledge.

Reitz, Jeffrey G., ed. 2003. *Host Societies and the Reception of Immigrants*. La Jolla, CA: Center for Comparative Immigration Studies.

Rosaldo, Renato. 1994. "Cultural Citizenship and Educational Democracy." *Cultural Anthropology* 9(3): 402–11.

Roseberry, William. 1993. "Beyond the Agrarian Question in Latin America." In *Confronting Historical Paradigms: Peasants, Labor, and the Capitalist World System in Africa and Latin America,* ed. Frederick Cooper, Alan Isaacman, Florencia Mallon, William Roseberry, and Steve J. Sterns. Madison: University of Wisconsin Press.

———. 1996. "The Unbearable Lightness of Anthropology." *Radical History Review* 65 (Spring): 5–25.

Rouse, Roger. 1992. "Making Sense of Settlement: Class Transformation, Cultural Struggle, and Transnationalism among Mexican Migrants in the United States. *Annals of the New York Academy of Sciences* 645: 25–52.

Sarker, Sonita, and Esha Niyogi De, eds. 2002. *Trans-Status Subjects: Gender in the Globalization of South and Southeast Asia*. Durham, NC: Duke University Press.

Scheper-Hughes, Nancy. 2004. "Dangerous and Endangered Youth: Social Structures and Determinants of Violence." *Annals of the New York Academy of Sciences* 1036 (December): 13–46.

Scheper-Hughes, Nancy, and Philippe Bourgois. 2004. Introduction to *Violence in War and Peace: An Anthology*. Ed. Nancy Scheper-Hughes and Philippe Bourgois. Malden, MA: Blackwell.

Seccombe, Ian, and Richard Lawless. 1986. "The Gulf Labour Market and the Early Oil Industry: Traditional Structures and New Forms of Organisation." In *The Gulf in the Early Twentieth Century: Foreign Institutions and Local Responses,* ed. Richard Lawless. Occasional Papers Series, no. 31. Centre for Middle Eastern and Islamic Studies, University of Durham, UK.

Seikaly, May. 2001. "Kuwait and Bahrain: The Appeal of Globalization and Internal Constraints." In *Iran, Iraq, and the Arab Gulf States,* ed. Joseph A. Kechichian. New York: Palgrave.

Sekhar, T. V. 1996. "Male Emigration and Changes in the Family: Impact on Female Sex Roles." *Indian Journal of Social Work* 57(2): 277–94.

Seymour, Susan. 1999. *Women, Family, and Child Care in India: A World in Transition*. Cambridge: Cambridge University Press.

———. 2002. "Family and Gender Systems in Transition: A Thirty-Five Year Perspective." In *Everyday Life in South Asia,* ed. Diana Mines and Sarah Lamb. Bloomington: Indiana University Press.

Sharma, Adrahana, and Akhil Gupta. 2006. Introduction to *The Anthropology of the State: A Reader,* ed. Adrahana Sharma and Akhil Gupta. Malden, MA: Blackwell.

Silvey, Rachel. 2004. "Transnational Domestication: State Power and Indonesian Migrant Women in Saudi Arabia." *Political Geography* 23: 245–64.

Slot, B. J. 1993. "The Dutch East India Company and Bahrain." In *Bahrain through the Ages The History,* ed. Abdullah bin Khalid al-Khalifa and Michael Rice, 497–503. London: Kegan Paul.

Smith, Michael P., and Luis Eduardo Guarnizo, eds. 1998. *Transnationalism from Below.* New Brunswick, NJ: Transaction Publishers.

Smith, Robert. 1998. "Transnational Localities: Community, Technology and the Politics of Membership within the Context of Mexico and U. S. Migration." In *Transnationalism from Below,* ed. Michael Peter Smith and Luis Eduardo Guarnizo, 196–240. New Brunswick, NJ: Transaction Publishers.

So, Alvin. 1990. *Social Change and Development: Modernization, Dependency and World-System Theories.* Newbury Park, CA: Sage.

Strobl, Staci. 2009. "Policing Housemaids: The Criminalization of Domestic Workers in Bahrain." *British Journal of Criminology* 49: 165–83.

Vertovec, Steve. 1999. "Conceiving and Researching Transnationalism." *Ethnic and Racial Studies* 22(2): 445–62.

Vora, Neha. 2008. "Producing Diasporas and Globalization: Indian Middle-Class Migrants in Dubai." *Anthropological Quarterly* 81(2): 377–406.

Wallerstein, Immanuel. 1974. *The Modern World-System.* Garden City, NY: Dolphin Books.

Walters, William. 2002. "Deportation, Expulsion, and the International Police of Aliens." *Citizenship Studies* 6(3): 265–92.

Warner, Michael. 2002. *Publics and Counterpublics.* Cambridge: Zone Books.

Weber, Max. 1947. *The Theory of Social and Economic Organization.* Trans. A. M. Henderson and Talcott Parsons. New York: Oxford University Press.

Weiner, Myron. 1986. "Labor Migrations as Incipient Diasporas." In *Modern Diasporas in International Politics,* ed. Gabriel Sheffer, 47–74. New York: St. Martin's Press.

Werbner, Pnina. 1998. "Diasporic Public Imaginaries: A Sphere of Freedom or a Sphere of Illusion?" *Communal/Plural* 6(1): 11–31.

Wheatcroft, Andrew. 1988. *Bahrain in Original Photographs, 1880–1961.* New York: Kegan Paul.

———. 1995. *The Life and Times of Shaikh Salman Bin Hamad al-Khalifa: Ruler of Bahrain, 1942–1961.* London: Kegan Paul.

Willen, Sarah S. 2007. "Toward a Critical Phenomenology of 'Illegality': State Power, Criminalization, and Abjectivity among Undocumented Migrant Workers in Tel Aviv, Israel." *International Migration* 45(3): 8–38.

Wilson, Peter W., and Douglas Graham. 1994. *Saudi Arabia: The Coming Storm.* Armonk, NY: M. E. Sharpe.

Wolf, Eric. 1982. *Europe and the People without History.* Berkeley: University of California Press.

———. 1999. *Envisioning Power: Ideologies of Dominance and Crisis.* Berkeley: University of California Press.

Wright, Steven. 2008. "Fixing the Kingdom: Political Evolution and Socio-Economic Challenges in Bahrain." Occasional Paper No. 3. Center for International and Regional Studies. Georgetown University School of Foreign Service in Qatar.

Yergin, Daniel. 1991. *The Prize: The Epic Quest for Oil, Money, and Power.* New York: Simon and Schuster.

Zahlan, Rosemarie Said. 1989. *The Making of the Modern Gulf States.* London: Unwin Hyman.

INDEX

al-Alawi, Dr. Majeed Mohsen, 161
Altorki, Soraya, 153–154, 157
Appadurai, Arjun, 72, 76, 79, 95, 97
applied anthropology, 160
Arab labor migration, 42
architecture
   monumental, 43–44, 123–125
   traditional, 137–140
auto-Orientalism, 4, 11

bachelor cities, 141
Bahrain
   agricultural production, 35–36
   early history, 31–33
   economic diversification, 42–43
   and Gulf liberalism, 46–47
   historical connections with India, 35–36
   legal institutions, 39–40
   and petroleum dependency, 42–43
   religious tolerance, 108
   villages of, 36
   work ethic, 149–153
   see also Manama
Bahrain Training Institute, 9, 15, 16, 17, 90, 151
Bahrainization, 52, 89–90, 92, 107, 112, 133, 142–143, 146–149, 150–152

Belgrave, Charles, 39–40, 168n13
Bhatias. See Sindhis
Bohra, Bohri, 77, 92
Bourdieu, Pierre, 80, 154–156
   see also habitus; social capital
Bourgois, Philippe, 6, 166n3
British Colonialism, 13, 20, 26–27, 37–40, 46, 107
   and the Bahraini court system, 39
   and Bahraini petroleum, 40
   and the British India Steam Navigation Company, 39
   discourse of, 35
   and English East India Company, 32
   and the Gulf Resident, 38–40
   and legitimacy of the state, 47
   and piracy, 38
   withdrawal/independence, 41

censorship, 120–122
citizenship, 44–45, 74, 80, 82, 87–88
   in Bahrain, 22, 87–88, 114, 142–146, 152
   and ethnicity, 81, 87–88, 166n9
   flexible 74, 94
   see also naturalization
Cole, Donald, 157
colonialism. See British Colonialism
contracts. See labor contracts

deportation, 21, 51–58, 62, 69–70
    as an industry, 68–69
diaspora, 14, 24–26, 75–77
    and the transnational polarity, 74
diasporization, 90–94
    and the public sphere, 96–98
    and social clubs, 113–114
domestic workers, 14, 19, 30, 66
Dresch, Paul, 44, 123, 140, 173n1
Dubai, 43, 45
Durkheim, Emile, 5

economic determinism, 157–158
economic diversification, 42–43, 46
Ecumenical Council of Charity, 63, 108–109, 114
ethnographic methods, 15–20

Farmer, Paul, 6, 143
Foucault, Michel, 82
Franklin, Robert Lee, 9, 102, 109, 156

Galtung, Johan, 6
Gamburd, Michele, 61, 73, 77
General Treaty of Peace, 38
Giddens, Anthony, 136
Gulf Daily News, 85, 119–122, 124, 125–133
    history of, 119–122
Gupta, Akhil, 31, 79, 119, 124–125, 170n3

Habermas, Jurgen, 96–98, 172n1
habitus, 72, 80–83, 88, 89, 115, 117, 137
Hamad Town, 1
hospitality, 137–140, 158, 160
housemaids. *See* domestic workers

identity
    Bahraini, 137–140, 138–140
    Bahraini exceptionalism, 45, 100, 163–164
    khaleeji identity, 44–45, 46
    Indian, 114–116
illegality, 51–58
    amnesty periods, 54

and the state, 62
India
    historical connections to Arabia, 26–28, 35–37
    and religious tension, 76–77
    wage levels, 74–75
Indian Club, 99, 101–103, 105, 117
Indian Ladies Association, 14, 16, 17, 109–112, 113, 172n9

Jews, 33, 35, 39

kafala, 20, 23, 29–30, 52–59, 60–62, 69–70, 83
    and business, 86–88
    as a cultural practice, 58–59, 162
    dismantling of, 30, 160–163
    and families, 85–86
    history of, 34–35, 37, 59–60
    and illegality, 52–54, 98
    inequality, 54, 63–64, 83
    and the labor market, 85
    and passports, 57, 58–59, 62–63, 108, 162
    self-sponsorship, 88
Khuri, Fuad, 32, 35, 38, 39, 40, 100, 155, 169n17
Knight Rider, 13

labor brokers, 30, 55, 58–59, 60–62
labor camps, 17, 19, 49, 53, 59, 64–67
labor contracts, 29, 60–62, 67–69, 83
labor court, 57
labor strikes, 42, 56–57, 63
language
    Arabic, 14, 23, 57, 58, 59, 63–64, 87, 151
    in Bahrain, 12–15, 17
    and citizenship, 14–15
    English, 13–14, 41, 101, 105–106, 119–120, 151
    Hindi, 14, 63–64
    Malayalam, 14, 63–64
    Persian, 14
    and power, 63–64

Leichtman, Mara, 73
Leonard, Karen, 16–17, 24, 75, 76, 77, 80, 86, 166n9
Lions Club, 16, 96, 106–108, 112, 117, 132–133
LMRA, 127, 161
localization. *See* Bahrainization
Longva, Anh, 26, 29, 45, 59–60, 64, 73, 81, 84–85, 162, 166n2, 167n4, 171n9, 173n1

Malinowski, Bronislaw, 12
Manama, 98, 140–142
   in the Indian Ocean world, 35–36
   multicultural history of, 35–36
   and petroleum revenues, 40–41
   urban space and power, 64–67, 140–142
merchants, 26–27, 77, 78, 92–94
migration
   Arab, 23, 42, 166n9
   and British Colonialism, 26–27, 41, 42
   chain migration, 30
   costs of, 59, 60–62
   Egyptian migrants, 23
   and ethnicity, 42
   for extra-economic reasons, 75–77
   and family, 28, 56, 57, 61, 85–86, 90–94
   and gender, 18–19, 30, 85–86
   and the OPEC embargo, 41, 42
   periods of, 26–28
   and the petroleum industry, 41, 42
   proportions of, 10–11, 12, 25–26, 43, 45
   and statistical data, 2, 9–10, 19, 25, 41, 165n1
Ministry of Labor and Social Affairs, 16, 56–57, 84, 86, 90, 142, 148, 161
Ministry of Social Development, 101
Mintz, Sidney, 5, 33
modernization, 27, 40, 43, 45, 122–125
   and petroleum revenues, 42

Nagy, Sharon, 11, 81, 96, 131, 143

nationalism, 44–45, 122–125, 145–146
   Bahraini, 79–80, 81–82, 132–133
   and neoliberalism, 80
naturalization, 14–15, 28, 87, 93, 166n9, 167n2, 171n9
   see also citizenship
neoliberalism, 4, 80, 82, 117, 123–124, 134, 143, 156–158
   and urban space, 140–142
Niezen, Ronald, 128

oil. *See* petroleum
Ong, Aihwa, 73–74, 79, 94
Onley, James, 13, 38–39, 168n15
OPEC embargo, 20, 27, 41–42, 44
Orientalism, 4, 11

pearls, 31, 33–36, 80
   social relations of pearl production, 34–35
petroleum, 37, 40–43, 44–46, 143–144
   discovery, 40–41
   economic dependency, 42–43, 44–45, 143–144
piracy, 38
power, theories of, 5–7, 82
public anthropology, 160
public sector 142–146, 151–153
   early history, 39
   and the legitimacy of the state, 44–45, 144
   and wasta, 152–157
   see also the welfare state
public space, 140–142
public sphere, 116–117, 133–135
   theories of, 96–98

rentier economy. *See* public sector; welfare state
Roseberry, William, 5–6

Saudi Arabia, 7–8
Scheper-Hughes, Nancy, 6, 70, 166n3
schools, 28, 85, 102–103

sectarianism, 33, 36, 66, 123–124, 156
   history in Bahrain, 33–35
   and wasta, 156–157
   and the workforce, 52, 144–145
segregation, 28–29, 81, 140–142, 168n9
   social, 81, 96–98, 100, 114–116, 129–132
   spatial, 100, 114–116, 140–142
Shia Islam. *See* sectarianism
Sindhis, 77, 103, 108
slavery, 34–35
   contract slavery, 58–59, 67–69
   new slavery, 58–59, 67–69
sleeping partners, 86–87, 93, 139
social capital, 152, 153–157
social clubs, 21, 28, 98–100
   and diaspora, 114–116
   and outreach to migrants, 98–100
   and transnationalism, 112–114
Special Economic Zones, 140–142
sponsorship system. *See* kafala
the state, 52, 62, 80, 82–83, 146–149
   and Bahrainization, 146–149
   and its complicity, 62
   theories of, 82–83
   and transnationalism, 52
   see also Bahrainization; the public sector; the welfare state
structural power, 7, 160

structural violence, 2–4, 5–7, 51–54, 58–60, 64, 67–69
structure and agency, 4, 7, 63, 72, 88–89
Sunni Islam. *See* sectarianism

TASCA, 99, 103–105, 106
Toastmasters, 16, 74, 96, 105–106, 116
transnationalism, 11–12, 24, 47–48, 51–52, 71–74
   and anthropology, 47–48
   diasporic elite, 24–25, 71
   and the global north, 69, 72–74, 94–95
   and the nation-state, 52
   strategic transnationalism, 89–95
   transnational proletariat, 24–25
tribalism, 34, 43, 44–45, 152–155, 160, 168n9

violence, 1–4, 5–7, 51, 58–60
   episodes, 2, 49–51, 78–79
   see also structural violence
Vora, Neha, 81

wasta, 153–157
welfare state, 80, 142–146, 150–151
   see also the public sector
Wolf, Eric, 5, 6–7, 33, 160
work ethic, 149–153
world system theory, 33